California Wine Country

California
Wine Country

John Doerper
Photography by Robert Holmes and
Charles O'Rear

COMPASS AMERICAN GUIDES
An imprint of Fodor's Travel Publications

Compass American Guides: California Wine Country

Editor: Paula Consolo
Designer: Fabrizio La Rocca
Compass Editorial Director: Daniel Mangin
Compass Senior Editor: Kristin Moehlmann
Compass Creative Director: Fabrizio La Rocca
Production Editor: Linda Schmidt
Photo Editor and Archival Researcher: Melanie Marin
Map Design: Mark Stroud, Moon Street Cartography

Cover photo (Niebaum-Coppola Estate): Robert Holmes

Fourth Edition
Copyright © 2004 Fodors LLC
Maps copyright © 2004 Fodors LLC

ISBN 1–4000–1264–3
ISSN 1547–7274

Compass American Guides, 1745 Broadway, New York, NY 10019
Printed in Singapore

10 9 8 7 6 5 4 3 2

To my wife, Victoria,
whose deep understanding of wines and words
has ever been of inestimable support.

CONTENTS

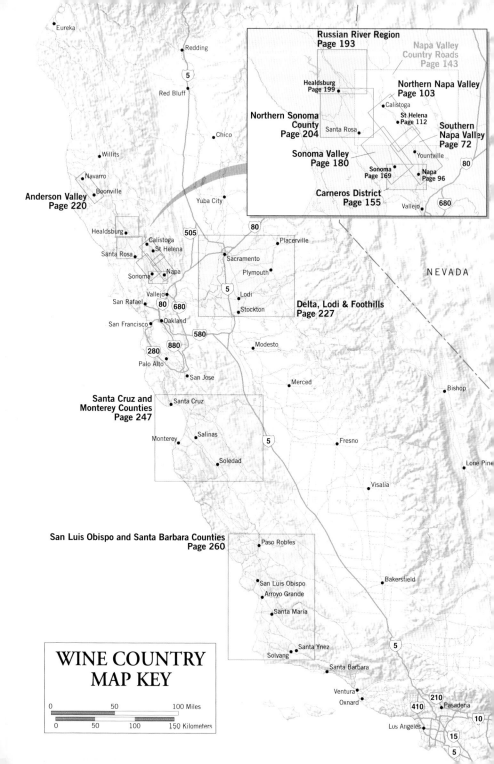

Eureka

Redding

5

Red Bluff

Chico

Willits

Navarro

Boonville

Anderson Valley
Page 220

Yuba City

Healdsburg

505

80

Placerville

Calistoga
St Helena

Sacramento

Santa Rosa

Sonoma
Napa

Plymouth

5

Lodi

Vallejo

San Rafael
80
680

Stockton

Delta, Lodi & Foothills
Page 227

San Francisco
Oakland

580

Modesto

280
880

Palo Alto

San Jose

Merced

Bishop

Santa Cruz and
Monterey Counties
Page 247

Santa Cruz

Salinas

Monterey

Soledad

5

Fresno

Visalia

Lone Pine

San Luis Obispo and Santa Barbara Counties
Page 260

Paso Robles

Bakersfield

San Luis Obispo
Arroyo Grande

Santa Maria

Santa Ynez

Solvang

5

Santa Barbara

Ventura
Oxnard

210
Pasadena

410

10

Los Angeles

15

5

Russian River Region
Page 193

Napa Valley
Country Roads
Page 143

Healdsburg
Page 199

Northern Napa Valley
Page 103

Calistoga

Northern Sonoma
County
Page 204

St Helena
Page 112

Santa Rosa

Southern
Napa Valley
Page 72

Sonoma Valley
Page 180

Yountville

80

Sonoma
Page 169

Napa
Page 96

Carneros District
Page 155

Vallejo

680

NEVADA

WINE COUNTRY
MAP KEY

0	50	100 Miles

0	50	100	150 Kilometers

Sidebars & Literary Extracts

Maps

INTRODUCTION

The patio lies in the deep afternoon shade of live oaks, but the vineyard across the road is lit up by the setting sun, which is giving the ripening cabernet grapes a final boost of sugars. I have returned to my favorite Wine Country cottage to relax, to taste the young, still fermenting wines of the current vintage, and to eat good food. Only an olive grove separates me from one of the Wine Country's busiest thoroughfares, yet everything here is peaceful. I listen to birds chirping in the blackberry thicket behind the winery and hear the splash of a heron as it lunges for fish in a pool left in the summer-dry creek. A hummingbird flits past, stalling intermittently to extract nectar; quail call from the vineyard. The heady aromas of fermenting must (crushed grapes used to make wine) waft through the air, mingling with the dusty smell of the vineyard and the perfume of autumn roses. Later that night, after dinner, I sit by the open window, sipping a glass of well-aged zinfandel. A screech owl calls, interrupted now and then by the unearthly howl of wandering coyotes. This is the Wine Country at its best.

During the past 40 years, the wine valleys of Napa and Sonoma have changed considerably, but in many ways the area has remained the same. There are more wineries now—many more—and more visitors, but the spirit of the land is intact. This is still one of the best places to visit, and though some locals decry the influx of "wine tourists," these visitors are a special breed. For the most part, they are eager to learn more about wine, they are willing to taste and evaluate, and they enthusiastically ask for advice from the staff at winery tasting rooms. There is an instant rapport, a communion of spirits, among lovers of fine wine. This club is open to all who embrace it, and its members readily and freely share information. No serious scholar of wine will keep secrets from fellow students. The discovery of a great wine is knowledge to be shared. Tasting rooms are places where anecdotes are told and tips are given.

I learned about California wines during my undergraduate years in southern California, where I belonged to a circle of friends who shared bottles of wine over dinner. We eagerly searched out the bottlings of now-closed local wineries in San Bernardino's Cucamonga and Guasti districts—always hoping for that truly special

A soft light illuminates a Domaine Chandon vineyard in the southern Napa Valley.

wine that would justify our efforts. We found it one day over lunch in a small Basque restaurant just off Route 66. The proprietor, after discussing the short wine list with us and listening to our wine talk, excused himself and vanished through a cellar door. He returned a short while later, carrying a pitcher of deeply colored red wine. He poured a little into our glasses, and we sipped, sniffed, and exclaimed. This wine, made by the restaurateur from local grapes, was some of the best red any of us had ever tasted straight from the barrel. I don't remember the name of the restaurant or the variety of grapes from which the wine was made, but I can still vividly recall its heady aroma and complex flavors.

When I first traveled to the northern California Wine Country in 1968, I was underwhelmed. Where I had expected a sea of vines, there was hardly a vine in sight. Prohibition and the Great Depression had pushed most wineries out of business in the 1930s, and only on the valley floor near Rutherford and north of St. Helena had some of them hung on. Still, the wines I tasted at the few wineries open to the public were very good. Food, however, was a real disappointment. You could get a hamburger, or greasy fried chicken, or unidentifiable meat smothered in brown sauce, but it was impossible to find a meal that would incite culinary passion.

In those days, few people had learned to appreciate cabernet sauvignon, and even fewer had heard of chardonnay, which existed in limited plantings in only a few vineyards—at rarefied places such as Stony Hill, high above the Napa Valley floor. Sylvaner (labeled "Riesling" by local custom), Green Hungarian, and carignane were varieties everyone drank. The latter might be labeled claret, "burgundy," or whatever name struck the vintner's fancy. The great red wines of California—cabernet sauvignon from Beaulieu and Inglenook, zinfandel from Ridge—were hard to find.

But change was in the air. Stately old wineries like Beaulieu and Christian Brothers, as well as Robert Mondavi's new place in Oakville, were attracting increasing numbers of visitors. Wine had become socially acceptable—not only to the so-called upper 10,000, who always drank good wine, but also to millions of middle-class American gourmets. New converts flocked to the wineries to learn more about wine and to taste the elixirs at their source. New wineries sprouted from the vineyards with every vintage. Old stone buildings, abandoned during Prohibition, were resurrected. Neglected farmhouses were saved from oblivion, restored, and turned into tasting rooms. Within a decade, the Napa Valley's focus shifted from mundane agricultural pursuits—such as walnuts, figs, olives, peaches, and prunes—to a search for excellence in wine making. Sonoma County was not far behind.

Soon there were outcries that too many wineries were ruining the pastoral valleys, but to my eyes the wine-producing valleys—Napa, Sonoma, Russian River, Alexander, Knights, and Dry Creek, as well as the gentle hills of the Carneros—are prettier than they were before. Vineyards have supplanted pastures and prune orchards, and beautifully designed and constructed wineries have replaced rusty equipment sheds.

As local wineries gained international respect for their wines, Napa and Sonoma took their rightful place among the great wine-producing districts of the world. Today, there is more good wine than ever, and the quality of food and lodging has caught up with the wine, making the valleys and mountains of Napa and Sonoma some of the best places to visit—anywhere.

The matching of local wines to food started in the home kitchens of vintners and gained international recognition when French master chef Madeleine Kamman started her program for professional chefs at Beringer Vineyards in the late 1980s. The quest for culinary excellence in the Wine Country received a major boost in 1995, when New York's Culinary Institute of America, one of this nation's premier schools for chefs, opened its West Coast campus in the old Greystone Winery building north of St. Helena.

The outlook for both local wine and food is bright. Napa Valley winegrower Andy Beckstoffer points out that the quality of the average wines produced in Napa and Sonoma Counties is now so high that the gap between them and premium wines has narrowed to where grapegrowers and winemakers must widen it—to keep distinctive wines truly distinct—by raising the quality of premium wines ever higher. I can hardly wait to taste them.

Wine is more than a beverage. To fully understand it, you must know its background. We are inviting you on a tour of the landscape where some of the world's best wines are produced. We shall give you a short history of the region and introduce you to the men and women who grow the grapes and make the wine, as well as to the chefs who create the dishes that enhance wine's place at the table. Pour yourself a glass of wine, sit back and relax, and we'll be on our way.

T H E   S E T T I N G

The northern California Wine Country is noted for its beautiful landscape and equable climate. It has tall mountains and sandy beaches; rocky, storm-tossed cliffs and quiet rivers; waterfowl marshes and redwood forests. Above all, it has vineyards that produce some of the finest wines in the world. Most of the wineries, even the famous ones, are open to visitors, and the small towns that dot the countryside make everyone feel welcome.

In the past two decades, food has taken its proper place next to wines in the area. Like many of the wines, the foods are Mediterranean in spirit, and like Mediterranean peoples everywhere, those in the Wine Country are ever willing to discuss their food—over a glass of wine, of course. They have every reason to be proud of it. Farmers' markets teem with fruits and vegetables. Cattle, goats, and sheep thrive in the hillside pastures and give rich milk, which is made into a greater variety of cheese than you'll find anywhere else in the United States. Figs and oranges can be eaten right off the tree. If this makes the Wine Country sound like

a veritable garden of Eden, that's because it is.

But there's more to the Wine Country than wine and food. You can walk quiet trails under ageless redwoods, stroll in sunny wildflower meadows, or silently glide over hills and vineyards in a hot-air balloon. You might explore an old Spanish mission and fortress, linger in Mexican plazas, or submerge yourself in the boisterous atmosphere of an old-fashioned stern-wheeler on the Napa River. In the Sierra foothills wine country, you can wander through old ghost towns, visit gold mines, and descend deep limestone caverns. You can raft on wild whitewater rapids or skip through alpine meadows. You can bask on rivers in the Delta and Lodi regions and navigate the twisting waterways and sloughs by boat, or you can picnic on the levees under the deep, cooling shade of ancient valley oaks.

If you visit Central Coast wineries, you might head for the old Spanish towns of Monterey, San Luis Obispo, and Santa Barbara or go surfing at Santa Cruz. You could linger on long sand beaches and investigate tidal pools, or watch sea otters, elephant seals, and, sometimes, migrating whales. There are giant redwoods to keep you humble, and the rugged Santa Cruz and Santa Lucia Mountains to hike and climb.

Throughout the region, you'll find numerous opportunities to join residents at small-town fiestas, community barbecues, and wine festivals. This book will guide you to some of the best wineries in California, but we hope you will also follow us as we explore the region's history, meet its wildlife, hike the trails, and drive the back roads. And we hope you'll join us for a picnic, as we sit on the ferny bank of a placid stream, with flowers in our hair, breaking our fast with a loaf of bread, a slice of cheese, and a bottle of wine.

(following pages) A worker at Buena Vista Vineyard in the town of Sonoma fills and records sparkling wine bottles in this circa-1870 stereographic image by Eadweard Muybridge.

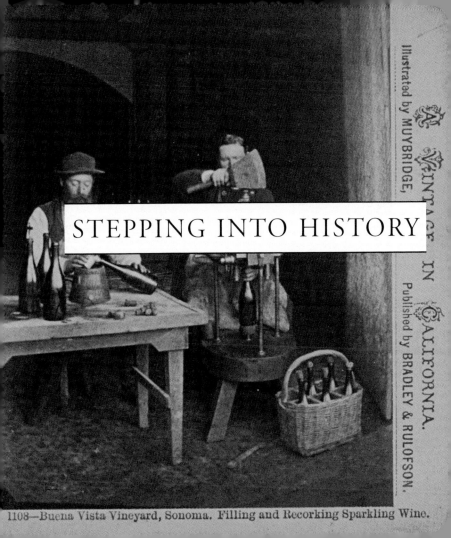

STEPPING INTO HISTORY

Illustrated by MUYBRIDGE, Published by BRADLEY & RULOFSON.

A VINTAGE IN CALIFORNIA.

1108—Buena Vista Vineyard, Sonoma. Filling and Recorking Sparkling Wine.

The afternoon has turned very hot and you search for a shady spot. You find it on rough-hewn wooden steps running from the balcony to the dusty patio. You sit down and look around. This is truly a courtyard that time forgot. Behind you rise the thick, whitewashed walls of an adobe building. In a gloomy passageway, you can just make out the silhouette of an old cannon. To your right, a white adobe wall, topped with red tiles, cuts off the outside world; to your left rises an exotic dome structure, also whitewashed: a beehive oven for baking breads and meats. It is flanked by an outdoor grill of two large *parilla* gridirons set into knee-high adobe walls. A prickly pear cactus, as tall as a small tree, sprawls over the far wall of the courtyard. The edges of its paddle-shaped stems are studded with the bright red fruit Mexicans call *tuna*.

The scents of countless flowers waft through the courtyard, and a mockingbird sings in a nearby tree. As you sample the smells and sounds of a Sonoma afternoon, you remember what you have learned about local history and you imagine yourself back a century and a half, when these adobe walls were part of the great fortress of the north—the *palacio* of the Mexican military commander Gen. Mariano Guadalupe Vallejo. A horse whinnies in the distance. You can almost hear—mingled with the singing of the birds and the rustling of the leaves—the creaking of leather saddles, the jingling of harness rings, and the muttering of Mexican soldiers, grumbling because they have been sent to this remote northern outpost.

They had reason to grumble. They had just returned from another fruitless chase after the Wappo of the upper Napa Valley and the Wintun of the Suisun marshes on the lower Sacramento River. With its soothing scenery and mild climate, Napa would be paradise, were it not for the native tribes who refused to surrender their ancestral lands without a fight.

■ EARLY SPANISH PRESENCE

This area of northern California was settled by Europeans half a century later than the lands south of San Francisco Bay. Spanish padres came first. Father José Altimira, a headstrong Catalan, founded San Francisco de Solano mission at Sonoma in 1823, at the very end of the mission period, without permission from his clerical superiors. Although he was censured, he allied himself with the secular authorities and managed to have the mission legitimized by the church. The Spanish had constant trouble with the native tribes, but the mission prospered, and the padres following in Altimira's footsteps established ranchos in the

Gen. Mariano Vallejo poses comfortably with his daughters and granddaughters, many of whom went on to marry prominent Californians.

Detail of the Blue Wing Inn, built in 1840 by General Vallejo, across the street from the Sonoma Mission.

Petaluma, Sonoma, and lower Napa Valleys, where they raised cattle and planted olives and grapes. Travelers of that time reported that the wine being made was indifferent at best. But it was good enough to be served at Mass, and it made decent *aguardiente* (brandy).

Wine was first made by the padres at Mission San Juan Capistrano in 1782 from grapes planted three years earlier. But secular wine was not far behind. According to John Melville's *Guide to California Wines,* the first wine-making layman of record was Gen. Pedro Fages, who planted a vineyard alongside his orchards in 1783, not far from his residence in Monterey, Alta California. In the early 19th century Dona Marcelina Felix Dominguez, the first known woman winegrower in California, planted at Montecito near Santa Barbara a fabulous vine that in good years would bear from four to six tons of grapes. (Known as La Vieja de la Parra Grande, or "The Old Lady of the Grapevine," she was said to be 105 years old when she died in 1865.) Production increased, but the quality of California wine did not improve much after the missions were secularized in the early 1830s, primarily because wine continued to be made only from the mission grape.

In Sonoma, Gen. Mariano Vallejo proved it was possible to get along with the natives. He made peace with the fiercest of his enemies, a Suisun leader known as Sem Yeto. Yeto was baptized, took the Christian name of Francisco Solano, and became one of Vallejo's most loyal friends and the leader of his native troops. Later, Solano took charge of the Sonoma *palacio* and its garrison.

General Vallejo was the first secular grapegrower in Sonoma. When he was put in charge of secularization in the North Bay country, he parceled out much of the former mission ranchos of today's Sonoma and Napa Counties—as far as the Dry Creek Valley and lower Lake County—to his relatives and friends, keeping prime properties like the Petaluma Valley and the rich lands bordering the lower Napa River for himself. He bestowed the lands bordering the tribes of the upper Napa Valley on Anglo adventurers, known to be at least as fierce as the indigenous people with whom they were to live.

■ ANGLO ADVENTURERS ARRIVE

George C. Yount, a mountain man who had come to Sonoma Mission in the 1820s and stayed to perform odd jobs, was granted Rancho Caymus, in the heart of the Napa Valley, in 1834. He built himself a block house—equipped with rifle ports—right smack in the middle of an Indian *ranchería,* and managed to keep his foothold. Edward T. Bale, an irascible British physician who had married one of Vallejo's nieces, was pushed off to the upper Napa Valley after he tried to shoot down Salvador Vallejo, the General's brother. Bale gave his rancho an oddly derived name when he changed the native name *Callajomanas* (a Wappo word of unknown meaning) to *Carne Humana* ("Human Flesh"). The grist mill Bale built on his ranch still stands. It has been restored, and on most weekends you can watch state park rangers grind by waterpower. Both Yount and Bale planted some grapes, but they were not instrumental in getting the Napa wine industry started. That was left to Bale's son-in-law, Charles Krug.

Back in Sonoma, on June 15, 1846, a ragtag band of American mountain men and adventurers surrounded the adobe fortress of Vallejo. After arresting Vallejo, his brother Salvador, and his secretary, Victor Prudon, the mountain men raised a makeshift flag decorated with a star, a badly painted bear, and a strip of red flannel. While their compatriots rushed Vallejo to John C. Frémont, who was camped on the American River near present-day Sacramento, the rebels, under the command of William B. Ide, declared California an independent republic. Neither side knew that the United States and Mexico had been at war for more than a month and that U.S. troops were about to land and take possession of all of California, including Sonoma.

Ide had made his declaration from the "Fortress of Sonoma," but Vallejo was kept prisoner in another fortress—that of John Sutter at Sacramento. This must have seemed like betrayal to many of the region's Hispanic citizens, especially since there is evidence that Vallejo had rigged the rebellion because he favored annexation of California by the Americans. En route to Frémont's camp, he refused to be rescued near Vacaville by a superior Mexican force under Juan Padilla, and he was certainly not shy about his continuing pro-American sympathies after his release. Holding no grudges, he did not object when his eldest daughter, Epifania, married Capt. J.B. Frisbie, U.S. Army, the commander of the barracks of Sonoma—which is what Vallejo's former *palacio* became under the new regime.

Since Vallejo had to move out of his fortress, he built himself an American-style mansion down the road, where he and his wife lavishly entertained visitors. This villa, named Lachryma Montis for the natural springs gushing from the ground, has been well preserved and is now part of Sonoma State Park. Later, he platted the city of Vallejo and offered it to the state as the site for the new capital. (Monterey, the old capital, was too far from the scene of the California Gold Rush and the most densely populated areas of

The Bale Grist Mill, just north of St. Helena.

the state: the San Francisco Bay Area, Sacramento, and the Sierra foothills.) The legislature ultimately preferred Sacramento, but it did grant Vallejo's wish and named the county in honor of Vallejo's Indian ally, Solano. Yet General Vallejo did not rest idly on his laurels. He continued making wines. Soon they were winning honors, and among proud relics of the old grandee are numerous premiums and medals, as well as a solid silver pitcher, a state fair trophy for his finest claret.

■ HARASZTHY FOUNDS BUENA VISTA

Vallejo was the first secular grapegrower in the Sonoma Valley, but the big push toward commercial production came from Agoston Haraszthy, a Hungarian immigrant encouraged by Vallejo (two of the general's daughters married Haraszthy's sons). Haraszthy, the founder of Sonoma's Buena Vista Winery, is often given credit as the first to plant European grape varieties in Northern California. That has since been disproved. Napa Valley vintners, among them George Beldon Crane and Sam Brannan, may have had more to do with introducing high-quality European vinifera grapes to the region than did Agoston Haraszthy.

Bottling wine in the 1870s at Buena Vista.

Nevertheless, Haraszthy deserves credit for two breakthroughs. During the mission and rancho periods, grapes were grown in the lowlands, close to sources of irrigation water. At Buena Vista, Haraszthy planted grapes on dry hillsides, proving that the climate was sufficiently moist to sustain grapes without irrigation. He was also the first to experiment with using redwood barrels for aging wine—an innovation that would become the most popular storage method of the California wine industry for almost 100 years. The adoption of inexpensive redwood over expensive oak went hand in hand with the boom in grape plantings in the Napa and Sonoma Valleys. Because the vines are very prolific, vintners were slow to replace the mission grape (a Spanish vinifera variety also known as *criolla*), which gives inferior wine, with better varieties of French, German, and Italian vinifera grapes.

In the 1860s, most Napa Valley wines still came from some 2,000 acres of mission grapes, and as late as 1876, Charles Krug ranted about the use of these inferior grapes for making wine. But a new red-wine grape was becoming popular, both because it made excellent claret (as good red wine was then called) and because it had adapted to the area's climate: the zinfandel.

Zinfandel, a grape of mysterious European origin, adapted well to the Napa and Sonoma climate.

THE VINTAGE IN CALIFORNIA—AT WORK AT

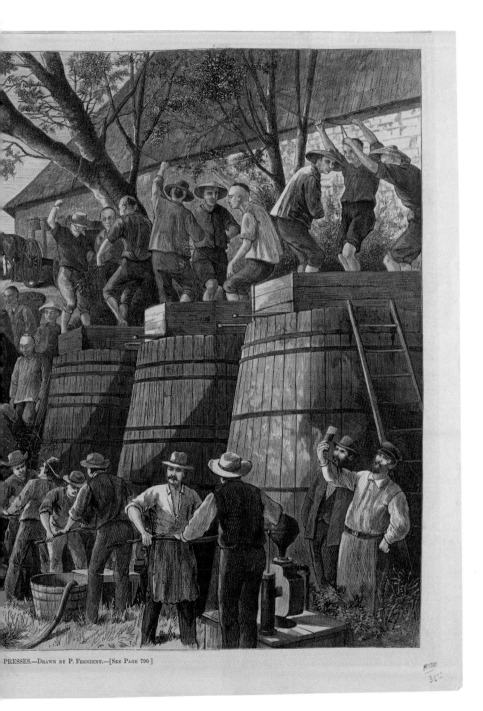

PRESSES.—Drawn by P. Frenzeny.—[See Page 790.]

■ 19TH-CENTURY IMPROVEMENTS

The second half of the century may be called Napa Valley's German age, because so many winemakers came from that country. German winemakers like Charles Krug and Jacob Schram set the tone for the style of wines made in the Napa Valley for years. The Italians, who also were very successful, came later. Many 19th-century vintners were immigrants from elsewhere in Europe, but Americans more than held their own. Charles Nordhoff wrote in 1872, "I was told that the Americans, where they attend to the business, become the most skillful and successful of all. . . ." Time has proved him right.

Wine-making methods had improved dramatically since the 1840s, when rancho Indians trod out the grapes in cowhide bags. J. J. Sigrist, whose vineyard was a few miles from Napa, distinguished himself by making "his wine from each variety of grape singly—Quite definitely a trend with a future." Pioneers such as Sigrist experimented with more than grapes and wine making; they also pioneered a new style of architecture. Most of the imposing stone wineries that still dominate hillsides in the Wine Country were built during this period.

When Gustave Niebaum built a new winery at Inglenook in Rutherford in the 1880s, he gave the quality of Napa wines a boost, not only by planting prime vinifera grapes and practicing meticulously clean methods of vinification, but also by bottling wines at the winery in large quantities for shipping, instead of having them bottled at the shipper's office in San Francisco. This ran counter to the prevailing practice of shipping the wine in barrels, or even railroad tank cars, to a shipper in San Francisco, the Midwest, or the East Coast, where the wine would be aged and bottled. (Not all of those shippers were honest, and some wine reached the market in adulterated form.)

Charles Krug and other California vintners traveling to the East Coast learned that what happened to the wine back East did not necessarily enhance the Napa and Sonoma Valleys' reputation, especially since some of the better vintages were bottled under fake European labels while indifferent wine was bottled as "California." The practice of shipping wine by the barrel allowed the shippers who stored the wine to set the purchase and sales prices of their wines and thus directly influence the money paid to the vintners. By speeding up or delaying the release of a vintage, the shippers could glut or starve the market. This ultimately led to com-

(previous pages) This engraving by 19th-century French artist Paul Frenzeny shows workers, many of them Chinese, crushing grapes with their feet and working the wine presses.

plete control of the market by the San Francisco wine houses, who in 1894 consolidated their power by forming the powerful—and monopolistic—California Wine Association. This monopoly would dominate the local wine industry until the onset of Prohibition.

■ VINEYARDS EXPAND AND SUFFER

During this formative time, vineyard plantings expanded into new territories. Jacob Schram planted grapes in Sonoma's Knights Valley, starting the link of that outlying Sonoma wine valley with Napa Valley producers. In Sonoma County, the Korbel Brothers established a successful sparkling-wine operation in the Russian River Valley; the Kunde family became major grapegrowers; and the Dry Creek Valley grew into a stronghold of Italian family wineries. Napa vintners planted grapes in the nearby Conn, Pope, and Chiles Valleys; on Howell Mountain; on the rolling green hills of the Carneros; and in Solano County's Green Valley (which should not be confused with Sonoma County's Green Valley).

Around the turn of the century, the vineyards were struck by phylloxera, a vine-destroying root louse (see "Glossary," page 342). The only way to fight this bug was to replant the vines on resistant root stocks—a process that was often uncertain. (The problem of dealing with phylloxera has not yet been satisfactorily resolved—in the 1990s, as in the 1890s, Sonoma and Napa vineyards were struck again.)

Once this was accomplished, the vineyards flourished. Many of the workers who dug the caves, constructed the stone wineries, and built the stone fences still snaking across the hillsides were Chinese. The Chinese had come to the American West to help build the transcontinental railroad, and when that job was done, they turned to agricultural pursuits. In the Napa and Sonoma Valleys, they not only helped build the wineries, but also cleared the land, tilled the soil, harvested the grapes, and in some cases, made the wine.

Most Chinese were driven out of California in the early 1890s because of anti-Asian agitation in San Francisco, and Napa Valley vintners hated to see them go. Immigrant workers from Italy and other regions of southern Europe took over the jobs vacated by the Chinese. Because of their heritage, the Italians, unlike their Chinese predecessors, had a keen interest in wine making. It was during this period that the first Italian family wineries were established in northern California, wineries that would make a major share of the region's wine for the next century.

(left) Barrel making has changed little since Roman times. (above) Howard C. Tibbetts, a San Francisco commercial photographer, documented wine making and bottling at a California winery in 1911.

Picking grapes in an Italian Swiss Colony vineyard in the 1880s.

■ ITALIAN SWISS COLONY

The most successful of the Italian enterprises was the Italian Swiss Colony, based in Asti, on the northern frontier of the Sonoma Wine Country. It was designed as a cooperative winery by San Francisco financier Andrea Sbarboro. Sbarboro had made a success in creating several self-help investment schemes, structured much like today's credit unions, and he thought it was time to provide work for the local Italian immigrants. In 1881, he rounded up Dr. Paolo de Vecchi and other investors to found a mutual aid society whose purpose would be to buy empty land, plant it to grapes, make wine, and turn a tidy profit. The workers involved in the scheme would receive wages at first; later they could invest part of their earnings and become stockholders.

The first part of the scheme worked. The society, incorporated as the Italian Swiss Colony (the "Swiss" was added to welcome Italian-speaking settlers from Switzerland's Ticino canton), bought land along the Russian River just south of Cloverdale in 1882, where the climate was like that of northern Italy. Although it was not "empty," part of it having been planted to grain, it seemed highly suitable for viticulture. The project made money right from the start. Much of the land had to be cleared of madrona, manzanita, and oak, but the workers turned the wood into charcoal, which was sold at a profit. Once the land was cleared, grape acreage increased rapidly. It became clear that the colony would be a financial success. It turned out, however, that the investors were not interested in working in the vineyards or winery, and the workers were not interested in becoming entrepreneurs, so the Italian Swiss Colony's by-laws were changed.

Pietro Carlo Rossi, an Italian immigrant, was hired as winemaker and general manager with free rein. In 1888, the winery made 130,000 gallons of wine from such classic Italian grapes as barbera, grignolino, nebbiolo, and sangiovese; by 1895 the capacity had reached a million gallons; in 1902, after the winery had expanded into other wine-growing districts, it reached 10 million gallons.

Quality mattered more to the Italian Swiss Colony than quantity. Following Rossi's maxim that "Pure wines are the gospel at Asti," the winery not only strove to make ever better wines, it also searched for improved ways to send them to market. Between 1904 and 1905, the colony began bottling wines in its San Francisco facilities and shipped the wine, in the bottle, up and down the coast—something almost unheard of at the time, despite Gustave Niebaum's earlier efforts. This new way of shipping wine was helped along by the Pure Food and Drug Act of 1906, which discouraged the altering of wines by the shipper. Even then, almost no wine was shipped to the East Coast in the bottle; it still went by tank car and barrel as before. All these wine tank cars came in handy during Prohibition, when no wine could be legally shipped, but it was perfectly legal to ship juice (and grapes) across the country for wine manufacture by home winemakers.

The Italian Swiss Colony was bought by the California Wine Association (CWA), but at the onset of Prohibition the CWA divested itself of its assets and sold the colony to several CWA employees, who kept the winery alive by selling grapes to home winemakers. After the repeal of Prohibition the Italian Swiss Colony never quite regained its former glory. In 1942—when the government outlawed the making of whiskey because grain was needed for the war effort—the Italian Swiss Colony was sold to National Distillers. After the war, it changed hands frequently until it became merely a label, like so many other old wineries.

■ Elsewhere in California

Vineyards came early to the Sierra foothills, because wineries were established during the Gold Rush to supply the gold miners with wine. Although most of these wineries fell victim to Prohibition, many of the vineyards survived. In the 1970s, some of these vineyards were resurrected, and their very old vines now produce very intense wines.

The Lodi area saw vineyards planted in the mid- to late 1800s, as did the Santa Clara Valley, where French immigrants such as Charles Lefranc noted that the soils and climate were perfect for raising grapes. Several vintners, most notably Paul Masson, moved into the Santa Cruz Mountains after loggers cleared the slopes of giant redwoods. A few of these wineries hung on through Prohibition and the Depression, but they fell victim to the rapid expansion of Silicon Valley in the late 1990s. Still, some of the highest mountain vineyards have survived and are being tended by new wineries.

In San Luis Obispo County, vineyards and wineries were established in the hills east of Arroyo Grande and west of Paso Robles in the 1880s. Of these, only a few wineries in the latter area survived until the late 1900s, when they joined the new wine revolution. By contrast, Santa Barbara County had few vines (except for those planted by mission padres to make sacramental wine) until the 1960s and 1970s, yet its Santa Ynez and Santa Maria Valleys have quickly joined the ranks of California's major viticultural regions.

■ Prohibition and Repeal

The National Prohibition Act, which passed in 1919 under the popular name of the Volstead Act, had an unlikely effect on Napa and Sonoma wineries. Several, such as Beaulieu, Beringer, and the Christian Brothers, stayed in business by making sacramental wines; others survived by shipping grape juice or grapes to home wine-makers. This, along with the rising demand for grapes, resulted in more grapes being grown in California at the end of Prohibition than at its start. Unfortunately, quality had declined. Growers had grafted over their vineyards to high-yielding red varieties such as the red-juiced alicante bouschet, which allowed home wine-makers to make more gallons of wine per ton of grapes than other grape varieties—especially if the juice was enhanced with a generous helping of cane sugar.

Many wineries shut down and growers planted their land with fruit and nut trees, but several wineries kept their inventories in bond, meaning it was put in a warehouse certified by the Department of Internal Revenue and guaranteed by a bonding agency until necessary duties or taxes could be paid. The wine magically flowed out the back door of these bonded warehouses into barrels and carboys brought by customers, and just as magically it seemed to replenish itself. Now and then a revenuer would crack down, but enforcement seems to have been lax at best.

After the repeal of Prohibition in 1933, restarting legitimate wine making proved difficult. During Prohibition, wineries had lost many of their traditional customers to bathtub gin and cheap cocktails. Those still drinking wine now preferred sweet wines to dry ones. The wine industry's struggle to gain back its customer base did not really end until the 1960s.

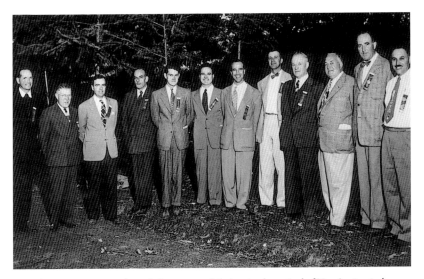

The "baggypants vintners brigade," movers and shakers in the revival of Napa's wine industry, included (left to right): Brother Timothy Diener of Christian Brothers; Charles B. Forni of Sunny St. Helena Co-op; Walter Sullivan and Aldo Fabrini of Beaulieu Vineyard; Michael Ahern of Freemark Abbey; Peter and Robert Mondavi of Krug; John Daniel Jr. of Inglenook; Louis M. Martini, Charlie Beringer, and Martin Stelling of Sunny St. Helena Co-op; and Fred Abruzzini of Beringer.

Old Vine *(1961), by Ansel Adams.*

Man Plowing Vineyard *(1961), by Ansel Adams.*

Man Looking at Bottle *(1961), by Ansel Adams.*

For 40 years after the repeal of Prohibition, much of the wine produced in Sonoma County was shipped in bulk, to be blended or bottled into generic brands. During this time, several Napa Valley wineries brought about a wine renaissance—almost in spite of themselves. To understand what happened, we must go back to the ancient grape-growing districts of Europe, where grapes and fruit trees also alternate in the mosaic of landscapes. In Europe these planting patterns were established centuries ago, with the richer soils always being reserved for fruit trees and the poorer soils assigned to grapes.

Sonoma County has greater patches of rich soil than does Napa, which made it possible for farmers to make a living from fruit trees without having to bother about grapes. With prices of grapes and wines at a Depression-era low, it did not pay to replant idle patches of grape lands, but it paid to harvest those vineyards that had supplied the home winemakers' market during Prohibition. The Napa Valley, on the other hand, is laced with rocky and gravelly slopes, bench lands, and alluvial fans where fruit trees grow poorly, but where grapes thrive. A Napa Valley farmer found it more difficult to make a living on tree fruit alone, so he had to find ways to make vineyards pay as well.

Fortunately, several major wineries had survived Prohibition and laid the foundation for new prosperity. These included Beringer, Beaulieu, Inglenook, Christian Brothers, Louis M. Martini, and, after the Cesare Mondavi family bought the winery in the 1940s, Charles Krug. Considering the all-time low demand for their product—and the state of the American palate—these wineries made some amazingly good wines during this period. But several more decades passed before the vintners' work really paid off, when Christian Moueix of Chateau Petrus tasted some well-aged Inglenook reds from this period and decided to become involved in Dominus Estate, one of the prestigious French/Napa wineries of the 1980s.

From 1947 until the early 1960s, Napa Valley's wine industry seemed to be running in place. In 1949, Idwal Jones published *Vines in the Sun,* a bubbly little book on California wine devoted primarily to the past, with historical anecdotes that may have owed more to fiction than fact. But his descriptions of the contemporary wine scene are lively and prove that wine was alive and well in the Golden Valleys:

> The road from Yountville to the [Robert Louis] Stevenson aerie
> on Mount St. Helena is the Grand Route for those curious about
> vineyards, which here seem to be numberless, and each has its
> "tasting room"—the parlor sometimes; and at the larger farms, the

office where the dossier on every barrel is kept in a metal cabinet. But the valley is not exploited on that account; the taverns or small eating places are ordinary, and the farms are not organized for tourists.

In an oral history, vintner Joe Heitz, one of the wine revolutionaries of the 1960s, blames himself for helping to start the tourist rush to the Napa Valley in the 1950s. It was he who convinced Beaulieu, his employer at the time, to open a tasting room. He nonetheless justifies his action by adding: "If there are no customers, there's no need for wineries."

California wine making, in the period from the end of Prohibition to the wine renaissance of the 1960s, was marked by confusion. Most wineries made drinkable wine, but much of it was marketed under generic names such as "sauterne" or "white burgundy" for whites. White wine came in three styles: dry, medium, and sweet. What passed as "white burgundy" in California was more often than not a blend of any white wine grapes at hand, just like the latter-day California whites known as "chablis" or "Rhine wine."

Red "burgundy" was blended in a similar fashion, but from red wine grapes, which included anything but pinot noir, the noble grape of France's Bourgogne (Burgundy) wine-growing district. "Claret" and "chianti" could also be made from any convenient red wine grape. The known style of an individual winery was more important than the generic name of the wine. To overcome this anarchy of meaningless proprietary and generic names, some wineries began labeling their finer wines with the name of the grape: what was once called "sauterne" became "sauvignon blanc," and "claret" became "cabernet sauvignon."

■ RENAISSANCE

The first proof of real change appeared in 1952, when Eleanor and Fred McCrea released the first of their now legendary chardonnays from Stony Hill Vineyard, a gravelly patch of land high up Spring Mountain, near a summer home they purchased in 1943. This wine set a new standard for California whites and may have inspired millionaire James Zellerbach to build Hanzell, a tiny Sonoma Valley winery dedicated to producing true Burgundian-style wines. Before he died in 1963, Zellerbach's winery had pioneered two methods that have become standard practice in California wine making: fermentation in stainless steel tanks rather than redwood or oak tanks, and the aging of chardonnay in small French Limousin oak barrels (the same oak from which Burgundian wine barrels are traditionally made).

Top row, from left: Robert Mondavi, Jacob Beringer, Frederick Beringer, Charles Krug.
Second row: Agoston Haraszthy, Jack Cakebread, Samuele Sebastiani, David Stare.
Third row: Zelma Long of Simi, Gustave Niebaum, Louis Kunde, Janet and John Trefethen.
Bottom row: Joe Heitz, Eleanor and Fred McCrea, Jim Bundschu.

Wine was about to make a comeback: American soldiers returning from France after World War II and the droves of college students who had traveled on the Continent in the 1950s and '60s brought back the belief that the enjoyment of wine was part of a sophisticated lifestyle. James Zellerbach had shown that it was all right for respectable folk to dabble in wine.

In 1965, Jack and Jamie Davies refurbished Jacob Schram's old cellars and began making first-rate sparkling wines from Napa Valley chardonnay grapes rather than from the colombard or Riesling used by other local producers. In 1966, after a quarrel with his brother Peter, Robert Mondavi left Charles Krug, the family winery, and built a place of his own in Oakville—the first new winery built in the Napa Valley since the repeal of Prohibition.

It was the right move at the right time, just as market demand for high-quality varietals was beginning to rise. He was emulated by Donn and Molly Chappellet on Pritchard Hill in 1969, by Charlie Wagner at Caymus in Rutherford and by David S. Stare at Sonoma County's Dry Creek Vineyard in 1972, by John and Janet Trefethen in Napa, by Fred Fisher on the Sonoma side of the Mayacamas range in 1973, and by many other vintners since. Napa Valley winemakers received a psychological boost in the early 1970s, when the renowned French champagne house of Moët & Chandon bought vineyards and platted a winery site to make French-style sparklers with Napa Valley grapes.

■ PARIS WINE TASTING OF 1976

The event that changed the Wine Country forever happened in Paris in 1976. To celebrate the American Bicentennial, Steven Spurrier, a wine merchant, sponsored a comparative blind tasting of California cabernet and chardonnay wines against Bordeaux cabernet blends and French chardonnays. The tasters were French and included journalists and producers. The 1973 Stag's Leap Wine Cellars cabernet sauvignon came in first among the reds, and the 1973 Chateau Montelena chardonnay edged out the French whites.

When the shouting died down, the rush was on. Tourists and winemakers streamed into the Napa Valley. Wine prices rose so much that they even helped revitalize the Sonoma County wine industry; in Sonoma as in Napa, prune orchards were supplanted by vines.

Barrels of aging wine are labeled in an old stone cellar.

■ PRECIOUS LAND

In the 1980s, the Napa Valley's rustic lifestyle seemed doomed by weekend home buyers who didn't mind plunking down a million dollars or more for a place amid the vines. But as the Valley's popularity increased, so did opposition to development that might threaten vineyards and wineries. By 1988, the battle lines had been drawn between pro-growth and farm-preservation factions. The pro-growth crowd won a hotly contested county-supervisor election in the fall of 1988, but when the newly elected supervisors granted too many land-use exceptions to developers, the pro-farm faction initiated a ballot proposition that would allow no modification of the Valley's agricultural preserve and watershed for the next 30 years without the voters' approval. The measure passed by a wide margin in 1990, and though challenged in court, it was declared legal in 1994.

Sonoma County also saw increased development, but it has more land: when suburban sprawl forced Landmark Vineyards out of the Windsor area, the winery moved into the upper Sonoma Valley. Other Sonoma wine regions are far enough from urban areas that they may not have to worry about encroachment for decades.

Stainless steel vats (above, at Domaine Chandon) are also used to ferment wine.

■ REAL CALIFORNIA WINES

Victory on the agrarian front has not brought complacency. As you travel through the Sonoma and Napa wine regions today, tasting the wines, talking to the wine-makers, you sense a change in the air. No longer are wineries going all out to make the best French-style wine they can: they are striving to make the best possible California wine. This involves harvesting grapes at the optimum time, not only for grape sugars (which will be fermented into alcohol) but also for freshness and complexity.

There used to be an almost desperate struggle to keep the alcohol level of California wines down to 12 percent by volume, which is the norm in France, where winemakers sometimes augment their fermenting must with sugar to reach even a 12 percent alcohol content. In California, where grapes ripen more fully than they do in France, keeping the alcohol content down meant harvesting grapes too young, before their complex flavors had fully developed. Today, it is accepted that California wines are different. Despite an alcohol content that may reach 14.5 percent, the wines are well balanced and do not seem overly alcoholic.

Fermentation, too, is undergoing a revolution. Instead of importing the European yeasts used to make Champagne, Montrachet (the finest white Burgundy), or Bordeaux reds, the winemakers try to capture the wild yeasts of their own vineyards to imbue their wines with the particular quality of the place.

But California vintners are no longer sure that undiluted cabernet sauvignon and chardonnay, the warhorses of the 1970s and 1980s, are the best grapes for the region. As a result, blends are back, many of them under the catch-all label "Meritage," or under a proprietary name. White Meritage is mostly a blend of sauvignon blanc and sémillon, for example, but red Meritage may be made from cabernet sauvignon with a liberal addition of merlot, cabernet franc, malbec, petit verdot, or other Bordeaux varieties. Other blends might not contain any cabernet at all, such as new reds based on red Rhône varieties, including mourvèdre, syrah, or grenache.

Traditional Italian varieties—barbera, grignolino, nebbiolo, and sangiovese, cousins of the grapes first planted by the Italian Swiss Colony at Asti 100 years ago—are also making a strong comeback. Even the Robert Mondavi winery, a leader in the promotion of inky cabernet sauvignons, is planting several varieties from the Rhône region and from Italy.

But don't worry if you've just learned to tell Howell Mountain from Carneros chardonnay or Dry Creek from Chiles Valley zinfandel. Change comes slowly in the Wine Country, and you'll still have all your old favorites to taste as you explore the new varietals.

Wooden vats for aging wine.

VISITING WINERIES
TASTING AND TOURING

Let us assume that you have parked your car under an arbor of blooming wisteria vines. The winery, a rambling building sheathed in naturally weathered redwood, rises to your left from thickets of roses in full bloom. Several climbing roses cover the entrance trellis. You pause before you enter, because the view down the valley across vineyards and oak copses is breathtaking. Mountains covered with a dark evergreen forest rise straight from the valley floor on the far side of the vineyards. Behind the winery, the vineyard abuts a rocky slope studded with blue oaks and gray pines. A pair of ravens circle overhead and a covey of quail chatter and cluck among the willows and cottonwoods lining a creek bed. A quail's distinctive call rises from a scrub oak thicket on the hillside and is answered by another from a willow tangle. A cow lows in the distance. You tear yourself away from this pastoral scene and enter the winery's tasting room.

■ INTO THE TASTING ROOM

Tasting rooms are very common among wineries in Napa and Sonoma Counties, and visiting them is essential to any Wine Country trip. They're generally well marked and easy to find—so much so that on a sunny weekend between April and October they're liable to be packed with tourists and Bay Area locals.

Don't worry if you know nothing about wine or the whys and wherefores of "tasting." Tasting rooms are very relaxed places. They're designed to introduce novices to the pleasures of wines as well as to give the more accomplished a chance to expand their knowledge. If you're a novice, everyone will be glad to help—wine is a very social beverage. Besides, there's no magic to tasting wine. All you need is a palate and a little common sense.

Wine is evaluated by appearance, aroma, and flavor, as follows.

■ THE WINE'S APPEARANCE

The first thing to judge when tasting wine is its appearance. No matter whether it's white, rosé, or red, a wine should be clear, without cloudiness or sediments when you drink it. Some unfiltered wines may seem cloudy at first, but they will clear as the sediments settle down. Such wines need to be decanted very carefully to avoid stirring up the sediments. Hold the wine up to a window to let more natural light flow through the glass and show up any cloudiness.

Signs point the way to some of the Sonoma Valley's leading wineries.

Natural light is best when checking wine for clarity and color.

Next, check the color. Is it right for the wine? A California white should be clear golden: straw, medium, or deep, depending on the type. The latter is acceptable in rich, sweet, dessert wine but out of place in a chardonnay or sauvignon blanc. A rosé should be a clear pink—not too red, and without touches of orange or brown. A brown tinge in white and rosé wines usually means that the wine is too old, over the hill, or has been stored badly. Reds may have a violet tinge when young, a hint of amber when well aged (at that stage it is permissible for reds to have deposits, but the wine should be decanted before being poured: a glass is not the proper place for settling out deposits). A definite brown color is a flaw in reds, as is paleness—unless you're looking at a pinot noir. Good wine made from this grape can be quite pale yet still have character.

■ THE WINE'S AROMA

After you have looked the wine over, swirl it gently in your glass and stick your nose into the glass. Aroma may well be the most important part of wine: your nose actually plays a larger role in tasting wine than your palate does, because the human palate can only perceive four basic tastes: salt, bitter, sour, and sweet.

Most of the aromas in wine are appealing. You might smell apricots, peaches, ripe melon, honey, and wildflowers in a white wine; black pepper, cherry, violets, and cedar in a red. Rosés are made from red wine grapes and thus have scents similar to those of a red wine, but on a more gentle scale and with hints of raspberry, geranium, and, sometimes, a touch of pomegranate. Each grape variety has its own distinct aroma. With experience you'll learn to recognize it. Wine with good varietal character is better than wine with indistinct aromas.

Of course, there are times when you are in the mood for a wine with a light aroma rather than a heavy, complex one. There's nothing wrong with this. A wine does not have to be "great" and complex to be thoroughly enjoyable. But the aroma of such a wine should be clean and pleasing. It should never be "off" or smell of such things as sauerkraut, wet cardboard, garlic, wet dog, or skunk—strange, unpleasant odors all listed on the official Wine Aroma Wheel of the American Society for Enology and Viticulture, along with such scents as moldy, horsey, mousy, and sweaty. If you're tasting a heavier wine, you'll want to sniff for such chemical faults as sulfur, or excess wood vanillin from the oak.

After you've judged the aroma, it's time to evaluate the acidity. All wine has acid, which is necessary to balance the fruit of the wine and give it backbone. But the acidity should be tasted and not smelled. If the wine smells like acetic acid, it has started turning into vinegar. Don't drink it. Use it to make salad dressing.

■ FLAVORS FOUND IN WINE

You're now ready to take your first sip of the wine. Does it feel pleasant? Do you like it? If not, don't drink it. You should never drink a wine you don't like. Although you may learn to appreciate a wine you don't understand, a wine will never really appeal to you unless you like it to begin with.

Now let's run through the four tastes the palate can process. The first, salt, is not a natural component of wine. And if you taste light bitterness in young reds, taste again. You'll soon discover that the wine's tannic tartness can fool the palate. True bitterness is a fault, and it's thankfully rare in wine. As for sourness, there is no such thing as a "sour" wine—at least not in the opinion of the experts. What you perceive as sour is called astringent, acidic, or tart by enophiles. Taste for sugar. Sweetness—perceived or real—is found in many wines, even in some wines claiming to be dry. Many wines have become sweeter in recent years, perhaps because the American consumer does have a sweet tooth. But it's a very light sweetness, barely at the threshold of perception. The traditional belief is that a dinner wine should have no perceptible sweetness; a dessert wine commonly has quite a bit.

As you taste wine you'll notice more than just the four basic flavors, because your nose continues to "taste" the aromas. A wine taster swirls the wine in his or her mouth, or chews it, to release more aromas, which the nose picks up and analyzes.

When you swirl the wine around in your mouth, how does it feel? Does it seem to fill your mouth, or is it thin and weak? It should be well balanced and feel good. Do you like the flavor? Does it relate to the aroma? If not, something is out of balance. Swallow. Does your throat feel like it's puckering up? Hopefully not.

Most importantly, you should ask yourself if you like the wine. Your appreciation of its general quality is just as important as the individual parts. A wine can be technically perfect but seem very boring nevertheless. Remember: you're the one to decide. It's your taste that matters.

Keep several other things in mind as you taste wine in a tasting room. First, don't overdo it, especially if you are driving. Those little sips add up. And don't feel like you have to buy a bottle of wine just because the winery has given you a taste or two—especially if you paid a tasting fee. You're not required to make a purchase, and though you might experience mildly overt pressure at some of the larger concerns to do so, tasting rooms have traditionally been set up to make customers familiar with a winery's name and product. Of course wineries will be happy, in these difficult economic times, if you buy a bottle or two at the source, and they'll be even happier if you buy a case or two of a wine you really like. You might want to stock up on hard-to-find vintages or varietals. Sometimes these can be bought only at the winery.

If you're an out-of-region visitor, ask about the winery's direct-shipment program. Most wineries now ship directly to consumers in the states that allow shipments of California wine to be received by residents.

■ MAKING WINE

If you have enjoyed your taste of wine, you might want to tour a winery and see how the wine is made. Such a tour will be most rewarding between August and October, when most of the grapes ripen and are crushed and fermented into wine. At other times of the year, winery work consists of monitoring the wine, "racking" it—that is, transferring it from one tank or barrel to another to leave deposits behind—or bottling and boxing the finished wine.

Stemmer-Crusher: Removes the grapes from their stems and crushes their skins so juice can flow off freely.

Juice that flows from crushed grapes before pressing is called "free-run."

Wine Press: An inflatable bag that gently pushes the grape pulp against a perforated drum.

Fermentation: The process by which the natural fruit sugars of grapes are converted, with the aid of yeasts, into alcohol. Takes place in large vats or tanks or small oak barrels.

White wines are not fermented with pulp and skins. The grapes are pressed before fermentation. White wines may be fermented in small barrels. They are often cool-fermented to preserve their fruitiness.

Racking: After fermentation, wine is racked, that is, moved to new, clean barrels, to aid clarification. It may be filtered or fined or allowed to settle naturally.

Aging: Many premium wines are aged in small oak barrels. Keeping wine in oak too long, though, kills delicate grape flavors and may make the wine taste "woody."

Red wines are fermented with pulp and skins. Some grapes are pressed after fermentation.

Bottling: After wine has been clarified it is ready for bottling. Very small wineries still bottle by hand, but most bottling is done by machine in the sterile environment of a special enclosure, to keep impurities out of the bottle.

Crushing grapes the old-fashioned way . . .

Winery tours can be exciting, but they are all pretty much alike. You can make tours more interesting by visiting different types of wineries. A large winery will make wine in a somewhat different fashion from a small family winery, and sparkling wine is made by a different process. Some wineries age their wines in warehouses, others have caves (pronounced "kahvz," from the French), which are long tunnels bored into the hillsides where the wine remains at an even temperature.

Even if you've taken tours before, you might take another now and then, to refresh your memory.

■ THE WINE CRUSH

Most winery tours start out at the **crush pad.** This is where the grapes are brought in from the vineyards. Grapes are brought to the winery in large containers called **gondolas,** which gently drop the grape bunches onto a conveyor belt. Grapes must be handled with care, so none of the juice is lost. Some wineries pick their grapes by machine, but others still pick by hand. It depends on the terrain and on the type of grape. Some delicate white varieties such as chardonnay are picked at night with the help of powerful floodlights.

. . . and the newfangled way.

Why at night? Because grapes contain natural fruit acids, which not only bring out the fruit but also give the wine its "backbone"—the element that holds it together during fermentation and aging. Grape acids are reduced during the heat of the day, when the sun warms the grapes, but they increase during the cool hours of the night. When white wine grapes are picked at night, they have their highest fruit-acid content. Nighttime picking is not a consideration with red wine grapes, because red wines depend upon acids from the grape skins. With white wines the acid is in the juice and pulp.

The conveyor belt drops the grape clusters into a **stemmer-crusher,** which has a drum equipped with steel fingers that knock the grapes off the stems, and pierce their skins, so the juice can flow off freely. The grapes and juice fall through a grate and are carried via stainless steel pipes to a press or vat. The stems and leaves drop out and are recycled to the vineyards as natural fertilizer.

■ FERMENTING AND AGING WHITE WINES

What happens to the crushed grapes at the next stage depends on what variety of grape has been crushed and what type of wine is being made—white, rosé, or red. The juice of white wine grapes is first sent to settling tanks, where the skins and grape solids settle to the bottom, separating from the clear free-run juice on top. From here the free run is pumped directly to a fermenter—either a stainless steel tank (which may be insulated to keep the fermenting juice cool) or to an oak barrel. The grape skins and other solids that have sunk to the bottom of the tank still contain a lot of juice. They are dropped into a press in which the juice is gently extracted by air pressure. Modern presses have a perforated drum with a Teflon-coated bag inside. As this bag is inflated slowly, like a balloon, it pushes the grapes against the outside wall—slowly and gently—and the liquids are squeezed from the solids and flow off.

Press juice and free-run juice are fermented separately, but a little of the press juice may be added to the free-run juice to give it added complexity. Because press juice tends to be too strongly flavored and may contain undesirable flavor components, winemakers are careful not to add too much of it. Press juice is always fermented in stainless steel tanks; free-run juice may be handled differently. In the case of chardonnay and some sauvignon blanc, free-run juice might be fermented in small oak barrels, in individual batches, with each vineyard and lot kept separate. That's the way some of the very best wine is made, and that's one reason why good white wines are so expensive. It's a very labor-intensive process.

Furthermore, the oak barrels, imported from France, are very expensive and can be used for a few years only. Following French wine-making tradition, California winemakers like to use French oak for aging wine, but some are experimenting with American oak as well. Three types of barrels are made: those of 100 percent American oak; those of 100 percent French oak; and those that are a blend of both.

Barrel aging rooms are kept dark, because electric lights generate heat, and wine does not like to be too warm. Nor does wine like bright light. If exposed to too much light, wine can change in unexpected ways. And if the cork dries out, it shrinks, allowing oxygen to enter the bottle and spoil the wine.

Large stainless steel tanks are used for fermenting wine and for storing white wine. They may be equipped with wraparound cooling sleeves. Sauvignon blanc and Riesling are commonly fermented cool to develop more fruit aromas and delicacy. Chardonnay, as well as some reds, may be fermented in small oak barrels, which makes for a richer wine. Fermentation in small barrels creates more depth and complexity, as the wine picks up vanilla and other harmonious flavors from the wood. When the wine is finished, several batches are blended together. Careful blending gives the winemaker an extra chance to create a perfect wine.

When the wine has finished fermenting, whether in a tank or barrel, it is racked—moved into a clean tank or barrel to separate it from the lees, that is the spent yeast and any grape solids that have dropped out of suspension. At this stage the wine may or may not be filtered, depending on how the winemaker feels about it. Sometimes chardonnay and special batches of sauvignon blanc are left on the lees for extended periods of time before being racked—at the winemaker's discretion—to pick up extra complexity.

If wine is aged for any length of time, it will be racked again and may be fined—clarified by the introduction of agents such as a fine clay called bentonite, or albumen from egg whites. Some wineries filter their wines, especially white ones, and others just fine them. Some reds are left unfined for extra depth. Wine may be filtered after fermentation, before bottling, or whenever the winemaker thinks it necessary. After the wine is bottled, most of it is not kept in storage for long. It goes to a cooperative warehouse from which it is shipped on demand. Many wineries age only their reserve wines in their own cellars.

■ FERMENTING AND AGING RED WINES

Red wine production differs slightly from that of white wine. Red wine grapes are crushed the same way white wine grapes are, but the juice is not separated from the grape skins and pulp before fermentation. This is what gives red wine its color. After crushing, the red wine must (juice) and the grape pulp and skins are pumped into vats where they are fermented together. The must is "left on the skins" for varying periods of time, depending on how much color the winemaker wants to extract. Reds are more robust than whites because the fermentation extracts not only color but also flavors and tannins (special acids that help the wine age) from the skins.

Red wine fermentation occurs at a higher temperature than that for whites—reds ferment at about 70°F to 90°F (21°C to 32°C). As the grape sugars are converted into alcohol, great amounts of carbon dioxide are generated. Carbon dioxide is lighter than wine but heavier than air, and it forms an "aerobic cover" that protects the wine from oxidation. As the wine ferments, grape skins rise to

THE FINE ART OF BARREL MAKING

Creating the oak barrels that age the wine is a craft in its own right. At Demptos Napa Cooperage, a French-owned company that employs French barrel-making techniques, the process involves several elaborate production phases. Below, the staves of oak are formed to the barrel shape using metal bands. At bottom left, semi-finishing takes place to smooth the rough edges off the bound staves. Finally, the barrels are literally toasted (bottom right) to give the oak "flavor," which will in turn be imparted to the wine.

the top and are periodically mixed back in so the wine can extract the maximum amount of color and flavor. This is done either in the traditional fashion by punching them down, or by pumping over the wine and the skins. The former method is preferable since it keeps the carbon dioxide cover intact and minimizes exposure of the wine to oxygen.

At the end of fermentation, the free-run wine is drained off. The grape skins and pulp are sent to a press where the remaining wine is extracted. As with the whites, the winemaker may choose to add a little of the press wine to the free-run wine—if he feels it will add complexity to the finished wine. Otherwise the press juice goes into bulk wine. After the wine has been

An enologist draws wine into a pipette to measure its acidity.

racked, it ages in oak barrels for a year or longer. Unlike many of the barrels used for aging and fermenting chardonnay, the barrels used for aging red wine are not always new. They may already have been used to age chardonnay, which has extracted most of their flavors. Oak, like grapes, contains natural tannins, and the wine extracts these tannins from the barrels. Oak also has countless tiny pores through which water in the wine slowly evaporates, making the wine more concentrated. To make sure the aging wine does not oxidize, the barrels have to be regularly topped off with wine from the same vintage. This increased amount of labor and the fact that some of the wine evaporates, resulting in lower yields, add to the cost of aged wine.

The only way even the best winemaker can tell if a wine is finished is by tasting it. A winemaker constantly tastes wines during fermentation, while they are aging in barrels, and regularly, though less often, while they age in bottles. The wine is released—or "sent to market"—when the winemaker's palate and nose say it's ready.

WINE COUNTRY GEOLOGY

The diverse patterns of soils below Napa Valley's crags befuddle even the most experienced geologist or grapegrower. Some of the soils are composed of dense, heavy sedimentary clays washed from the mountains; others are very rocky clays, loams, or silts of alluvial fans. You'll find similar soils in the wine-growing valleys of Sonoma County. These soils are best for growing grapes when they are composed largely of rocks and pebbles and are thus very porous. Grapes do not like their feet wet. But even here you will find that different grape varieties thrive under different conditions: cabernet sauvignon does best on well-drained, gravelly soils. If the soils are too wet or contain too much heavy clay or organic matter, the wines will have an obnoxious vegetative quality that even the best wine-making techniques cannot remove. Merlot grapes, on the other hand, can take more clay and still be made into wine that tastes rich and complex. Sauvignon blanc grapes do quite well in heavy clay soils, but the winegrower has to prune back vines and leaves to let sun reach the grapes and cut back on irrigation to rid the grapes of such vegetative flavors as green pepper and asparagus—once thought to be varietal characteristics of this white grape, but now considered unacceptable.

A streak of light-colored, almost white soil runs across the Napa Valley from the Palisades to St. Helena and in Sonoma County from the western flanks of the Mayacamas Mountains to Windsor. This soil has been described as limestone—which would be a desirable rock in any wine country, because vines prefer basic soils to acidic ones. But it is actually comprised of volcanic ashes, tufas or tephras, of plutonic (volcanic) rather than neptunic (oceanic) origin. The "limestone" into which Napa Valley wine caves were dug in the 19th century and the pale building stone of Beringer's Rhine House and other Wine Country mansions and wineries was born of volcanic activity, and is thus not limestone at all.

Volcanic ash can be seen in several road cuts along the Napa Valley's Silverado Trail. A particularly good cut is near its northern end, below Glass Mountain, where broad bands of light-colored ash are speckled with flecks of black obsidian. Curiously, volcanic ash, obsidian, and rhyolite rock all have the same chemical composition—even though their outward appearance differs dramatically. They also have the same composition as the light-colored granite—also of plutonic origin—of the Sierra Nevada. These various rocks differ in appearance because the igneous granite slowly cooled under the earth, allowing its minerals to settle out, while the volcanic rocks of the Wine Country cooled rapidly above the earth, keeping the minerals in suspension. Like the Sierra Nevada, the mountains of the Wine

Old zinfandel vines at the Sonoma Valley's Kunde Estate Winery.

Country have produced quantities of silver and gold. The Silverado Mine on Mount St. Helena was made famous by writer Robert Louis Stevenson, but the less romantic Palisades Mine east of Calistoga produced a greater amount of silver and gold and was, for a short time, one of the richest mines in the country. It closed in 1941, but there's still enough of the precious metals in the soil to reopen the mine if the price of silver rises.

As you drive through the mountains of the Wine Country, you may notice almost barren patches of landscape where scrub oak and gray pine predominate, even though nearby slopes are blanketed by lush meadows or woods. These sere patches are underlaid by a gray-green to blue-green rock with a smooth, almost soapy surface. This is serpentine, a rock rarely seen elsewhere on the surface of our planet. If you look closely, you may notice that this odd-colored rock—with a color like petrified essence of ocean waves—does not merge into neighboring rock, but is cut off from it along a fairly sharp edge. That is because serpentine is a rock originating deep within the earth's crust that has been squeezed, unchanged, from its native matrix like paint from a tube. Why? How? No one knows. Unweathered serpentine contains chemicals noxious to most plants and will thus support only a limited number of trees and shrubs. But its nature changes as it weathers. When serpentine is exposed to the air for long periods of time, it turns red and eventually decomposes into soil that supports the growth of trees and—best of all—vines.

■ MAKING ROSÉ WINES

Rosé or blush wines are also made from red wine grapes—but the juicy pulp is left on the skins for a matter of hours, not days. The winemaker decides how long. When the juice has reached the desired color, it is drained off and filtered. The yeast is added, and the juice, or must, is left to ferment. Because the must stays on the skins for a shorter time than the must of red wines, fewer tannins are leached from the skins, and the resulting wine is not as heavy-flavored as a red. You might say that rosé is a lighter, fruitier version of red wine, not a pink version of white. If it is made right, it will have some of the flavors of the grape. Rosé can be a great food wine—if it is not too sweet. It is also great for sipping on the back porch on a hot afternoon or warm summer evening.

■ GROWERS, WINEMAKERS, AND THE LAND

Is wine made in the vineyard or in the winery? French winemakers, who believe in the importance of the *terroir* (the soil, the microclimate, the growing conditions), would argue the former. California winemakers—not all of whom grow grapes of their own—generally claim the latter. California winemakers do, however, recognize that growing regions play a role in the quality of grapes. When a specific region has unique soil, climate, and other growing conditions, it can be designated by the Alcohol and Tobacco Tax and Trade Bureau as an American Viticultural Area (AVA), more commonly called an **appellation.** Until recently, this was the job of the Bureau of Alcohol, Tobacco and Firearms.

Different appellations—there are more than 80 AVAs in California, and more than a dozen in the Napa Valley alone—are renowned for different wines. It is common to find an appellation mentioned on a wine label, though this can be done only if 85 percent of the grapes used to make the wine were grown in that appellation. In this book, we have color-coded each winery according to its physical location, but keep in mind that the appellation listed on a label always refers to where a wine's grapes were grown. Many Sonoma County wineries buy grapes from Napa Valley growers—and vice versa—so it is quite possible for the wine of a Sonoma winery to be labeled, for instance, a Napa Valley cabernet. California winemakers have also begun to acknowledge that grapes grown in particular vineyards differ widely in quality, and the best vineyards also are frequently mentioned on wine labels.

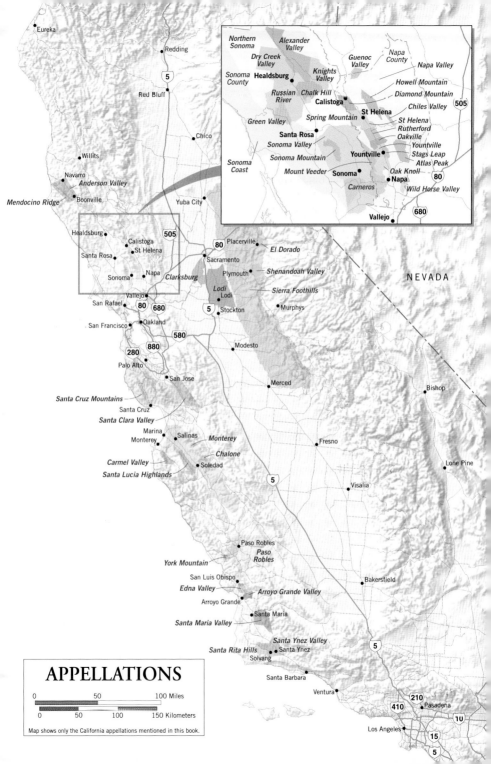

APPELLATIONS

| 0 | 50 | 100 Miles |

| 0 | 50 | 100 | 150 Kilometers |

Map shows only the California appellations mentioned in this book.

Andy Beckstoffer, lord of his realm.

Ideally, all winemakers would grow the grapes they need, but that's not always possible—especially in the Wine Country, where prices for prime vineyard land have soared in recent decades. Though the vineyard was once the first investment of every winery, few of the wineries that have opened since Prohibition began their operations with a vineyard. Instead, many winemakers purchase their grapes from independent growers. Unfortunately, winemakers are not always able to buy grapes from the same grower year after year, so consumers must check every year to see if the wine is made from the same grower's grapes. Some wineries have negotiated long-term contracts with top growers, but this locks the wineries into high grape prices even in times of falling sales. Not surprisingly, growers have become key players in the wine industry, and an understanding of their complex, ever-changing relationship with winemakers is helpful information for any lover of wine.

■ GROWERS AND VINEYARDS

Andy Beckstoffer, a prominent Napa Valley grower, estimates that only about 50 percent of the grapes harvested in the Wine Country are grown by wineries; the other half come from independent growers. Where grape quality is concerned, the growers may have the edge over many wineries, because they must be in the forefront of viticultural innovation in order to sell grapes to finicky winemakers.

And right now, everything is being questioned—even the soils in which the vines are planted. According to vineyard specialist Beckstoffer, from 30 percent to 50 percent of Napa Valley vineyards are planted in bottomland soils that are too rich: vines are among the few plants that give their best fruit when they grow in poor soils. Ideal vineyard soils, says Beckstoffer, drain well. "You need lots of things," he says, "but permeability is on top. The permeability of the soil is more important than its mineral content. You can always change the mineral content."

Another challenge for growers is the phylloxera root louse, which is slowly killing local vines. Most of the region's vineyards will have to be replanted within the next decade. As a grower replants, he has to carefully select vine clones and match the most desirable clones to the best root stocks. Since growing is all they do (and the main source of their income) independent growers tend to react more quickly to problems in the vineyard than do wineries (who can buy grapes from other growers, if necessary). Still, even when replanting, growers must continue to anticipate the needs of their winemaker clients. For example, **Robert Young Vineyard,** the Alexander Valley vineyard famous for its chardonnay grapes, had to be uprooted because of phylloxera. The vineyard is being replanted not just with chardonnay, but with cabernet sauvignon, merlot, cabernet franc, and even sangiovese, because the Youngs discern a market trend toward red wines.

In San Luis Obispo and Santa Barbara Counties, **Central Coast Wine Services,** owned by Bob and Steve Miller, supplies wineries from as far away as Napa and Sonoma Counties with grapes from its French Camp (Paso Robles) and Bien Nacido (Santa Maria Valley) Vineyards. The Millers have a custom crush facility where they produce bulk wine for various wineries, but they do not have a label of their own. They do not think it is a good idea to compete with their customers. By providing space in their large facility to small local wineries, they have created, instead, a unique wine-making community of friendly competitors who have improved the wines of the region through an unusual cooperative arrangement.

Well-known **Sangiacomo Vineyards** lies to the south of the city of Sonoma, along Sonoma Creek. The Sangiacomo family owns no winery. Farming more than 1,000 acres of grapes in the cool Carneros region, the Sangiacomos are best known for the chardonnay grapes their vineyards produce. But they also grow pinot noir and a few merlot vines. It may be the latter that will ultimately produce the best wine. One indicator is the intense 1993 Ravenswood merlot, made from Sangiacomo grapes. Besides Ravenswood, the Sangiacomos sell their grapes to such top wineries as Chateau Souverain, Clos du Bois, Domaine Chandon, Gundlach-Bundschu, Matanzas Creek, Saintsbury, and Simi. Even Buena Vista, the Carneros district's biggest winery and grapegrower, buys some grapes from the Sangiacomos.

(following pages) A medley of wine labels: the wines of Napa (top row),
Sonoma (middle), and other regions (bottom).

Without producing a single bottle of wine, large growers such as Sangiacomo are pivotal to the success of the region's wine industry.

Small wineries with only a few acres of grapes are limited in their scope, because different grape varieties like different types of soils and microclimates. This is the reason why so many small wineries buy grapes, even if they have vineyards of their own. Chardonnay likes well-drained vineyards but will take heavy soil, and merlot likes clay with gravel. Sauvignon blanc will grow in much richer soil but needs special handling, such as leaf-pulling and other viticultural techniques, to make up for the richness of the soil (which can give the grapes and wine a "weedy" flavor).

If, on the other hand, a small winery has the right location and grows only those grapes best suited to its special soil and microclimate, it can produce spectacular wines from small vineyards. That's what Stony Hill does with chardonnay, Storybook Mountain with zinfandel, and Livingston with cabernet sauvignon. If such a small winery wants to expand production, it needs to buy another vineyard or buy grapes from other growers.

A misty autumn morning at Stony Hill Vineyard.

HOW TO READ A WINE LABEL

Vintage: All the grapes in the wine were harvested in 2000.

Appellation: At least 85 percent of the grapes were grown in the Napa Valley appellation.

Vineyard name: The grapes were grown in Mondavi's To Kalon Vineyard.

Varietal composition: At least 75 percent of the grapes in this wine are sauvignon blanc. (Robert Mondavi invented the fanciful name fumé blanc.)

Reserve: An inexact term meaning "special," this can refer to how or where the grapes were grown or how the wine was made.

Filtration: This wine has not been filtered to remove sediments and other elements; with this strategy a winemaker often achieves deeper color and richer flavors than with filtered wines.

Winery name

Alcohol content: By law, this must be listed.

2000
NAPA VALLEY
TO KALON VINEYARD
FUMÉ BLANC
RESERVE
UNFILTERED
ROBERT MONDAVI WINERY
ALCOHOL 13.5% BY VOLUME

Winery name

No vintage date: The grapes could have come from more than one year's harvest.

Wine name: "Le Mistral" is the winery's name for this red-wine blend.

Appellation: The grapes could have come from anywhere in California.

Additional label terms
Estate grown: The grapes came from vineyards the winery owns or operates.

Estate bottled: The grapes were estate grown, and the wine was bottled at the winery, with both winery and vineyard in the same appellation.

JOSEPH PHELPS
Le Mistral
CALIFORNIA

A RED TABLE WINE
JOSEPH PHELPS VINEYARDS
ST. HELENA, CALIFORNIA

PRODUCED AND BOTTLED BY
POST OFFICE BOX 1031
ALC. 13.5% BY VOLUME

No varietal: No single grape made up 75 percent or more of the wine.

Production: Phelps did not grow the grapes; it bought them.

Alcohol content: Table wines can be between 7 and 14 percent alcohol.

GRAPE VARIETIES

■ WHITE

CHARDONNAY
This noble white grape variety from Burgundy can be made into great wine in California when grown in austere soils of cool vineyards.

MARSANNE
A white-wine grape from France's Rhône Valley, marsanne makes good, fragrant wine in California.

PINOT BLANC
When cultivated in well-drained soils of cool vineyards, this white grape can create a wine that rivals chardonnay.

RIESLING
Also called Johannisberg Riesling or White Riesling, this cool-climate grape has been upstaged by chardonnay, but it can make great wine in California—when conditions are right.

SAUVIGNON BLANC
This white grape does very well almost anywhere in the Wine Country—even in fertile bottom lands—and often makes more interesting wine than chardonnay.

VIOGNIER
This white grape from France's Rhône Valley makes distinguished wines with fruity bouquet.

■ RED

CABERNET FRANC
Cabernet franc can produce aromatic red wines, soft and more subtle than those of the closely related cabernet sauvignon.

CABERNET SAUVIGNON
This noble red wine grape of Bordeaux has long been made into great wine in California, when grown in austere, well-drained soils.

MERLOT
This dark, blue-black grape is quickly becoming California's most popular red wine grape, because its wine is soft yet complex, even when young.

PINOT NOIR
This finicky grape is being turned into great wine in the cool growing regions of the Carneros District and the Russian River Valley.

SANGIOVESE
This versatile Tuscan wine grape grows well in Sonoma County and can be used to create light-bodied as well as long-lived, very complex reds.

ZINFANDEL
When grown in the austere red soils of northern Sonoma or Napa, this "native" California grape can be transformed into complex, well-balanced wines that age as well as the best French clarets.

■ WINEMAKERS

Buying grapes from a grower doesn't necessarily reduce a winemaker's labors, but it may change the type of work he or she does. A good winemaker carefully monitors the grapes from different growers' vineyards throughout the season. Spring pruning determines the vigor of the vines; fruit thinning makes the remaining grapes more intense in flavor; leaf-pulling gives the grapes even exposure to the sun. The winemaker will even help determine the proper day for picking. If the vineyards from which a winemaker buys grapes are spread out over several appellations—as often happens—a winemaker will spend a considerable amount of time on the road, traveling back and forth between the different plots of vines. The winemaker's presence is especially critical at harvest, when he or she will regularly check the grapes' ripeness by tasting and testing sugar levels.

Winemakers try to sign long-term contracts with reliable growers to control the consistency and quality of the fruit—as though they had their own vineyard run by a vineyard manager. But that's not always possible, especially when a grower sells to more than one winery.

Paradoxically, the winemaker also faces the problem of making wine that is too good and too popular. As the demand for a wine—and its price—rises, so will the price of the grapes used to make it. Other wineries sometimes bid up the price of the grapes, with the result that a winemaker can no longer afford the grapes that made a wine famous. This competitiveness among winemakers for a specific batch of grapes brings us back to the French notion that great wine is made in the vineyard. Which might lead us to believe that the grower is at least as important as the winemaker. Yet when you taste wines made by different winemakers from grapes produced in one vineyard, you'll notice right away that there's more to making wine than growing grapes. The quality of these wines may range from merely good to truly great. Wine making is more than an agricultural pursuit. It is an art.

Wild mustard blooms in late winter between the vines at Opus One.

SOUTHERN NAPA VALLEY

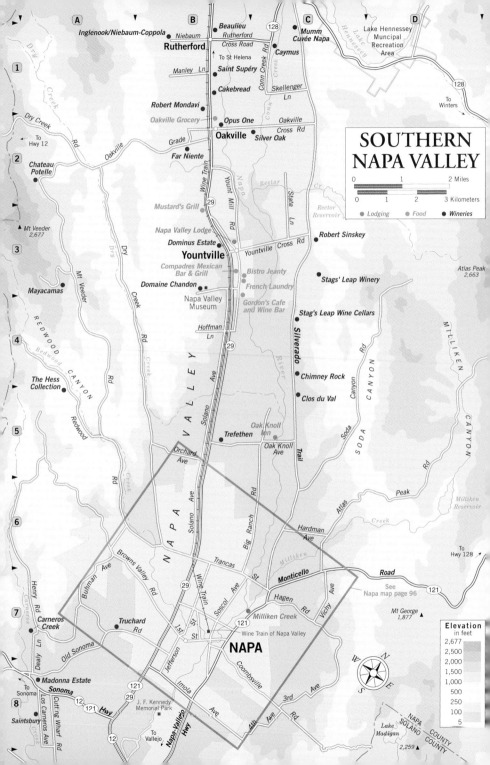

■ OVERVIEW OF THE NAPA VALLEY

The Napa Valley is a long, narrow trough between mountain chains, with more wineries per mile than any other place in America. Because there is so much to see and taste, this books divides the valley into two drives, each of which makes for a fine day of self-guided touring.

The first drive, described below as the southern valley, follows a loop route, heading north from the city of Napa, visiting Yountville and Oakville, and turning east at Rutherford Cross Road to return south by way of the Silverado Trail and the Stags Leap District. The second drive, described in the "Northern Napa Valley" chapter, starts with a visit to Rutherford, and includes wineries found along the route to St. Helena and Calistoga before rambling down the Silverado Trail back to Rutherford. Keep in mind that the southern valley is close to tidewater and thus stays cool on a hot summer day. The northern valley can get very hot in summer, but the weather is pleasant in spring and autumn.

On both of these drives, you must be selective. You cannot possibly visit every winery, nor would you want to. A tour of three or four per day is plenty to keep you busy, and such a tour is manageable in terms of alcohol consumption. Plan ahead but also leave time to pay a spontaneous visit to a winery not on your list. Tours of Robert Mondavi, Opus One, and other wineries fill up quickly except in winter, so it's wise to make a reservation.

Highway 29, the Napa Valley Highway, heads north from Vallejo first as a busy four-lane highway with traffic lights, then as a freeway, and finally as a two-lane highway. At the intersection where Highway 29 becomes a freeway heading north into the Napa Valley, a sign points the driver north to "Napa" along Highway 121. This sign refers to the town of Napa; ignore it and continue north on Highway 29 to reach the main part of the Napa Valley.

At one point the state of California had plans to convert Highway 29 into a freeway all the way to Calistoga. Local winemakers stopped that plan by turning the Napa Valley into an agricultural preserve. And so, Highway 29 is a freeway only until Yountville. Beyond that it is a two-lane road, congested with visitors eager to see the Napa Valley and taste its fabled wines. The road's narrow width hasn't stopped the tourists, but it has stopped most development, and except for a new winery or two, the valley looks much as it did a quarter of a century ago.

In the 35-mile drive from tidewater to the foothills of Mount St. Helena, you will pass through several different climate zones; driving into the mountains to the

east and west will add a few more. The variety of the grapes grown is indicative of the changing soil conditions, and the variety of the soils is why the valley makes so many different wines and makes them so well. Almost the entire county, east to Lake Berryessa, is known as the Napa Valley AVA, but several areas within that AVA have been designated as AVAs themselves. Three of these, Oakville, Rutherford, and St. Helena, stretch clear across the valley floor. Stags Leap encompasses a small district on the east side of the valley, and Mount Veeder, Spring Mountain, and Howell Mountain each encompass parts—but not all—of the mountains from which they take their names. The Atlas Peak AVA lies east of Stags Leap, and the Wild Horse Valley appellation is a small area south of Atlas Peak. The Carneros overlaps both the Napa Valley and Sonoma Valley appellations.

Most of the wineries grow grapes in several of the regions or buy them from growers in other appellations. Thus Mumm Cuvée Napa gets the grapes for its sparkling wines from the cool Carneros region, while the grapes in the vineyards surrounding the winery are sold to other wineries. As you taste the wines, ask where the grapes came from. It's a part of understanding wine.

■ ENTERING THE NAPA VALLEY

Because Highway 29 passes through unpleasant urban sprawl as it leaves the town of Napa, many visitors rush north to Yountville, where some feel the real valley starts. Those who do are missing one of the Napa Valley's most important wineries, Trefethen Vineyards.

Trefethen Vineyards   *map page 72, B-5*

The big Tuscan-red building here is the old Eshcol Winery, built in 1886. This huge three-story gravity-flow winery is built from wood rather than stone, making it somewhat of a rarity. It has weathered the last century well, although the upper floors were strained when a budding Domaine Chandon used it for storing sparkling wine. Eshcol closed during Prohibition and was reopened for a short time after Prohibition was repealed. Then the vineyards were leased to Beringer.

A horse-drawn cart delivers grapes to the Eshcol Winery for crushing.

Gene Trefethen, the executive vice president of Kaiser Industries, and his wife, Catherine, bought the property in 1968 as a retirement home. Like so many folks retiring to the Napa Valley, they began replanting the vineyards and restoring the winery. They started making wine sometime around 1973.

Around the same time, Moët-Hennessy (M-H), the French champagne house, decided to open a winery in the Napa Valley and settled on Yountville as the facility's location. While plans were made for building the winery, Moët-Hennessy's master of champagne was eager to make wine from local grapes to learn which would be best for sparkling-wine production. But making commercial wine requires a bonded winery, that is, one designated as such by the federal government, which wants to be sure winery owners pay the proper taxes on all the wine they produce.

As historian Jamie Laughridge tells it, Robert-Jean de Vogüé, the chairman of M-H, and John Wright, the project manager, met Catherine Trefethen at a party. She invited them to lunch the next day. The Trefethens had vineyards and a splendid old winery building and had applied for a license to make wine commercially,

but they did not yet have wine-making equipment. Moët-Hennessy needed grapes and a bonded winery to press and ferment them. M-H struck a deal with the Trefethens, offering to equip their empty winery building in exchange for its use until M-H's Yountville facility was completed. The deal made everyone involved happy, and M-H kept some of its operations at Trefethen until 1977.

The Trefethen winery, by this time run by Gene and Catherine's son, John, and his wife, Janet, gained early recognition for the excellence of its wines: a 1976 chardonnay placed first in a 1979 tasting held in Paris by Gault Millau. Trefethen continues to make superb chardonnay, cabernet sauvignon, and merlot, as well as Riesling. The two proprietary wines are Eshcol chardonnay and Eshcol cabernet sauvignon. In the late 1990s, Trefethen Vineyards applied to have the federal government create Napa Valley's 14th appellation, the Oak Knoll District. A dispute with a winery in Oregon over the name has held up the designation, though it will likely have been approved by the time you read this. *1160 Oak Knoll Avenue; 707-255-7700.*

Domaine Chandon *map page 72, B-3/4*

A few miles up the road, to the west of Yountville's only freeway underpass, sprawls the expansive, sparkling-wine complex of Domaine Chandon. The winery here is built into a hillside, blending into the landscape like no other. You can hardly see it from the highway even though it's just off the road, but its south side of windowed arches is dramatic. When the winery was built, the ancient oaks on the property were spared, and decades later, they are more beautiful than ever. Unfortunately, Domaine Chandon recently violated its aesthetic standards by erecting an unappealing concrete-slab warehouse north of the old winery.

Sparklers here are made only by the labor-intensive—and costly—*méthode champenoise,* meaning the wine is fermented individually in the bottle and individually disgorged (see page 128 for more about disgorging). All of the wines are *cuvées* (blends); the top of the line Etoile is a cuvée of older vintages. It is a splendid accompaniment for the exquisite dishes served at Domaine Chandon's restaurant—a Wine Country first that was an instant hit when it opened in 1977. This winery is especially nice to visit. *1 California Drive; 707-944-8844.*

(opposite) Domaine Chandon's dining room has been a Napa Valley star for more than a quarter century. (following pages) Harvesting grapes for Chandon's sparkling wines.

Dominus Estate   *map page 72, B-3*

Founded in 1983, Dominus Estate is the Napa Valley venture of Christian Moueix, owner of Bordeaux's prestigious Château Pétrus. In *Guide to the Best Wineries of North America,* André Gayot comments on the creation of Domaine Chandon, Opus One, and Dominus that "collectively these three joint ventures signaled the Napa Valley's unassailable eminence in the wine world." Dominus now occupies an ultra-modern winery designed by Swiss architects and finished in 1997 at its historic Napanook Vineyard, northwest of Yountville. Dominus makes two wines: its signature Dominus Bordeaux-style blend (cabernet sauvignon with small amounts of merlot, cabernet franc, and petit verdot) and a second label wine called Napanook. Dominus wines, which have been very austere, even harsh, have both fervent adherents and critics. The winery is not open to the public, but its wines are worth seeking out. *Near Highway 29 and Dwyer Lane; 707-944-8954.*

■ YOUNTVILLE   *map page 72, B-3*

Yountville became a wine-growing center back in 1870, when wealthy San Francisco immigrant Gottlieb Groezinger built a large winery here. The brick winery building still stands, but it has been turned into a shopping complex called Vintage 1870. The town was founded a few decades earlier by George Calvert Yount, a mountain man from North Carolina. Yount changed his name to Jorge Concepcion Yount when he converted to Catholicism so that he could obtain the grant of Rancho Caymus from Mariano Vallejo in 1836.

Yountville has several of the Valley's best restaurants, including the French Laundry, Bistro Jeanty, and, north of town, Mustard's Grill. The town's lodging facilities match the quality of the food. Yountville Market, on Washington Street, dates back to 1916. It's a good place for local bread, produce, wines, and take-out lunches. You can picnic at either the **Yountville Park** (tables, barbecue grills, public rest rooms) at the north end of town or at the **Napa River Ecological Reserve** off the Yountville Cross Road (no tables), where you can sit on a grassy bank or gravelly beach and dangle your feet in the river, when it has water. While strolling through Yountville, you might want to visit the Pioneer Cemetery and Indian Burial Ground, off Jackson Street, which were established in 1848. George Yount is buried here, and the cemetery is still used by the remaining members of the local Wappo tribe.

Ripe tomatoes ready for preparation at the French Laundry.

The design of the Opus One winery combines space-age and Mayan elements.

The Veterans Home southwest of Domaine Chandon was established in 1881 for disabled veterans of the Mexican War and the Grand Army of the Republic. The marvelous **Napa Valley Museum** has been built on Veterans' Home property. Its permanent exhibit, *California Wine: The Science of an Art,* explains how the sciences of geology, agriculture, and wine-making technology join forces with the inspiration, creativity, and experience of the winemaker to create a memorable bottle of wine. The user-friendly museum is accessible directly through the Veterans Home or by gate from the Domaine Chandon winery. *55 Presidents Circle; 707-944-0500.*

■ OAKVILLE APPELLATION

Just north of Yountville lies the hamlet of Oakville. Stop here and check out the local deli fare. The **Oakville Grocery,** on the east side of the road, just north of where Oakville Cross Road meets the main highway, has a great selection of local bread, cheese, olive oils, and wines, as well as sandwiches and other picnic fare.

Far Niente *map page 72, B-2*

Just west of town, this prominent Oakville winery occupies a stone building erected in 1885 and restored from 1978 to 1982 by Gil Nickel. Its 15,000 square feet of caves were dug in 1990. The winery, which produces a much-loved chardonnay and cabernet sauvignon, is not open to the public. *1 Acacia Drive; 707-944-2861.*

Silver Oak Wine Cellars *map page 72, B/C-2*

Take the Oakville Cross Road east and look for this small winery on the right. Started by Ray Duncan and former Christian Brother Justin Meyer, Silver Oak makes nothing but cabernet sauvignon. The grapes come from Sonoma County's Alexander Valley, from the small Bonny's Vineyard in Oakville, and from other Napa Valley vineyards. The wines age well, but the prices do not necessarily reflect the quality of the wines. *915 Oakville Cross Road; 707-944-8808.*

Opus One *map page 72, B-2*

Built into a hillside amid vineyards just off Highway 29, this winery with a stone facade is a joint venture of the Napa Valley's Robert Mondavi and France's Baron Philippe Rothschild. Opus One, whose modern design incorporates classical

Robert Mondavi (foreground) joins friends for a fund-raising event in his vineyards.

references, was planned as a semi-subterranean facility, where the cool earth would keep the aging cellars at constant temperature. But the builders found a hot spring, so the winery is cooled by mechanical rather than natural air-conditioning. Visitors sign in and are directed to the tasting room "as space is available." The cost of a glass is steep: $25. Up on the roof terrace is a fine view, where big spenders sip and the plebs mill about. *7900 St. Helena Highway; 707-944-9442.*

Robert Mondavi Winery *map page 72, B-1/2*

A short distance north of Oakville Cross Road, on the west side of the highway, rise the tower and large entrance gate of the Napa Valley's best-known winery. Earlier in this century, the huge To-Kalon Winery dominated this part of the Napa Valley, both with the quantity and the quality of its wines. Today, its place—and some of its vineyards—have been taken over by Robert Mondavi Winery. No other winery has done more to promote the excellence of Napa Valley wines throughout the world (even though Mondavi wines were absent from the 1976 Paris tasting that brought the Napa Valley such fame).

Since its inception in the 1960s, the Robert Mondavi Winery has been one of the Napa Valley's preeminent producers of premium wines.

Robert Mondavi forever changed the nature of the wine known as California sauterne by taking sauvignon blanc grapes, leaving them on the skins after the crush, fermenting the juice in stainless steel, and aging it in French oak barrels. He called his creation fumé blanc (a play on blanc fumé, the steely-crisp wine made from sauvignon blanc in France's Loire Valley, and on Pouilly-Fumé, a dry white from the same area). Both the style and the name caught on: dozens of wineries in both Napa and Sonoma Counties now make fumé blanc. But though the fumé blanc has been Mondavi's most copied wine, it is the reserve reds that have made the winery's reputation.

Recently, the Mondavi operation, now a publicly owned corporation, has crossed another frontier by experimenting with wines made from Italian and Rhône grape varieties. If you've never been on a winery tour before, the one here provides a good introduction to the wine-making process, including past methods and the many Mondavi innovations. *7801 St. Helena Highway; 707-963-9611.*

■ RUTHERFORD APPELLATION

You will not notice a change in the scenery or the vineyards as you cross from the Oakville AVA into the Rutherford one, yet Robert Mondavi lies in the former, and Cakebread, just a stone's throw up the road, lies in the latter. To keep this tour manageable in a day, skip the tiny town of Rutherford and choose from the Rutherford wineries listed here. Other Rutherford wineries are covered in the "Northern Napa Valley" chapter.

Cakebread Cellars   *map page 72, B-1/2*

This great winery is run by one of the nicest and most creative families in the business. Jack Cakebread, who founded the winery in 1973 with his wife, Dolores, is also a renowned photographer; Dolores is a superb cook who has played a major role in making the Napa Valley a food as well as a wine region. Her kitchen garden—where she grows vegetables and herbs for entertaining important guests—occupies a prominent (and perhaps symbolic) spot between the winery and the vineyards. Their son Bruce makes the wines, a sauvignon blanc of great character and depth, a beautifully complex cabernet sauvignon, and a luscious chardonnay. The winery, which was designed by William Turnbull, is truly beautiful, with an attention to detail in the woodwork and brickwork that's unmatched anywhere else. But see for yourself. The tasting room is open to the public. Tours are by appointment. *8300 St. Helena Highway; 707-963-5221.*

Saint Supéry Vineyards & Winery   *map page 72, B-1*

Set well back from the road, Saint Supéry is a study in contrast. The first building you see after you park your car is the beautifully restored Atkinson farmhouse. The next building is a vast concrete edifice that looks like a cross between a college hall and a factory. Ignore the ugly exterior. Inside, you'll find one of the most thoughtfully appointed visitors centers in the Wine Country. Besides a relief map of the Napa Valley and other displays, you'll appreciate the sniffing station, an ingenious contraption that lets you smell some of the elements that determine the character of red and white wines—the cherry, black pepper, bell pepper, and cedar aromas of reds, and the wildflower, new-mown hay, green olive, and grapefruit of white wines. It's a good way of checking up on your nose; one of the peculiarities of human physiology is that not everyone smells the same things. You can go on a self-guided tour or take the formal tour, which includes the 1881 farmhouse.

The beautiful Cakebread Cellars was designed by William Turnbull.

Saint Supéry is owned by Skalli, a large French food corporation and *negoçiant*—a special type of French wine shipper that buys wines from small wineries soon after they are made, matures them in its cellars, and bottles and ships them when they are ready. In 1982, Skalli purchased the Dollarhide Ranch in Pope Valley; the company planted grapes in 1983 and built the winery in 1989. The winery takes its name from Edward St. Supéry, a French winemaker who lived in the farmhouse from the early 1900s until Prohibition.

Primarily a "red wine house," Saint Supéry makes very good cabernet sauvignon and merlot from its Pope Valley grapes, wines that will get even better as the vines mature. A 35-acre vineyard next to the winery is planted exclusively with cabernet sauvignon. There's also a well-structured chardonnay, as well as a limited edition Dollarhide Ranch sémillon, an excellent sauvignon blanc, a red Napa Valley Meritage, and a white Napa Valley Meritage. *8440 St. Helena Highway; 707-963-4507.*

■ STAGS LEAP DISTRICT

Make a right on Rutherford Cross Road and follow Highway 128 east; turn right onto the Silverado Trail and drive south. A sign by the road marks the beginning of the Stags Leap District, but even without the sign you would probably notice the change in the landscape. Towering volcanic palisades and crags hover over the vineyards here, and the special ecosystem has unique soils and a singular microclimate. There are several versions of how these rocks got their name: In one a stag, pursued by hunters, leaped off the rocks to safety; in another, he leaped to his death. A third version has several stags leaping. Take your pick.

The Stags Leap District (no apostrophe) is close to Yountville, connected by Yountville Cross Road. It is home to two wineries whose names may pose some confusion. Because of a trademark battle, the Stag's Leap Winery moved its apostrophe one space to the right to become the Stags' Leap Winery, while the winery down-valley is called Stag's Leap Wine Cellars. Seem a trifle picky? Remember, these distinctions were decided on by winemakers, who spend their lives judging nuances.

Robert Sinskey Vineyards   *map page 72, C-3*

The first winery you'll come upon on the Silverado Trail is Robert Sinskey Vineyards, off to your left and as austere as the landscape. The building looks like an oversized horse barn, which is fitting because the grapes here grow on old pasture land. The quality of Robert Sinskey wines is amazingly high, but take note that the grapes used are grown in the Carneros District. Thereby hangs a tale. As Rob Sinskey tells it, his father, Robert Sinskey, M.D., got together with two friends, Mike Richmond and Jerry Goldstein, and became limited partners in Acacia Winery. Robert Sr. became seriously bitten by the wine bug, so in 1982 he bought 32 acres along Las Amigas Road in the Carneros. In 1985, by the time the vines in the Carneros were ready to bear fruit, the partners had decided to sell Acacia to Chalone. Sinskey had his vineyard—all he needed was a winery to put his grapes to use. He bought land in Stags Leap and construction began. The first two Sinskey vintages were crushed across the valley at Flora Springs, while his winery was under construction. The first crush in this winery occurred in 1988.

Newlyweds, their cow, and a friend pose at Stag's Leap Vineyard in 1888.

Warren Winiarski is the proprietor of the world-renowned Stag's Leap Wine Cellars.

Sinskey's son, Rob, took some time off to help in the winery. "I think a week had passed," he says, "when I discovered that my father's avocation had become my obsession." Rob is now the winery's president.

At first sniff and sip, you will know you are on to something good in Sinskey's pinot noir. The merlot is even better. Rob Sinskey explains that the Carneros is cool by California standards but still warmer than some of the world's other growing regions such as St. Emilion and Pomerol, where some of the greatest merlots are produced. As for the grapes he has planted in Stags Leap, he is confident they will also produce great wine. *6320 Silverado Trail; 707-944-9090.*

Stags' Leap Winery *map page 72, C-3*
One winery you can't see as you pass by on the Silverado Trail is Stags' Leap Winery. This is home to a very special petite sirah, a grape variety grown in a vineyard atop the alluvial fan that slopes downhill from the Stags Leap palisades. The vineyard lies in a small side valley, between the Stags' Leap Winery and the mansion built here in 1888 by Horace B. Chase, a Chicago financier. Mr. Chase lost his fortune shortly thereafter, and his winery soon lay in ruins. The mansion had a somewhat checkered career as the Stag's Leap Hotel (and establishments of

less repute) until Carl Doumani rescued it in the early 1970s and reopened the winery as well. During the rebuilding, the workmen found a deep wine cave that had been dug into the hill behind the winery. No one had suspected its existence under the mound of rubble that hid its entrance. It now serves as an aging cellar.

Stags' Leap Winery's estate-grown petite sirah produces a wine that is intense, well-rounded, and complex, on par with the best of France's Rhône wines. The winery also produces a cabernet sauvignon that is lean and complex, yet restrained—like a first-rate red Bordeaux. Stags' Leap Winery is now owned by Blass Wine Estates, the winery division of the Australian beverage conglomerate Foster's Group. It is not open to the public. *6150 Silverado Trail; 707-944-1303.*

Stag's Leap Wine Cellars   *map page 72, C-3/4*

Farther south on the Silverado Trail, you'll see on your left the plain, low earth-colored buildings of Stag's Leap Wine Cellars, which look more like they house a modern country school than a winery of such eminence. But flowers liven up the place, and there's a small picnic area in a garden.

Warren and Barbara Winiarski's winery is the home of the 1973 cabernet that won the red wine section of the famous 1976 Paris tasting; it is also the home of the famed "Cask 23" cabernet sauvignon. Because of this, the place tends to be overrun with serious enophiles. Relax. Let the snobs show off their winespeak. Taste the wines: not just the cab, but also the sauvignon blanc and chardonnay. This is good wine.

In 1964, Warren Winiarski left a job as a lecturer at the University of Chicago and moved his family to California. He apprenticed with Lee Stewart, of the original Souverain Winery, and André Tchelistcheff of Beaulieu Vineyards, before becoming assistant winemaker at the newly established Robert Mondavi Winery from 1966 to 1968. In 1970, he acquired a vineyard in the Stags Leap District, named it Stag's Leap Vineyard, and replanted its 44 acres of French prune trees and alicanté bouschet and petite sirah grapevines with cabernet sauvignon and merlot.

In 1972, he built a winery just off the Silverado Trail and named it Stag's Leap Wine Cellars. Winiarski's winery catapulted to international fame in 1976, when his 1973 cabernet sauvignon, the first wine produced at the new winery, bested four top-ranked Bordeaux entries, including first-growths Château Mouton-Rothschild and Château Haut-Brion. This tasting not only placed Winiarski in the ranks of the world's most respected winemakers, but it also changed the wine world's perception of California wines. *5766 Silverado Trail; 707-944-2020.*

Bernard Portet (left) and winemaker Kian Tavakoli (right) in the Clos du Val vineyards.

Chimney Rock Winery   *map page 72, C-4/5*

As you continue south on the Silverado Trail, you can't help noticing a low white building to the east—unless the poplar trees surrounding it are in full leaf, hiding it from view. In the somewhat ornate Cape (as in Cape of Good Hope) Dutch style of the 17th century, it seems a bit out of place amid the austere Stags Leap landscape. This is Chimney Rock Winery. You have to love a winery that was built on part of a golf course, putting the land to a much nobler use. In 1984, Hack Wilson, a former soft drink executive, bought the Chimney Rock Golf Course, decided that part of the land had just the right soils for a vineyard, and sent in the bulldozers. The golf course still exists, but it has only nine holes. All Chimney Rock wines are estate-grown. The cabernet is more elegant than wines of its caliber tend to be hereabouts, and there's also a very fine fumé blanc. Chimney Rock has a very pleasant tasting room. *5350 Silverado Trail; 707-257-2641.*

Clos du Val   *map page 72, C-5*

With the exception of Chimney Rock, architectural understatement seems to be the rule in the Stags Leap District. The next winery down the road, Clos du Val, has the plain, severe lines of a *Bordelais chais* (wine-aging cellar) and does not at all look like a château. The winery, built in 1972, is owned by French-American businessman John Goelet. It was started by Bernard Portet, a French winemaker whose father was technical director at Château Lafite-Rothschild. Portet, who is also the winery's president, began with the intention of making only cabernet sauvignon and zinfandel, but Clos du Val has since branched out into merlot, pinot noir, chardonnay, and Bordeaux blend white wines. Clos du Val's wines are French in character and structure, not revealing their complexity until after they have been aged in the bottle for considerable time. Taste the reserve if you get the chance—it is produced only in exceptional years. *5330 Silverado Trail; 707-259-2200.*

■ TOWN OF NAPA   *map page 96*

Not many years ago, Yountville could rightly be considered the southernmost wine commune of the Napa Valley, because the city of Napa had turned its back on the Wine Country. That is no longer true—and it was certainly not the case before Prohibition. Today, with the revitalization and expansion of the Carneros vineyards, Napa suddenly finds itself in the heart of the Wine Country, which makes it a perfect stopping-over place, especially since hotel rates are considerably lower than those in Yountville, St. Helena, and Calistoga.

Napa, the oldest town in the Napa Valley, was founded in 1848 in a strategic location on the Napa River, where the Sonoma-Benicia Road (Highways 12 and 29) crossed at a ford. The first steamship arrived in 1850, and according to one historian, "the *Dolphin* was very small—about the size of a whaleboat." It was so small, he comments, "It is said that when coming up the river, the Captain (who is very tall) came in sight before the smoke stack." The first wood-frame building, a saloon, was built in 1848. Before then, a few Mexican adobes were the only houses in the region. One of these, built in the 1840s, survives at the corner of Soscol Avenue and the Silverado Trail as a restaurant.

The first commercial Napa Valley wine was made by a Britisher named Patchett in the 1850s from grapes planted in a vineyard in what is now downtown Napa. Patchett also built the first stone cellar in the Napa Valley and shipped wine regularly from 1857 on. Although Napa's first cash crops were cattle and wheat, by the late 1800s large wineries like the Uncle Sam Wine Cellars lined the river. Large wineries dominated the trade until Prohibition, but unlike the small family-owned wineries up-valley, they never recovered.

(following pages) The Napa River snakes south through Napa on this 19th-century map.

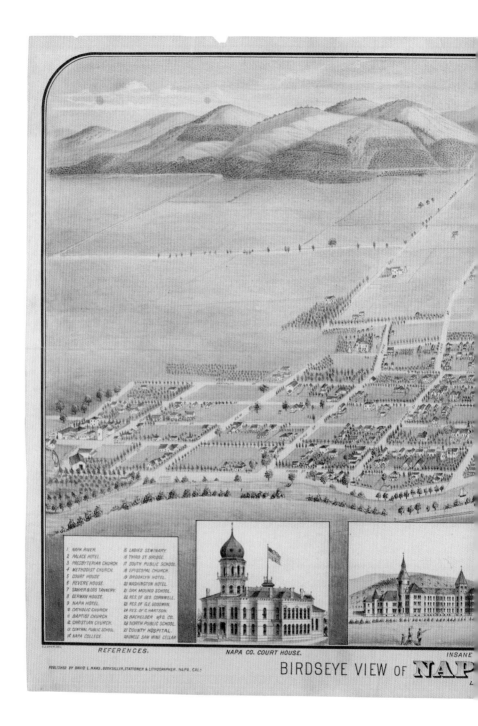

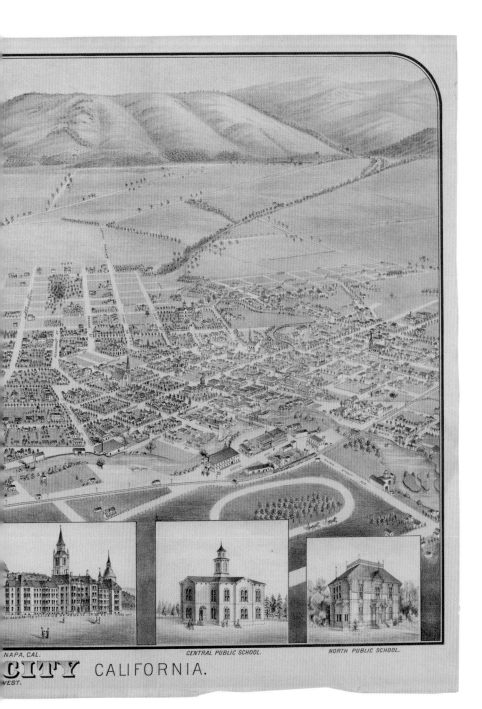

NAPA, CAL.

CENTRAL PUBLIC SCHOOL.

NORTH PUBLIC SCHOOL.

CITY CALIFORNIA.

WEST.

But Napa is not exactly a small town anymore, and gone are the days when sailboats tacked up the river on weekend excursions from San Francisco and riverfront saloons—many of which had gotten their start catering to the Sierra Foothills gold miners who wintered here—were a major industry. But downtown still preserves an old river-town atmosphere. The early residential areas, in which many Victorian houses survive, evoke a simpler, less hectic time. Within the original business district, a few historic buildings have been preserved, including the Opera House from 1879, the century-old courthouse, and several riverfront warehouses.

Napa County Landmarks will set you on the right trail for a self-guided tour of the town's older buildings. *1026 Brown Street; 707-255-1836.*

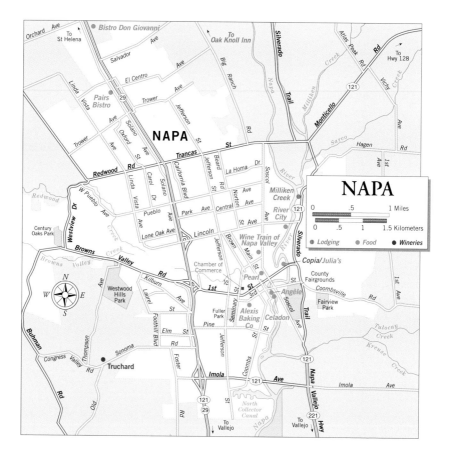

The brainchild of Robert Mondavi, **Copia: The American Center for Wine, Food and the Arts** aims to pull together the most important elements of the Napa Valley lifestyle—wine and food—and enhance them with exhibits and performing arts programs. Opened in 2001 on the banks of the Napa River, the 80,000-square-foot building includes a theater, a museum, a show kitchen, a gallery, and restaurants. The complex was jump-started by a $1 million donation from Garen Staglin, a businessman and winery owner who also raised additional funds from various corporate heads.

Copia—named for the goddess of abundance—presents exhibitions, educational programs, art shows, and cooking demonstrations. These are often successful as individual events, but the center as a whole does not always work as a harmonious unit. Part of the problem is the design of the ultra-modern facility, which resembles a soda-bottling plant on the outside and a train station on the inside. Made of concrete, stainless steel, and glass, Copia has a stark feel—disappointing to those who love the sensuous, vine-covered stone edifices elsewhere in the Napa Valley.

Still, Copia is a symbol of the city of Napa's full admission to the Wine Country's community of beautiful people. The city's transformation has been gradual. Its motels and coffee shops are slowly being replaced by B&Bs, luxury hotels, and fancy restaurants; and the Napa River, neglected for more than a century, is being cleared of weeds and snags. Restaurants are popping up along the riverbanks, and it is no longer gauche to dine, shop, or sleep in this formerly blue-collar town. Though the famed Wine Auction held up-valley every June has deteriorated into an ostentatious gathering of wealthy outsiders fawned over by local vintners, the valley's residents come to Napa instead. They drop by Copia to see a show, hear a lecture, or watch a cooking demo. *500 First Street, Napa; 707-265-5900; tickets 707-259-1600.*

■ MOUNT VEEDER APPELLATION

The wineries in this southwestern Napa Valley AVA can be reached from the town of Napa and Highway 29 by taking Redwood Road to Mount Veeder Road; or from the north via the top of the Oakville Grade, then Dry Creek Road to Mount Veeder Road.

South of the Oakville Grade, the Mayacamas Range is deeply cut by several creeks that flow from northwest to southeast; farther south, the mountains break

Gaining a sense of scents at Copia.

up into a series of hillocks, ridges, and mountain glades. Even though this region gets more rain than the Napa Valley (as witnessed by surviving stands of redwoods), soils are poor and rocky and the water runs off quickly, forcing any grapevines planted here to grow deep roots. Vines thus stressed produce grapes of exceptional character, as proved by the sparkling wines made from Domaine Chandon's Pickle Canyon vineyard as well as by the cabernet sauvignons and chardonnays produced by the handful of wineries whose owners eke out a living in this austere terroir.

The Hess Collection *map page 72, A-4/5*

Not all the wines made by the Hess Collection are austere, because grapes from other growing regions are used as well. Still, when the Swiss brewer and soda merchant Donald Hess took over the Christian Brothers Mont LaSalle winery in 1986, he planted vineyards on ridges and mountaintops. Some of these sites are so steep the grapes have to be picked by hand and brought down to the winery in a four-wheel-drive pickup truck. This extra care taken in growing the grapes definitely shows in the quality of the estate wines.

Johanna II, *by artist Franz Gertsh, is part of the Hess Collection.*

The Hess Collection offers free guided tours of its world-class modern art collection, but it charges a fee for tasting its wines. Although the wines are worth paying for, you will probably remember the art more than the cabernets or chardonnay. It is hard to forget Leopold Maler's striking *Hommage 1974,* a literally flaming typewriter, created as a protest piece against the repression of artistic freedom by totalitarian regimes. There are some spectacular views from the terrace here into the heart of the Mayacamas Range, with hills as tortured as those in a Chinese landscape painting. And yes, those green patches on the mountaintops are vineyards. *4411 Redwood Road; 707-255-1144.*

Mayacamas Vineyards   *map page 72, A-3/4*
The drive to the Hess Collection may be convoluted, but the drive up Mount Veeder Road to Mayacamas Vineyards has been known to try the faint of heart. The old Fischer stone winery, built in 1889, was resurrected in 1941 by Jack and Mary Taylor, pioneers of the Napa Valley wine renaissance who demonstrated that great wines can be made from cabernet sauvignon and chardonnay grapes grown high in the mountains. The winery, owned by Bob and Elinor Travers since 1968, now makes sauvignon blanc as well, plus a little pinot noir. The wines are big, flavorful, and concentrated. Production is limited to about 5,000 cases a year. Call ahead for an appointment before you visit. *1155 Lokoya Road; 707-224-4030.*

Chateau Potelle   *map page 72, A-2*
The road to this small winery is steep, but the wines are worth every inch of the 1,800-foot elevation. The winery uses only natural fermentation for its estate and Napa Valley grapes. The splendid estate zinfandel proves that even the French (owners Jean-Noel and Marketta Fourmeaux de Sartel are from France) can make a great wine from California's native grape. *3875 Mount Veeder Road; 707-255-9440.*

A vineyard at Schramsberg.

NORTHERN NAPA VALLEY

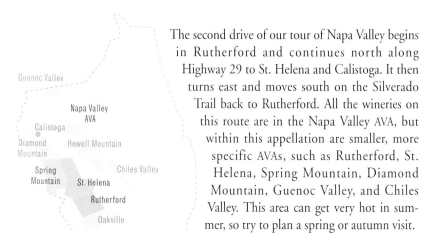

The second drive of our tour of Napa Valley begins in Rutherford and continues north along Highway 29 to St. Helena and Calistoga. It then turns east and moves south on the Silverado Trail back to Rutherford. All the wineries on this route are in the Napa Valley AVA, but within this appellation are smaller, more specific AVAs, such as Rutherford, St. Helena, Spring Mountain, Diamond Mountain, Guenoc Valley, and Chiles Valley. This area can get very hot in summer, so try to plan a spring or autumn visit.

■ RUTHERFORD APPELLATION

The tiny community of Rutherford is made up of a few houses near the intersection of two Wine Country roads, but this may well be one of the most important wine-related intersections in the United States. For here, on either side of the highway, stand the ivy-clad wineries of Inglenook and Beaulieu. The former was founded in 1879 by Gustave Niebaum, a Finnish sea captain; the latter, by the French vintner Georges de Latour in 1900. Together they kept the reputation of California wines alive during Prohibition.

Two wineries in the Rutherford AVA, Cakebread and Saint Supéry, are covered in the "Southern Napa Valley" chapter, and you can visit a few more in this appellation toward the end of this tour when we swing south on the Silverado Trail.)

Inglenook and Niebaum-Coppola Estate *map page 103, B-7/8*
Although the once-venerated Inglenook label has been reduced to a Central Valley bulk wine label, the winery building and vineyards are now part of the Niebaum-Coppola Estate. Inglenook's founder, Gustave Niebaum, had made his money in the Alaska fur trade after his Russian employers sold that territory to the United States. Having traveled widely in Europe, Niebaum was familiar with fine wines, and when in 1880 he purchased two farms, one of which had been named Inglenook by its former owner, Niebaum set out to make California wines that would rival the best in Europe. He learned everything he could about wine making—through books, magazines, and trips to great vineyards and wineries.

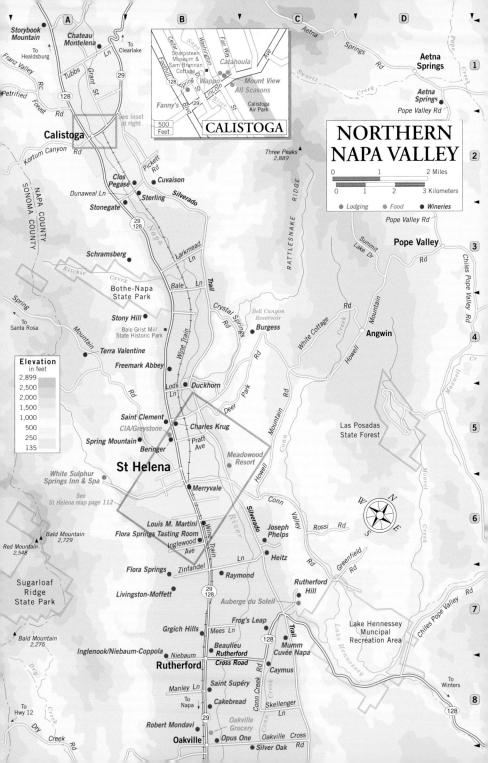

NORTHERN NAPA VALLEY

CALISTOGA

- Lodging
- Food
- Wineries

Elevation
in feet
- 2,899
- 2,500
- 2,000
- 1,500
- 1,000
- 500
- 250
- 135

St Helena

Rutherford

Oakville

Pope Valley

Angwin

Aetna Springs

Calistoga

Storybook Mountain
Chateau Montelena
To Healdsburg
Franz Valley Rd
Petrified Forest Rd
Tubbs Ln
Grant St
To Clearlake

NAPA COUNTY
SONOMA COUNTY

To Santa Rosa

Kortum Canyon Rd
Pickett Rd
Clos Pegase
Cuvaison
Dunaweal Ln
Sterling
Silverado
Stonegate
Schramsberg
Ritchie Creek
Bothe-Napa State Park
Stony Hill
Bale Grist Mill State Historic Park
Terra Valentine
Freemark Abbey
Wine Train
Lodi Ln
Duckhorn
Saint Clement
CIA/Greystone
Charles Krug
Spring Mountain
Beringer
Pratt Ave
White Sulphur Springs Inn & Spa
Merryvale
Louis M. Martini
Flora Springs Tasting Room
Inglewood Ave
Flora Springs
Zinfandel
Livingston-Moffett
Raymond
Heitz
Grgich Hills
Frog's Leap
Mees Ln
Beaulieu
Inglenook/Niebaum-Coppola
Niebaum
Cross Road
Saint Supéry
Manley Ln
Cakebread
Robert Mondavi
Opus One
Silver Oak
Oakville Grocery
To Napa
To Hwy 12

Bale Ln
Larkmead Ln
Crystal Springs Rd
Bell Canyon Reservoir
Burgess
Deer Park Rd
Conn Creek Rd
White Cottage Rd
Howell Mountain Rd
Meadowood Resort
Howell
Conn
Silverado
Napa River
Joseph Phelps
Valley Rd
Rossi Rd
Greenfield Rd
Rutherford Hill
Auberge du Soleil
Caymus
Mumm Cuvée Napa
Trail
Skellenger Ln
Oakville Cross Rd
Conn Creek Rd

Three Peaks 2,889
RATTLESNAKE RIDGE
Summit Lake Dr
Pope Valley Rd
Chiles Pope Valley Rd
Maxwell Cr
Las Posadas State Forest
Moorel Creek
Lake Hennessey Muncipal Recreation Area
Lake Hennessey
To Winters
Chiles Pope Valley Rd

Bald Mountain 2,729
Red Mountain 2,548
Sugarloaf Ridge State Park
Bald Mountain 2,275
Dry Creek Rd
Dry Creek Rd

Aetna Springs Rd
Aetna Springs
Pope Valley Rd
Swartz Creek
Pope Creek

0   1   2 Miles
0   1   2   3 Kilometers

N
W   E
S

See inset at right
See St Helena map page 112

CALISTOGA
Sharpsteen Museum & Sam Brannan Cottage
Catahoula
Wappo
Mount View All Seasons
Fanny's
Calistoga Air Park
Cedar St
Foothill
Spring St
Washington
Lincoln Ave
Fair Way
Napa River
Wappo Ave
500 Feet
128
29

Gustave Niebaum in 1880, the year after the Finnish sea captain completed his purchase of the Inglenook farm.

By 1887, construction on the state-of-the-art Niebaum winery had been completed, and by 1889, he was producing wines of such excellent quality that they won prizes at an exposition in Paris. Niebaum required that all Inglenook wines be bottled in glass, which was not required by law for another half century.

During Prohibition the winery was closed, and the estate concentrated on producing prunes. After the repeal of Prohibition, John Daniel, a grandnephew of Niebaum, took over the winery and restored it to its former eminence, producing red wines of very high quality. In 1964, he sold the winery to Allied Grape Growers, who after forming an entity called United Vintners promptly transferred wine making to a larger facility the company owned nearby. In 1969, United Vintners was sold to Heublein, a producer of spirits. Later that year, Heublein bought Beaulieu, Rutherford's other venerable winery. Heublein made some halfhearted attempts to keep up the quality at Inglenook, but the winery's reputation continued to deteriorate. The Inglenook label was eventually sold to the New York–based wine company, Canandaigua, and the building itself was purchased by filmmaker Francis Ford Coppola in 1995.

Two decades earlier, Coppola and his wife, Eleanor, had purchased the Niebaum mansion and grounds, west of the Inglenook winery, from Inglenook. They converted the old stables to a winery and started making wine as Niebaum-Coppola Estate. It was obvious from the beginning that this was going to be a high-quality operation. The first wine, from the 1978 vintage, was not released until 1985. The wine, named Rubicon, showed that it was in the same class as the old Inglenook reds—of which the 1887, 1888, and 1889 vintages are still alive and well, although you can hardly expect to find a bottle.

Japanese plum trees bloom along the road leading to the Niebaum-Coppola Estate.

According to Coppola, local residents who wanted to see Inglenook restored to its former glory helped him persuade Heublein to sell the winery to him. To thank them, he threw the biggest block party the Napa Valley has ever seen. Coppola restored the old Inglenook winery and now uses part of it to produce Niebaum-Coppola Estate wines. The winery also houses paraphernalia from Coppola movies. Tours and tastings are offered. *1991 St. Helena Highway; 707-968-1100.*

Beaulieu Vineyard   *map page 103, G-2*

The ivy-covered edifice of Beaulieu Vineyard sits prominently in the center of Rutherford. The winery was founded by Georges de Latour, but his wife, Fernande, had much to do with the winery's success. A Californian of French parentage, she introduced de Latour to the San Francisco social circles in which his wine became fashionable. According to the novelist Gertrude Atherton, Fernande de Latour, not Georges, named the winery Beaulieu ("beautiful site"), and the winery stayed open during Prohibition, making "wines for sacramental and governmental purposes" (throughout Prohibition the government served wine at functions at which foreign dignitaries were present). After her husband's death in

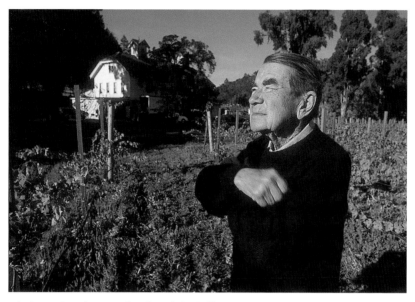

The late and much respected André Tchelistcheff, the doyen of the California wine industry.

1940, Fernande de Latour kept the winery going. Her heirs sold it to Heublein in 1969, and it is now owned by Diageo/UDV Guinness.

The late André Tchelistcheff, Beaulieu's winemaker from 1936 to 1973, placed Beaulieu among the world's great wineries and may well have been the most influential American winemaker ever. Not only did he set an example by making great wine, he also advised winemakers from California to the Pacific Northwest. Look at the historical records of the West Coast's most successful wineries, and Tchelistcheff's name is sure to pop up. The style of the wine you drink with your dinner is more likely than not influenced by his ideas and ideals, from varietal selection to fermentation techniques to barrel construction.

Despite Beaulieu's corporate ownership, the integrity of its top wine, the Georges Latour Private Reserve cabernet sauvignon, first created by Tchelistcheff in the 1930s, has been maintained. The winery also makes good cabernet sauvignon, chardonnay, and pinot noir. The "Beautour" reds are good wines at reasonable prices. By all means, take the tour offered here. *1960 St. Helena Highway; 707-963-2411.*

Grgich Hills Cellar   *map page 103, B-7*

Just north of Rutherford center, look for Grgich Hills, a small ivy-covered winery on the west side of the highway. In 1977, shortly after his Chateau Montelena chardonnay bested several top French white Burgundies at the famous 1976 Paris tasting, Miljenko (Mike) Grgich opened a winery of his own in partnership with Austin Hills, an heir to the Hills Brothers coffee fortune. It's almost too bad that Grgich won early fame with chardonnay, a grape that has almost been turned into a Napa Valley cliché, because the cabernet sauvignon, fumé blanc, and zinfandel that Grgich makes are every bit as good, if not better. Taste them at the winery, then surprise your friends by planning a meal around a Grgich Hills fumé and zinfandel. You might also want to lay away a few bottles. Wines made by Grgich in the early 1970s are still very good and are aging well; a few could even go a bit longer. Tastings are offered daily, but tours are by appointment only. *1829 St. Helena Highway; 707-963-2784.*

Raymond Vineyards & Cellars   *map page 103, B-6/7*

Roy Raymond Sr. went to work for Beringer as winemaker in 1933; in 1936 he married Martha Jane Beringer, the granddaughter of one of the founders. After spending some 30 years at Beringer he retired, and in 1971 he established his own 80-acre vineyard on Zinfandel Lane east of Highway 29. His sons, Roy Jr. and Walt, joined him in the winery, which made its first wine in 1974. Today, Roy Jr. manages the vineyards at Raymond Vineyards & Cellars, and Walt makes the wine. The wines are still good, but not as exciting as the cabernets made by Raymond in the early 1980s. Perhaps it was the special touch of Roy Sr., who died in 1998, that made those wines so distinct. Or the winery may have suffered when the Raymonds sold it to Kirin Breweries of Japan in 1989 (the Raymonds are now managing partners with a minority interest). But who knows? Upcoming vintages might surprise us all. Keep tasting. Recent vintages of Raymond sauvignon blanc have been quite nice. The winery is open daily for tastings; recent vintages are complimentary, but a fee is charged for older and limited-production wines. Tours are offered in the morning, by appointment. *849 Zinfandel Lane; 707-963-3141.*

Livingston-Moffett Wines   *map page 103, B-7*

Several of the valley's top red wine vineyards lie in the small Rutherford Bench area, roughly 3 miles of deep, well-drained alluvial soils west of Highway 29 between between Rutherford and Oakville. This is some of the Wine Country's

Merlot grapes just before harvest.

best grape-growing land and is home Livingston-Moffett Wines, a small winery that makes truly great cabernet sauvignon. Some of the grapes used to produce Livingston wines come from the Moffett Vineyard right on the property, and others come from gravelly patches of vineyards up and down the valley. These gravelly patches are chosen by John Livingston, a geologist by training, who has a knack for finding small pockets of exceptional grapes and convincing vineyard owners to sell those grapes to Livingston. (The wines created from these grapes are labeled as Stanley's Selection.)

Livingston is managed by John's wife, Diane. One son handles much of the sales, marketing, and strategic planning for the winery; another son oversees the cellar operations. Just south of the family home and the old barn that serves as the winery's office stand the stone wall ruins of the H. W. Helms Winery of 1883, which the Livingstons plan to restore. Wine caves dug in the hill will connect with the winery when the restoration is complete. The Helms winery was famous in its day for the quality of its wines, and Livingston wines exceed the Helms standard. Tastings and tours are by appointment only. Call to buy a few cases for a special occasion. *1895 Cabernet Lane; 707-963-2120.*

■ St. Helena Appellation

North of the Rutherford AVA lies the St. Helena AVA, which encompasses the town of St. Helena.

Flora Springs Wine Company   *map page 103, B-6/7 and B-6*
Off Zinfandel Lane west of Highway 29 and right next to Livingston is the Flora Springs Wine Company. This old stone winery, built in the 1880s by the Scots Rennie Brothers, served as home for Louis M. Martini from 1930 to 1976 and was purchased in 1977 by Jerry and Flora Komes as a retirement getaway. In 1979, their adult children joined them in making the first wine from grapes growing on the property, a chardonnay. In recent years, Flora Springs has made more of a splash with its reds, especially a sangiovese and a red Meritage called Trilogy because it is blended from three traditional Bordeaux grape varietals: cabernet sauvignon, cabernet franc, and merlot. There's a good reason for the quality of the wines: the grapes grow in some of the best soils of the Rutherford appellation. The winery itself is not open to the public, but the tasting room in St. Helena is. *Winery: Zinfandel Lane; 707-963-5711. Tasting Room: 677 St. Helena Highway South; 707-967-8032.*

Louis M. Martini   *map page 103, B-5/6*
Back on Highway 29, head north toward St. Helena. Just before you reach town, look for the Louis M. Martini winery on the right side. This winery, founded in 1922 by the late Louis M. Martini as a grape-growing farm, started making wines under his name after the repeal of Prohibition. Martini's son Louis P., who died in 1998, brought the winery to prominence. Although it is now owned by Gallo, Louis P.'s daughter Caroline runs it, and her brother Michael makes the wine. Known primarily for "sound wines and honest prices," as one guidebook states it, this winery has always kept a low profile, both in its physical plant and in its public image, causing a lot of credit owed Louis M. Martini to go to others. Truly one of the Wine Country's pioneering wineries, Louis M. Martini was among the first to identify and propagate vinifera clones and to release vintage-dated varietal wines. Martini's was the first large winery to invest in Carneros and Mayacamas vineyards. The winery's best wines are its reds, especially the barbera and zinfandel. Both profit from bottle aging. Tastings and tours are offered. *254 St. Helena Highway South; 707-963-2736.*

The late Louis P. Martini inspects grapes in one of his vineyards.

■ **TOWN OF ST. HELENA**   *map page 103, B-5/6, and page 112*

At the **Bale Grist Mill State Historic Park,** north of St. Helena off Highway 29, you can watch grain being ground by water power on weekends and buy some freshly milled flour. But unlike many other parts of the Napa Valley, which focused on milling grain until the very late 19th century, St. Helena took to vines almost instantly. The town got its start in 1854 when Henry Still built a store. Still wanted company and donated lots on his town site to anyone who wanted to erect a business house. Soon his store was joined by a wagon shop, a shoe shop, hotels, and churches. In 1857, the town was large enough to be officially recognized.

Dr. George Crane planted a vineyard in 1858 and was the first to produce wine in commercially viable quantities. A German winemaker named Charles Krug followed suit a couple of years later, and other wineries soon followed. At the same time that phylloxera began its destruction of France's vineyards, Napa Valley wines caught the world's attention. At the 1889 World's Fair in Paris, Napa Valley wines walked away with an impressive array of awards, and demand for them increased exponentially. In St. Helena, rapid business growth spawned a building frenzy. Many of the mansions still gracing the town's residential neighborhoods were built

PROUD OF ITS WINE

St. Helena . . . is proud of the great quantity of rich wine-grapes grown in the district it serves and of its many old wine cellars. Many of the inhabitants of St. Helena and environs are Swiss, Germans, and Italians from vineyard sections of Europe. Here as abroad they hold their new-wine festivals each fall—with certain American additions in the form of floats with figures of Bacchus and his followers. Beside State 29 on the northern outskirts is the **Beringer Brothers Winery** (*open*), in whose underground storage cellars . . . hundreds of thousands of gallons of wine are aging in great casks.

—*WPA Guide to California,* 1939

during this decade. Many homes also served as wineries, and many basements were designed as wine cellars. Today, several old stone wineries have been converted into private homes: the 1886 Dowdell Winery, 1870 Edge Hill Vineyard winery, 1880 Castner winery, and 1876 Weinberger winery.

What gives downtown St. Helena its special ambience is the warmth of the sun-mellowed stone buildings on Main Street, mostly between Adams and Spring Streets, and along Railroad Avenue. Of these, Steve's Hardware dates back to 1878, the I.O.O.F. Building to 1885, and the very elaborately decorated Masonic Lodge to 1892. Other notable structures include the Noble Building at Main and Spring Streets and the *St. Helena Star* offices on Main Street. Several buildings sport modern facades, but you can study the old structures by strolling the back alleys. The St. Helena Hotel, built in 1881, has a room dedicated to the British actress Lillie Langtry, who is said to have stayed here on her way to visit her ranch at Guenoc, in Lake County. (Other accounts claim she stayed at the Miramonte near the railroad tracks.)

In the late 1800s, there were some attempts at turning St. Helena into an industrial center to supply specialized machinery to local viticulturists. Several stone warehouses were built near the railroad tracks downtown, and in 1884 the firm of Taylor, Duckworth, and Company put up an impressive stone building to serve as a foundry for building wine presses, and as a planing mill and factory for grape boxes. By 1890 the enterprise had failed, and the structure was subsequently used as an electric plant, glove factory, storage shed, and hatchery. For a while, it housed the Robert Louis Stevenson Museum, which moved adjacent to the public library in 1979. The old foundry building is now occupied by offices and the restaurant Terra.

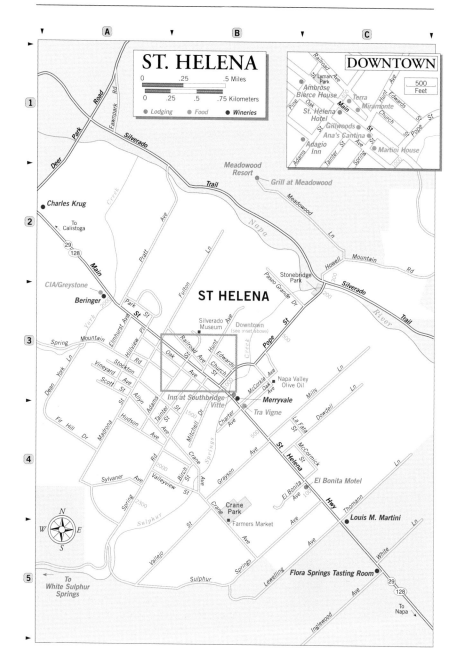

ST. HELENA

0 .25 .5 Miles
0 .25 .5 .75 Kilometers

● Lodging   ● Food   ● Wineries

DOWNTOWN

500 Feet

Lyman Park
Ambrose Bierce House
Terra
Miramonte
St. Helena Hotel
Gillwoods
Ana's Cantina
Adagio Inn
Martini House

Meadowood Resort
Grill at Meadowood

Charles Krug
To Calistoga

CIA/Greystone
Beringer

ST HELENA

Stonebridge Park

Silverado Museum
Downtown (see inset above)

Napa Valley Olive Oil
Inn at Southbridge
Vitte
Merryvale
Tra Vigne

El Bonita Motel

Crane Park
Farmers Market

Louis M. Martini

To White Sulphur Springs

Flora Springs Tasting Room

To Napa

(left) Robert Louis Stevenson, who visited Jacob Schram's winery north of St. Helena in 1880. (right) Ambrose Bierce, who lived in St. Helena for a time at the end of the 19th century.

The **Ambrose Bierce House** (1515 Main Street), built in 1872, has been restored. It now serves as an inn and has a collection of memorabilia of the cantankerous writer of *The Devil's Dictionary* and other works, who lived here for 13 years before vanishing in Mexico in 1913.

The **Silverado Museum,** east of downtown at the public library on Library Lane, has one of the best collections of Robert Louis Stevenson memorabilia in the world. The collection is so good that Scottish television crews have come several times to shoot documentaries here. *1490 Library Lane; 707-963-3757.*

Many visitors never get away from Main Street and its wineries, restaurants, and shops, but leave it behind to stroll through quiet residential neighborhoods. A few blocks to the west you are surrounded by vineyards that merge into the ragged wilderness edge of the Mayacamas Mountains. A few blocks to the east on Pope Street is the Napa River, which separates St. Helena from the Silverado Trail and Howell Mountain. Don't be surprised if a deer comes down to the edge of the road, or if a heron rises from a riparian pool.

The hardest part about dining in St. Helena is choosing a restaurant. The public parking area on Railroad Avenue is within walking distance of many places, including Terra, which has superb food and an outstanding wine list, and Martini House, a somewhat fancy establishment where it can be difficult to get a table. Tra Vigne is a longer walk to the south. For casual fare, drop in at Ana's Cantina on Main Street near Spring, or pick up the makings for a picnic at the Napa Valley Olive Oil Mfg. Co., at the east end of Charter Oak Avenue. You can settle down at one of the picnic tables just outside the white barnlike structure, amid grapevines and orange trees, or head for **Lyman Park** downtown, or to **Stonebridge Park,** where the stone-arch Pope Street Bridge, built in 1890, crosses the Napa River.

■ St. Helena and Spring Mountain Appellations

The St. Helena AVA stretches from Flora Springs north to Freemark Abbey and east to the Silverado Trail. The Spring Mountain AVA includes land to the west and north of St. Helena. All the wineries in this section of our tour are in the St. Helena appellation except for Spring Mountain Vineyards, Terra Valentine, and Stony Hill, which are in the Spring Mountain appellation.

Merryvale Vineyards   *map page 103, B-5/6*

Shortly after you enter downtown St. Helena, you'll see the pastel-colored stone buildings of the Tra Vigne restaurant complex on your right. Just beyond is Merryvale Vineyards, founded in 1983 by Robin Lail (a daughter of John Daniel, of Inglenook fame) and other investors at what was originally the Sunny St. Helena Winery (which gave the Mondavis their Napa Valley start). Among the wines a red Meritage blend called Profile is worth tasting, as is a white Meritage. The tasting room is an easy stroll from Tra Vigne and offers a pleasant diversion while you wait for a table. *1000 Main Street; 707-963-2225.*

Beringer Vineyards   *map page 103, B-5*

North of St. Helena, on the west side of Highway 29 just before a tunnel of elm trees, is the entrance gate to Beringer Vineyards, the Napa Valley's oldest winery in continuous operation. Founded in 1876 by Rhine Valley emigrants

Tra Vigne restaurant is one of several that have transformed St. Helena into a gourmet's paradise.

Jacob and Frederick Beringer, the winery made sacramental wines as well as a little brandy for "health purposes" during Prohibition. Beringer had fallen on hard times when it was rescued by the Swiss Nestlé corporation in 1971. Nestlé proved that corporate ownership of a winery does not necessarily mean a decline in quality. The company hired the legendary Myron Nightingale as winemaker and supplied him with everything he needed to produce first-rate wine. It also renovated the old Beringer mansion, updated the winery and wine-making equipment, restored the caves, and invested in excellent vineyards.

Nestlé sold its wine interests in late 1995 to American investors, and Beringer is now owned by Blass Wine Estates, the winery division of the Australian beverage conglomerate Foster's Group. The Napa Valley cabernet and chardonnay—especially the reserve wines—put Beringer in the ranks of California's top wineries; the Knights Valley cabernet and sauvignon blanc are in a class by themselves.

The tour of Beringer should not be missed, especially the stone tunnels dug by Chinese laborers in the 19th century, which now serve as storage cellars for the reserve cabernets. A guide may tell you that the tunnels were cut into limestone,

(above) Frederick Beringer (fifth from right) poses in front of his winery.
(opposite) A candlelit banquet in the cask room of Merryvale Vineyards.

The Beringer estate and winery is probably the biggest tourist attraction in the Napa Valley.

but the "stone" here is actually compacted volcanic ash. The old winery, built from squared stones, is much too small for current operations, but a state-of-the-art winery, not open to the public, is located across the street.

The winery's grounds are beautifully landscaped, and its two mansions have been meticulously restored. The Rhine House, built in the 1880s to resemble the Beringers' ancestral home, was Frederick's residence and now contains the tasting rooms. Jacob and his family lived north of the redwood grove in the Hudson House, built by the property's first settler. For a few years, Hudson House was home to the Beringer's School for American Chefs, a program that brought professional chefs to the winery for an intense two-week course taught by the renowned cooking teacher and writer Madeleine Kamman. Through her courses, Kamman did more than anyone else to put the Napa Valley on the national food map. On the north side of the Hudson House, near the overflow parking lot, look for an old mission fig tree. If you visit in autumn when the figs are ripe, be sure to take at least one delicious bite. *2000 Main Street; 707-963-7115.*

CULINARY INSTITUTE OF AMERICA

Across the street from Charles Krug is a huge stone building known as Greystone. Built in 1889 by William Bourn II, an investor who had made his money in gold mines, Greystone was intended as a cooperative winery for Napa growers, but was never used as such and was not even equipped as a winery until Christian Brothers bought it in 1950. In 1995 it became the West Coast campus of the CIA, which restored the stone edifice, installed teaching kitchens, planted a 2-acre organic garden, and opened a diverting museum of corkscrews and a 125-seat classroom restaurant. The emphasis of the restaurant is on foods from countries on the Mediterranean Sea. A scholarship program set up by Jack and Jamie Davies of Schramsberg allows chefs to study wine, wine making, and the matching of wine and food. Late on a warm afternoon, the terrace here is a fine place to enjoy a glass of wine and vineyard views. *2555 St. Helena Highway; 707-963-4503.*

Greystone being built in 1889. The massive structure became Christian Brothers Winery in 1950 and now accommodates the Culinary Institute of America's West Coast campus.

Cesare Mondavi and his sons rescued the Charles Krug Winery in 1943.

Charles Krug Winery   *map page 103, B-5*

The Napa Valley's oldest surviving winery was founded by Charles Krug in 1861 and quickly rose to prominence. Unfortunately, Krug had a tendency to overspend, and he went bankrupt before his death. His huge, ostentatious carriage house is now used to store wine. Charles Krug was closed during Prohibition and did not reopen until it was rescued by Cesare Mondavi and his sons, Robert and Peter, in 1943. The quality of the wines made by the Mondavis put Charles Krug back in the limelight; however, after Robert Mondavi left in the 1960s to set up his own operation, Charles Krug lost its luster. Still, under Peter Mondavi's stewardship, the winery has continued to make good wine, especially reds. Tours and tastings are offered. *2800 Main Street; 707-963-2761.*

Saint Clement Vineyards   *map page 103, B-5*

Just north of the CIA on the same side of the road is Saint Clement Vineyards. A hospitality center with tasting room occupies a Victorian mansion built here in 1876 as a family home by Fritz Rosenbaum, who made wine in the small stone winery beneath the house. He called his property Johannaberg. The mansion was bonded in 1968 by Mike Robbins, a southern California real estate speculator, as Spring Mountain Vineyards. Robbins sold the Rosenbaum mansion in 1975 to Dr. William Casey, a San Francisco eye surgeon, who renamed it St. Clement and continued to make wine here. He built a larger winery adjacent to the mansion in 1979. Saint Clement is now owned by Beringer Blass and is worth visiting for a tour of the stone cellar, a taste of the sauvignon blanc and merlot, and for its splendid views. *2867 St. Helena Highway; 707-963-7221.*

Spring Mountain Vineyards   *map page 103, A/B-5*

In 1974 Robbins bought Tiburcio Parrott's old Miravalle estate on Spring Mountain. In 1976, he built a new winery beside the mansion and named it Spring Mountain Vineyards. This was once the best-known winery in the Napa Valley, not because its chardonnay came in fourth in the famous Paris tasting, ahead of three renowned white burgundies, but because it served as a setting for the television soap opera *Falcon Crest.* Robbins even released a Falcon Crest wine in 1982. Unfortunately, in the end the *Falcon Crest* association hurt the winery's reputation, and the bank foreclosed on the winery. It was rescued by the Good Wine Company, headed by Tom Ferrell, formerly the president of Sterling Vineyards. The first-rate wines here include a Spring Mountain Reserve red (a blend of cabernet sauvignon, merlot, and cabernet franc), a Spring Mountain Estate red (a blend of cabernet sauvignon and merlot), a syrah, and a sauvignon blanc. The winery is closed to the public. *2805 Spring Mountain Road; 707-967-4188.*

Terra Valentine   *map page 103, A-4/5*

Farther up Spring Mountain Road is Terra Valentine, in the resurrected Yverdon winery. Yverdon was founded in 1970, at an elevation of 2,100 feet above the Napa Valley, by eccentric Fred Aves, a self-taught winemaker. He designed this two-story stone and concrete winery with stained glass, wood carvings, bronze doors, and statues. The building had stood empty since the early 1980s, but entrepreneur Fred Wurtele bought the property in 1999 and restored the winery and its two vineyards, one of which has been planted primarily in cabernet sauvignon, with smaller plantings of traditional Bordeaux blending grapes (merlot, cabernet franc, petit verdot, and malbec). So far, Terra Valentine has made only two wines, both cabernet sauvignons and both superb. Tastings are by appointment. *3787 Spring Mountain Road; 707-967-8340.*

Freemark Abbey *map page 103, B-4/5*

Old-time Napa Valley vintners and friends established Freemark Abbey in 1967 in a stone winery erected in 1886 by Josephine Tychson after her husband, John, committed suicide. Taking over the project the couple had planned together, Josephine became the first woman to oversee the building of a winery in California. In 1900 it was acquired by Antonio Forni, who renamed it Lombarda and produced wine until Prohibition shut him down in 1919. Eventually, the winery was sold to three investors—Charles Freeman, Mark Foster, and Albert Ahern, whose boyhood nickname had been Abbey. The trio operated Freemark Abbey from 1940 to 1959. Then, for eight years, no wine was produced here, although parts of the building served as a candle factory and a restaurant.

The current owners started making great wines from the first vintage, and the winery has been noteworthy for its cabernets ever since. All the wines are made from estate-grown grapes, with the exception of a cabernet whose grapes come from the Bosché vineyard of the Rutherford Bench and which is bottled separately. The winery has also gained notice for its late-harvest Riesling. Its visitors center is open daily. *3022 St. Helena Highway North; 707-963-9694.*

Stony Hill Vineyard *map page 103, A/B-4*

A narrow unmarked road leads up Spring Mountain to Stony Hill Vineyard, a wine-making legend that preceded others by some 30 years. This is another Napa Valley winery that started out as a weekend retreat. Eleanor and Fred McCrea fell in love with a goat farm on Spring Mountain and bought it as a summer home in 1943. They planted chardonnay vines in 1948, when that grape was virtually unknown in the Wine Country, and sold their first wines in 1954. Fred McCrea died in 1977, Eleanor in 1991, so the winery is now run by their descendants. Production is still minuscule, and quality has not suffered. The winery makes a little Riesling, which, sip by sip, is as good as the chardonnay. If you have not tasted a Stony Hill wine, find a way to do so. You might go to one of the Napa Valley restaurants where Stony Hill wines are served, among them Auberge de Soleil and the French Laundry.

Stony Hill Vineyard occupies one of the Valley's loveliest spots, with perhaps the most perfect integration of farm and nature. You must call ahead for a tour or tasting appointment. *3331 St. Helena Highway North; 707-963-2636.*

(top) The Freemark Abbey stone winery dates back to 1886.
(bottom) Drying trays at Stony Hill Vineyard.

Jacob Schram built this mansion for his wife after she complained about the small cabin they had been living in since the vineyard's founding in 1862.

■ NAPA VALLEY APPELLATION

Traveling toward Calistoga, you move out of the St. Helena AVA. Head north on Highway 29 and turn east on Dunaweal Lane to reach the Silverado Trail. The wineries along the way are in the Napa Valley AVA and do not fall into any other appellation. This route includes two of the splashiest wineries in the Napa Valley: Sterling Vineyards and Clos Pegase.

Schramsberg Vineyards   *map page 103, A/B-3*
On the southern edge of Calistoga, tucked into an idyllic dell on the slope of a mountain, is Schramsberg, a famed maker of sparkling wines. Founded in 1965 by Jack and Jamie Davies, the winery occupies the 19th-century cellars, stone winery, and home of Jacob Schram. Schram had founded a winery here in 1862, a year after Charles Krug started his. He made many different wines, including a first-rate Riesling, but he did not make sparklers. His winery gained literary fame when Robert Louis Stevenson visited in 1880 to taste the wines and wrote about his experience in *Silverado Squatters*.

Annie Schram (seated above) poses with vineyard workers and family members in front of a new wine cellar.

The Davies family's excursion into sparkling-wine production was unique not because they made their wine by the traditional *méthode champenoise*—others, such as Hanns Kornell, on Larkmead Lane, had done that before—but because they insisted on using the traditional grapes of Champagne: chardonnay and pinot noir, very few of which had been planted in the Napa Valley at that time. Schramsberg has not looked back since President Richard Nixon served Schramsberg sparkling wine at a state dinner he gave for the Chinese premier Chou En-lai in Beijing in 1972. Production has increased, but the quality is still as good as ever.

Tours and tasting at this especially charming winery are by appointment only. You will learn a lot about how sparkling wine is made, but perhaps best of all is the delightful bubbly you'll get to sip at the end of the tour. Travel 5 miles north of St. Helena on Highway 29; turn left onto Peterson Road and then right onto Schramsberg Road. The road is very narrow and winding; watch for wildlife and other cars. *1400 Schramsberg Road; 707-942-4558.*

CHAMPAGNE AND SPARKLING WINES

If you don't like dry Champagne say so. A moderately sweet (or moderately dry) Champagne is a human kind. A Brut is not. It is an acquired taste.

—Hilaire Belloc

Sparkling wines are, despite the mystique surrounding them, nothing more or less than wines in which carbon dioxide is suspended, making them bubbly. Sparkling wines were perfected in Champagne, France's northernmost wine district, where wines tend to be a bit acidic because grapes do not always fully ripen. That's why sparkling wines have traditionally been naturally tart, even austere.

Because of their progenitor's birthplace, many sparkling wines are often called "Champagne." However, this term designates a region of origin, so it really shouldn't be used for American sparkling wines. That's not to say that Napa and Sonoma County sparkling wines are in any way inferior to French ones—some are even better. The French Champagne houses are fully aware of the excellence of the California product and have been quick to cash in on the laurels gathered by such pioneers as Hanns Kornell, Schramsberg, and Iron Horse by establishing sparkling-wine cellars in Sonoma and Napa with American partners.

Keep in mind that although we no longer need to drink pricey imported Champagne, quality American sparklers don't come cheap. Good sparkling wine will always be expensive because a great amount of work goes into making it.

Harvest

It starts with the harvest. White sparkling wines are made from white and black grapes, which allows them to achieve complex flavors. Growers pick the black grapes carefully to avoid crushing them. The goal is to minimize contact between the inner fruit and the skins, where the purply-red color pigments reside. The grapes are rushed to the winery, crushed very gently, and the juice is strained off the skins right away, again, to prevent the juice from coming in contact with pigments and turning red. (The juice of the black grape's inner fruit is usually white.) Even so, some sparklers have more of a pink tinge to them than the winemaker intends.

Sparkling wines are traditionally made from pinot noir (and, in France, from pinot meunier as well) and chardonnay grapes. In California, pinot blanc, Riesling, and other white wine grapes may also be used.

Man Riddling Bottles of Champagne *(1961) by Ansel Adams.*

Fermentation

The freshly pressed juice and pulp, or must, is fermented with special yeasts that preserve the wine's fruit, the characteristic fruit flavor of the grape variety used. Before bottling, this finished "still" wine (wine without bubbles) is mixed with a *liqueur de tirage,* a blend of wine, sugar, and yeast. This mixture causes the wine to ferment again—in the bottle, where it stays for 6 to 12 weeks. Carbon dioxide, a by-product of fermentation, is produced and trapped in the bottle, where it dissolves in the wine (instead of escaping into the air, as happens during fermentation in barrel, vat, or tank). This captive carbon dioxide transforms the still wine into a sparkling wine. The second fermentation also raises the wine's alcohol content by about one percent. This is one reason why grapes for sparkling wines are picked at low sugar levels: they must ferment out initially to 11 percent alcohol instead of the 12 percent (or more) of regular wines.

Aging

Bottles of new sparkling wine are stored on their sides in deep cellars. The wine now ages *sur lie*, or "on the lees" (the dead yeast cells and other deposits trapped in the bottle). This aging process enriches the wine's texture and embellishes the complexity of its bouquet. The amount of time a sparkling wine ages *sur lie* bears a direct relation to its quality: the longer the aging, the more complex the wine.

Riddling

The lees must be removed from the bottle before a sparkling wine can be enjoyed. This is achieved in a process whose first step is called "riddling." In the past, each bottle, head tilted slightly downward, was placed in a riddling rack, an A-frame with many holes of bottleneck size. Riddlers gave each bottle a slight shake and a downward turn, every day if possible. This continued for six weeks, until each bottle rested upside down in the hole and the sediment had collected in the neck, next to the cork. Simple as this sounds, it is actually very difficult to do. Hand-riddling is a fine art perfected after much training. Today, most sparkling wines are riddled in ingeniously designed machines called gyro palettes, which riddle up to 500 or more bottles at one time. The machines do the work in as little as a week to 10 days. Yet some bottles resist the caressing touch of the machines and must still be riddled by hand.

Disgorging

After riddling, the bottles are "disgorged." The upside-down bottles are placed in a deeply chilled brine solution, which freezes the sediments in a block that attaches itself to the crown cap sealing the bottle. The cap and frozen plug are removed, the bottle is topped off with a wine-and-sugar mixture called "dosage," and recorked with the traditional champagne cork. The dosage determines the final sweetness of a sparkling wine.

Brut to Doux

Sparkling wines with 1.5 percent sugar or less are labeled "brut"; those with 1.2 to 2 percent sugar are called "extra dry"; those with 1.7 to 3.5 percent are called "sec"; and those with 3.5 to 5 percent, "demi-sec." "Doux" (sweet) sparkling wine has more than 5 percent sugar. Most sparkling-wine drinkers refuse to admit that they like their bubbly on the sweet side, and this labeling convention allows them to drink sweet while pretending to drink dry. It's a marketing ploy invented in Champagne at least a century ago. A sparkling wine to which no dosage has been added will be bone dry (and taste "sour" to some) and may be called "extra-brut" or "natural."

Vintage Dating

Most sparkling wines are not vintage dated but are "assembled" (the term sparkling-wine makers use instead of "blended") to create a *cuvée,* a mix of different wines and sometimes different vintages consistent with the house style. However, sparkling wines may be vintage dated in very great years.

Bulk or Charmat Process

Sparkling wine may also be made by time- and cost-saving bulk methods, although this is not done with Champagne. In the bulk or Charmat process, invented by Eugene Charmat early in the 20th century, the secondary fermentation takes place in large tanks rather than individual bottles. Each tank is basically treated as one huge bottle. After the bubbles have developed, the sediments are filtered from the wine and the wine is bottled. But at a price: while the sparkling wine may be ready in as little as a month, it has neither the complexity nor the bubble quality of the more slowly made sparklers. In the United States, sparkling wine made in this way must be labeled "Bulk Process" or "Charmat Process."

Sparkling wines made in the traditional, time-consuming fashion may be labeled "méthode champenoise" or "wine fermented in this bot-tle." But read carefully. One sparkler labels itself "wine made in the bottle." There's quite a differ-ence in methodology here between "this" and "the." The latter is sparkling wine made in the transfer process, in which the second fermentation of the wine takes place in a bottle, but in which all the bottles of a particular batch—instead of being disgorged individually—are emptied into large tanks, under pressure. The sediments are filtered out, the wine is rebottled, corked, and shipped to market.

The different processes of making sparkling wine have an effect not only on the quality and complexity of the wine itself but also on the quality of the bubbles. Filtered wines are not as complex as unfiltered ones: their bubbles are more sparingly distributed, and they do not last very long. But that doesn't really matter, since most wines made like this are drunk quickly, at parties or weddings.

Stonegate Winery   *map page 103, A/B-2/3*

On Dunaweal Lane, just east of Highway 29, look for tiny Stonegate Winery, founded by Jim and Barbara Spaulding in 1973. The Spauldings planted their first grapes on Spring Mountain in 1969, before the Napa Valley became world famous. Stonegate's wines, now from grapes grown in the Diamond Mountain AVA, are consistently good, especially the cabernet sauvignon and merlot made by the couple's son, David, who is the winemaker. The sauvignon blanc is also worth tasting. Tours are by appointment, but tastings are offered daily. *1183 Dunaweal Lane; 707-942-6500.*

Sterling Vineyards   *map page 103, A/B-2/3*

When Sterling Vineyards opened in 1969, few enophiles expected the wines to be good. This was a huge white spectacle dominating a hillside. It was set up by some unknown investors and seemed more of a tourist attraction than a place for making serious wines. But the wines were good, especially the reds. In 1977, the original partners sold the winery to Coca-Cola, which was not a good wine steward. Joseph E. Seagram & Sons bought the winery in 1983 and quality began to improve. Diageo/UDV Guinness bought Seagram and thus Sterling in December 2001, and these days the chardonnay and pinot noir are very good. They are made from Carneros grapes, grown in the renowned Winery Lake Vineyard, which Seagram had bought from René di Rosa in 1986 amid the outcry of winemakers who had depended on those grapes for the excellence of their own wines. The cabernet and merlot are also good but will benefit from bottle aging.

The Sterling winery, built in the stark white style of an Aegean monastery, sits atop a 300-foot-high knoll. You must ride a tram to reach the top, but the fee you pay includes a wine tasting, and your tram ticket is good for a discount on the first bottle of wine you buy. *1111 Dunaweal Lane; 707-942-3344.*

Clos Pegase   *map page 103, A/B-2/3*

Just after the valley had gotten used to Sterling's white monastery-like presence, art book publisher Jan Shrem raised everybody's blood pressure with his plan for an Egyptian temple of a winery—across the street from Sterling. Clos Pegase opened in 1987 with modifications, say those who have seen the original design. The work of the postmodernist architect Michael Graves, Clos Pegase's winery is outrageously individualistic and loaded, but not overloaded, with art objects collected by Jan and Mitsuko Shrem.

Jan Shrem wants people to feel the connection between wine and art, and he most certainly succeeds. Best of all, the wines are as interesting as the art and architecture, and they're getting better with every vintage. *1060 Dunaweal Lane; 707-942-4981.*

Cuvaison Winery   *map page 103, B-2*

Continue east on Dunaweal Lane to the Silverado Trail. Turn right and look for the mission-style arches of Cuvaison Winery on the left. This small winery struggled after it was founded in 1969 as a tax write-off by two engineers. It was rescued in 1979 by Swiss investors who own Tobler Chocolates, among other products. The new owners upgraded the facilities and bought estate vineyards in the Carneros, clear on the other end of the Napa Valley. Somehow this works, especially for cabernet sauvignon, which is odd considering that the Carneros is a cool growing region and cabernet likes warmth. But don't quibble. Enjoy the wine. Tastings are offered daily; tours are in the morning by appointment. *4550 Silverado Trail; 707-942-6266.*

Cuvaison's estate vineyard in the Carneros.

■ CALISTOGA   *map page 103, A-2*

Traveling north on Highway 29/128, consider overshooting your turn onto Dunaweal Lane to stop in the small town of Calistoga. From Lincoln Avenue, Calistoga's main street, you can see Mount St. Helena rising to the north, some 4,000 feet above the valley floor, along with other tall mountains to the west and east. It is hard to believe that you are a mere 365 feet above the level of the Napa River tidewater. The false-fronted shops, old hotels, and quaint stone buildings look like those of a cattle town tucked into a remote mountain valley, where a posse might show up looking for a fugitive desperado. A hundred years ago there were holdups of the stagecoach line that ran across the shoulder of Mount St. Helena to Clear Lake carrying the payroll for the quicksilver mines dotting the mountains. There was even a gold mine here, high above Calistoga, but the town's true claim to fame came from its waters, which bubbled from natural hot springs.

When Sam Brannan—Mormon missionary, San Francisco vigilante, entrepreneur, and vineyard developer—learned in 1859 that a place in the upper Napa Valley called Agua Caliente by the settlers did indeed have hot springs and even an "old faithful" geyser, he bought up 2,000 acres of prime property and laid out a resort. Planning a place that would rival New York's famous Saratoga Hot Springs, which Brannan had visited on a proselytizing trip, he built an elegant hotel, bathhouses, cottages, stables, an observatory, and a distillery (a questionable choice for a Mormon missionary). The distillery proved to be the only moneymaker; its brandy was shipped as far as Europe.

The resort remained unprofitable even after the railroad reached Calistoga in 1868. When the railroad too proved a loser, interest in the resort waned. Brannan left Calistoga in 1877, and the bank holding the mortgage sold the place to Leland Stanford, who intended to build his college here. But the college was built elsewhere, and Stanford sold his interest in 1919. Folks continued traveling to Calistoga to "take the waters," and though the town never achieved the status of a world-class resort, the springs supported a sprinkling of small hotels and bathhouses, built wherever a hot spring bubbled to the surface. You can still take soothing mud baths in a hot paste mixed from mineral water, peat, and volcanic ash, or you can submerge yourself in the naturally hot—and rather muddy—water of a whirlpool bath. You might finish up with a full-body massage.

(previous pages) Barrels large and small at Sterling Vineyards.

The bathhouse at Calistoga Springs, by Eadweard Muybridge (1830–1904), a pioneer of stop-action series photography. In 1874 he was acquitted of killing his wife's lover in Calistoga.

Despite its fame, Calistoga remains an understated sort of place, with quiet tree-shaded back streets where Calistogans live and where some run bed-and-breakfasts. The Napa River flows right through town, but you'll be hard-pressed to find a sign directing you to the places where you can dangle your feet in its cold waters. Park at Pioneer Park on Cedar Street, just north of Lincoln Street, walk past the white gingerbread bandstand, and take the short trail down to the river.

The trail continues across the river—merely a creek at this point—on a concrete walk that leads to two sites you should not miss: the **Sharpsteen Museum** and the adjoining **Sam Brannan Cottage.** The museum was founded by Ben Sharpsteen, an award-winning Walt Disney animator, after Sharpsteen had retired to Calistoga. It contains detailed dioramas showing how the resort looked in its heyday. Quarterly special exhibits have included antique silverware, model ships, and musical instruments of old. The cottage, one of three in town to survive from town founder Sam Brannan's day, has been restored to its original appearance. *1131 Washington Street; 707-942-5911.*

Calistoga has remained more of a spa than wine town, but its vineyards produce some of the Napa Valley's best wines. **Chateau Montelena,** renowned for its chardonnay and cabernet sauvignon, lies at the edge of town (see page 144 for details.) To the northwest, at the head of the valley, rises the steep mountain vineyards that grow Storybook Mountain's superb zinfandel. The All Seasons Cafe, besides serving great food, may well have the best list of local Napa Valley wines of any restaurant in the valley. Several other restaurants in town, most notably Wappo and Catahoula, have also gained widespread fame for the quality of their cookery.

■ SOUTH ON THE SILVERADO TRAIL

From Calistoga, backtrack south on Highway 29/128 and turn left on Dunaweal Lane to reach the Silverado Trail. Turn right again to travel south back through the St. Helena and Rutherford AVAs to the tiny town of Rutherford.

Duckhorn Vineyards   *map page 103, B-4/5*
You will need to look closely to find the buildings of Duckhorn Vineyards. They are below the level of the road and easy to miss. But do as other pilgrims do: take off your hat and bow your head in homage to merlot. This winery, in the St. Helena appellation, also makes cabernet and sauvignon blanc. It was founded in 1978 by a Napa Valley banker and his wife, along with a group of investors. Duckhorn struggled for the first few years, but its wisely planted vineyards assured a reliable supply of great grapes, and the wines soon gained public and critical attention. Duckhorn is now among the Napa Valley's most respected producers. It is open daily for sales and tastings, and for tours by appointment. *1000 Lodi Lane; 707-963-7108.*

Joseph Phelps Vineyards   *map page 103, C-6*
About 4 miles south of Duckhorn, after you pass the Pope Street Bridge, look to the left for a green schoolhouse with white trim. The next left is the turnoff to Joseph Phelps. Turn left again at a big redwood gate to reach the winery, which is up a slope to the north in Spring Valley, part of the St. Helena appellation.

Phelps, a top-rate Colorado contractor, came to the Wine Country to build wineries for Pillsbury (namely, the wineries now known as Rutherford Hill and Chateau Souverain). He fell in love with the area, and in 1973 he bought the

A huge redwood gate marks the entrance to
Joseph Phelps Vineyards.

Connolly Hereford Ranch and built himself a winery. The winery attracted attention right away, especially the wines made by Phelps's initial winemaker, Walter Schug, who left in 1982 to found his own winery. Phelps's best wines in the past were Rieslings; today they are reds: the superb Meritage blend called Insignia, the cabernet sauvignon, and the Rhône-style blends sold as Vin du Mistral and Le Mistral. A tasting room was added in 1995; you'll need to call ahead for an appointment. *200 Taplin Road; 707-963-2745.*

Heitz Wine Cellars   *map page 103, C-6*

Also in Spring Valley, to the south of Phelps, is Heitz Wine Cellars, housed in the old stone winery of Anton Rossi. Joe Heitz, one of the Napa Valley's wine pioneers, opened his first winery in 1961, just south of St. Helena (it is now a tasting room), but he quickly outgrew the original space and bought this property in 1964. Heitz replanted the original vineyard almost exclusively with grignolino, an Italian grape of which he is uncommonly fond.

Successes with his powerful cabernet sauvignon have spurred on other winemakers, but his wines have been a bit uneven in recent years. Taste carefully. Winery tours are by appointment. The tasting room and sales office are open daily. *Winery: 500 Taplin Road; 707-963-3542. Tasting Room: 436 St. Helena Highway; 707-963-3542.*

Rutherford Hill Winery   *map page 103, C-7*

Turn west off the Silverado Trail on Rutherford Hill Road to reach Rutherford Hill Winery, which was at one time the home of the Napa Valley division of Souverain. This Rutherford-appellation winery has one of the most extensive systems of wine caves of any California winery—nearly a mile of tunnels and passageways that were drilled with a special English drilling machine. It took almost a year and a half to complete the project. Rutherford Hill, owned these days by Paterno Imports of Chicago, may well become the leading quality producer of merlot in the United States. It also makes very good cabernet sauvignon and chardonnay. Tours and tastings are offered. *200 Rutherford Hill Road; 707-963-1871.*

Mumm Cuvée Napa   *map page 103, C-7*

Drive south on the Silverado Trail until you see a low barnlike structure on your right, below road level. That's Mumm Cuvée Napa. You don't realize how large this unobtrusive, beautifully designed winery is until you walk right up to it and find yourself walking and walking.

The old stone winery of Anton Rossi now belongs to Heitz Wine Cellars.

Built in 1986, long after other French winemakers had become entrenched in the Napa Valley, Mumm—originally a joint endeavor of Seagram and the French champagne house Mumm but now owned by Allied Domecq—had some catching up to do. It did so with the winery's intelligent layout and with the quality of its sparkling wines. The winery contains an art gallery, which has a permanent exhibit of Ansel Adams photographs commissioned by Seagram to document the wine-making process. There are hourly tours. Be sure to taste the sparklers; they are worth the fee. *8445 Silverado Trail; 707-967-7700.*

Frog's Leap   *map page 103, C-7*

Backtrack north on the Silverado Trail and turn west on Highway 128 (called Conn Creek Road at this point); when you see a leaping-frog weathervane on a huge red barn, you have found Frog's Leap. This Rutherford appellation winery should be on your must-see list, not only because the wines are great—especially the zinfandel, sauvignon blanc, and cabernet sauvignon—but also because this is a winery run by people who make you feel welcome.

The grapes used in Frog's Leap wines are organically grown, and the wines are as good as ever. In 1994, after splitting up with partner Larry Turley, owners John and Julie Williams took their leaping-frog label from the old frog farm north of St. Helena, where it was founded in 1981, to this Rutherford location, the site of the Adamson Winery from 1884 to 1896 (when phylloxera ate the vines). The Williamses have restored the big red barn, the oldest board-and-batten building in the Napa Valley, and turned it into their winery. It is surrounded by gardens, with flowers, shrubs, and olive trees. There's even a frog pond with lily pads. How can a winery go wrong that has a great enough sense of humor to name one of its wines Leapfrögmilch? And you can buy yourself a T-shirt with the famed leaping frog logo. Tours and tastings here are by appointment only. *8815 Conn Creek Road; 707-963-4704.*

Caymus Vineyards *map page 103, C-8*
Continue south on Highway 128 to visit Caymus, a winery with a special quality. The Wagner family began farming in the Napa Valley in 1906, when it grew prunes as well as grapes. In 1972, Charlie Wagner converted an old barn into a winery and started making wine. After he hired Randy Dunn as winemaker, Caymus cabernet sauvignon gained national stature. Dunn left in 1986 to run his own winery on Howell Mountain, and Charlie's son took over the wine making—with no discernible drop in quality. The Caymus reds—the concentration here is solely on cabernet sauvignon these days—are as good as ever. Tasting is by appointment only, and no tours are given. *8700 Conn Creek Road; 707-967-3010.*

At 4,344 feet, Mount St. Helena is the region's highest peak.

NAPA VALLEY
COUNTRY ROADS

What could be more romantic than driving through rolling hills and peaceful valleys along a Wine Country back road, where oak forests, vineyards, and wildflower meadows are still largely undisturbed by the hectic pace of our times? When planning a tour of Napa Valley wineries, consider setting aside a day or two to explore some that are off the beaten path. You will need to change your mindset for this. Don't be in a hurry. Pull over to let hot-rodders pass. Be patient with lumbering pieces of farm machinery and with the occasional herd of cattle slowly mooing down the road. These pauses will give you time to see the sights: strange rock formations, uncommon trees such as tanbark oak and cypress, wildflowers in an assortment of colors, and wildlife, on the ground and in the air.

Watch for wildlife in unexpected places. Deer, for example, have a way of popping up behind blind curves, and hawks and eagles, in pursuit of prey, will skim across the road at breakneck speed. Turkey vultures, the large birds with dingy brown-black plumage and bare heads, live on carrion; they are nature's way of disposing of reckless drivers' roadkill.

On several back roads you might venture down steep trails to creeks and rivers. Beware of poison oak, rattlesnakes, and "No Trespassing" signs. Stay on established trails, being careful not to trample fragile vegetation, and never pick wildflowers. Some of them will not grow back; they should be left for bees, hummingbirds, and the next wayfarer to enjoy.

This trip begins in Calistoga. It takes you over the flanks of Mount St. Helena via Highway 29 to Middletown, where you continue southeast on Butts Canyon Road through the Guenoc and Pope Valleys before returning to the Napa Valley via Chiles Valley. Allow a whole day, so you'll have time for both a hike on Mount St. Helena and stops at a few wineries.

■ OUTSIDE CALISTOGA

Drive north on Highway 128/29 from Rutherford. At Calistoga, Highway 29 takes a hard right and heads east through downtown toward Mount St. Helena and Clear Lake, north of Middletown. Before heading east on Highway 29, consider taking the short drive north on Highway 128 to Storybook Mountain Vineyards.

Storybook Mountain Vineyards *map page 143, A-2*

The tiny winery at Storybook Mountain is tucked into the rock face of the mountain and hardly visible, but the vineyard is one of the most dramatic in the Wine Country, with vines rising steeply from the winery in theatrical tiers. Zinfandel is king here, and those produced by Jerry (Dr. J. Bernard) and Sigrid Seps are deep red in color, full-flavored, and richly complex, with a unique peppery spiciness. (There's talk of cloning a special Storybook Mountain zinfandel grape.) These well-structured wines age beautifully.

The winery itself dates from 1888, when Jacob Grimm, a gentleman farmer from San Francisco, had Chinese workmen dig three deep hillside tunnels to age wine and house a distillery. Storybook's tasting room, in a vaulted cavern connecting two of the tunnels, may well be the most romantic in the Napa Valley. The tunnels are among the best-preserved ones in California, perhaps because a facade of solid concrete—an uncommon building material at the time they were constructed—fronts them. You must make an appointment for tours and tastings. *3835 Highway 128; 707-942-5310.*

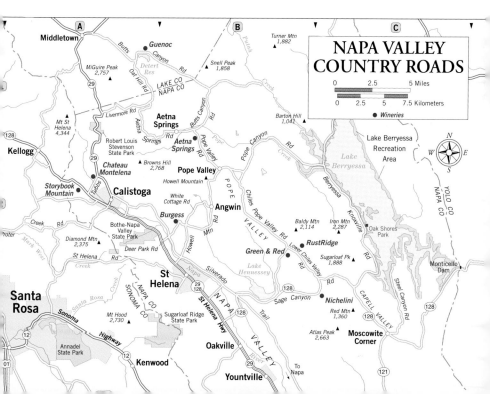

The vineyards of Guenoc Winery.

Chateau Montelena   *map page 143, A-2*

Heading southeast on Highway 128 toward Calistoga, turn left at Tubbs Lane, shortly before town. Continue past the Old Faithful Geyser, which is not worth the stop (it pauses nearly an hour between blasts that are hardly dynamic). Chateau Montelena, just up the road, is something of a curiosity: a French château of hewn gray stone rising above an artificial lake where swans glide among islands topped by Chinese pavilions. It was built by California senator Alfred L. Tubbs in 1882, when the California wine industry was booming because the phylloxera root louse had sucked France's vines dry. A Chinese engineer who had made a lot of money building the Manchurian Railroad added the lake and the Chinese touches in the 1950s.

Los Angeles attorney Jim Barrett rescued the property from hard times in the early 1970s, restored the winery, and hired Miljenko "Mike" Grgich as winemaker. Enlisting Grgich proved to be a stroke of genius: his 1973 chardonnay took first place in the famous 1976 Judgment of Paris tasting of top French and Californian wines. Grgich has since left to open his own winery, but the Chateau Montelena wines, now made by Bo Barrett, are still world-class. Be sure to taste the chardonnay, the estate-grown cabernet sauvignon, and the zinfandel. Tastings are offered daily, but tours are by appointment only. *1429 Tubbs Lane; 707-942-5105.*

(above) This house was occupied by the British actress Lillie Langtry when she owned Guenoc Ranch, from 1888 to 1906. (following pages) The view from Langtry House.

■ OVER MOUNT ST. HELENA TO GUENOC LAKE

As you leave Chateau Montelena, turn left to reach Highway 29. Turn left again (watch for fast-moving downhill traffic) toward Mount St. Helena. The road climbs steeply through curves and switchbacks, but it's splendidly scenic.

At 4,344 feet, Mount St. Helena is the tallest peak in the Bay Area. Drive slowly. Note the changing vegetation and the variety of rock formations. Middletown, at an altitude of about 1,300 feet, lies exactly midway between Lower Lake and Calistoga, in the heart of the Loconomi Valley. At the end of town, turn right onto Butts Canyon Road. The white plumes rising in the hills to the west are steam plumes from volcanic fumaroles, which operate in principle much like a geyser, except that the water turns to steam before it reaches the surface. When you come to Detert Reservoir, slow down. You may see ducks, geese, and swans here, in season, and perhaps a blue heron or one of the resident bald eagles. Black beef cattle graze in the pastures; as do, on occasion, black wild boars, which abound in this valley.

Guenoc Winery   *map page 143, A/B-1*

Look for the sign on the left and drive up the rocky road to this hilltop winery, which opened in 1981 and looks like a large barn. The tasting room entrance is to the right. Of the different wines made by Guenoc, you may want to sample the Genevieve Magoon reserve chardonnay as well as the red and white Meritage wines. The white manor in the distance, half hidden by huge valley oaks, is the house where the British actress Lillie Langtry stayed when she owned Guenoc Ranch in the late 19th century. Her profile graces the winery's label. *21000 Butts Canyon Road; 707-987-2385.*

■ POPE VALLEY, CHILES VALLEY, AND SAGE CANYON

Toward the top of the ridges to your right, you should be able to see a vineyard. Grapes were first planted here in 1854, when stagecoaches ran from St. Helena across the ridges separating the Guenoc and Napa Valleys. Today, the forest has reclaimed formerly cultivated land, but you can still tell the course of the old road by the moss-covered stone walls along its margins. Here and there in the woods you'll discover the ruin of an abandoned winery, and you may stumble over an ancient vine maintaining itself among the oaks, laurels, and pines. As you drive south from Guenoc on Butts Canyon Road, the valley narrows dramatically and becomes densely overgrown with oaks, laurels, cypresses, gray pines, and chaparral scrub. If you're lucky, you'll see a deer or wild boar foraging among the trees.

After a few miles of winding about, the road enters a large grassy glen: you have arrived in Pope Valley. For more than 100 years, some of Napa County's best grapes have been grown here and in neighboring, slightly higher, Chiles Valley—the reason both are included in the Napa Valley AVA. But you'll see few grapes on this tour; most of the vineyards are to the south and east. Instead, you'll find grasslands studded with great oaks—some of the most magnificent of their kind in the state.

Although there are few signs of civilization in Pope Valley, it does have its oddities, such as "Hubcap City," a ranch where almost every fence post and tree has been decorated with hubcaps. Litto, the old man who collected these caps, has passed away, and his daughter discourages the trading the old man was so fond of, but you can still stop and look.

Trail up Mount St. Helena

Drive up Highway 29 north of Calistoga to the crest of the road, where there are two large dirt parking areas on either side of the highway. A trail starting at the eastern parking area leads to the palisades—steep-sided cliffs of volcanic origin—and into very scenic backcountry. A grassy flat above the western parking area was the site of a tollhouse used in the days when the highway was a toll road frequented by stagecoaches, miners, and highwaymen. Stairs mark the trail leading to the top of the mountain. This trail passes the site of the cabin occupied by Robert Louis Stevenson and his bride, Fanny Osbourne, in the summer of 1880. A monument, carved in the shape of an open book, commemorates the couple's stay. The 5.5-mile trail continues uphill to connect with the fire road that runs all the way to the top. Look for the mouth of the abandoned Silverado Mine high in the hillside above a skirt of reddish cinnabar rock tailings.

As you near the top, a ray of sun cleaves the clouds, and the wind pushes them apart. Suddenly, to the south, the Napa Valley stretches from the foot of the mountains to the salt marshes of San Pablo Bay; to the west, the sun illuminates the hills and vales of Sonoma County. North and east of the mountain, valleys and mountains stretch to distant horizons. The average person will need about four hours to hike leisurely to the top of Mount St. Helena and back.

Aetna Springs Cellars   *map page 143, B-1/2*

Follow Pope Valley Road to Aetna Springs Cellars, a family-run winery opened in 1990. Aetna Springs grows cabernet sauvignon, cabernet franc, and syrah grapes on its Pope Valley ranch and chardonnay and merlot in vineyards in the Rutherford appellation. The two main wines produced, a chardonnay and a merlot, are both intense and fruity. Tastings and tours are by appointment only. There's a nine-hole golf course here. *7227 Pope Valley Road; 707-965-2675.*

Green & Red Vineyard   *map page 143, B-2/3*

From Aetna Springs turn right onto Pope Valley Road to reach the Pope Valley gas station and store. Stay to the left and continue on Pope Valley Road (which now becomes Chiles Pope Valley Road). The Green & Red Vineyard, opened in 1977, is on the left, after the junction with Lower Chiles Valley Road. This winery makes a splendid zinfandel from its steep 16-acre hillside vineyard, which is hidden away in Chiles Canyon. Unfortunately, it is not open to the public. *3208 Chiles Pope Valley Road; 707-965-2346.*

RustRidge Winery   *map page 143, B-2/3*

Backtrack to Lower Chiles Valley Road and turn right. The road skirts a hillside and gives you some nice views of vines, pastures, and wooded hills. RustRidge Winery, opened in 1984, is on the left. Chardonnay, sauvignon blanc, late-harvest Riesling, cabernet sauvignon, and zinfandel are the favored wines here. RustRidge also grows grapes that are sold to other wineries.

The property—now owned by Susan Meyer and her husband, Jim Fresquez—was purchased by the Meyer family in 1972 as a Thoroughbred horse ranch, and Thoroughbreds continue to be raised here. It is also a bed-and-breakfast. There are miles of trails, but you must bring your own horse if you want to ride. *2910 Lower Chiles Valley Road; 707-965-9353.*

Nichelini Winery   *map page 143, B/C-3*

Continuing on Lower Chiles Valley Road, turn right on Highway 128, which leaves Chiles Valley and plunges into rock-walled Sage Canyon. The family-owned Nichelini Winery, which dates from about 1890, clings to a steep embankment where the road skirts a cliff. The buildings are old and sit, very scenic, by the edge of the road. There is a picnic area here—a pretty place to while away an afternoon with a bottle of wine, a loaf of bread, a book of verse, and a "thou" sitting underneath a bough. The wines to taste are the zinfandel and the crisp and very

---

BOTTLED POETRY

Wine in California is still in the experimental stage; and when you taste a vintage, grave economical questions are involved. The beginning of vine-planting is like the beginning of mining for the precious metals: the wine grower also "prospects." One corner of land is tried with one kind of grape after another. This is a failure; that is better; a third best. So, bit by bit, they grope about for their Clos Vougeot and Lafite. Those lodes and pockets of earth, more precious than the precious ores, that yield inimitable fragrance of soft fire; whose virtuous Bonanzas, where the soil has sublimated under sun and stars to something finer, and the wine is bottled poetry: these still lie undiscovered; chaparral conceals, thicket embowers them. . . .

—Robert Louis Stevenson, *Silverado Squatters,* 1883

---

refreshing sauvignon vert. The latter grape was once commonly planted in California but has fallen out of favor, and Nichelini is the last winery to make a varietal wine from it. The winery is open for tastings on weekends only. It is so small, there is no need for tours. The tasting counter is in a barrel room, and most of the equipment sits outside. *2970 Sage Canyon Road; 707-963-0717.*

■ HOWELL MOUNTAIN APPELLATION

From Nichelini take Highway 128 back to Highway 29 and travel through St. Helena, turning right north of town onto Deer Park Road. Cross the valley floor and the Silverado Trail at the blinking red light, then climb to the forested heights of Howell Mountain, a grape-growing area that is quite a bit cooler than the Napa Valley floor and is distinct enough with its austere soils and cold nights to be considered an individual AVA. As you ascend the mountain, look for Burgess Cellars on the left.

Burgess Cellars   *map page 143, B-2*
This old stone winery, built in 1875 by a Swiss winemaker named Carlo Rossini, is a real cliff-hanger, hugging the steep western flank of Howell Mountain. It is the site of the original Souverain Cellars, which opened here in 1942, and it shared in the post-Prohibition Napa Valley wine resurrection. Tom Burgess bought the winery in 1972, just in time to share in another renaissance,

and he has consistently made superb zinfandel, cabernet sauvignon, and chardonnay. The wines became less tannic and more elegant in the mid-1980s, but that did not diminish their aging capability. A mature Burgess red is truly a great experience. Tours and tastings are by appointment only. *1108 Deer Park Road; 707-963-4766.*

■ LAKE BERRYESSA

After visiting Burgess, turn left and drive uphill on Deer Park Road, which becomes Howell Mountain Road further up the hill, to the alcohol-free Seventh Day Adventist community of Angwin and through its college campus. East of Angwin, Howell Mountain Road winds downhill. Drive carefully—the road is very steep (up to 10 percent grade), with many switchbacks. It runs through beautiful forests of tanbark and black oak, ponderosa pine, and Douglas fir before reaching a very rustic barn, gas station, and country store in Pope Valley.

Follow the road as it curves to the right and becomes Chiles Pope Valley Road; then look for Pope Canyon Road on your left. Follow this scenic road to the northwest shore of Lake Berryessa. En route you will drive through forests of native pines and oaks and see—in season—meadows and cliffs covered with wildflowers. The submerged canyon where Pope Creek enters the lake is a favorite local swimming hole. Turn right onto the Berryessa-Knoxville Road. Much of Lake Berryessa's western shore is included in vast Oak Shores Park, a region of grassy glens and wooded draws.

You'll reach Highway 128 at Turtle Rock, at the northern end of Capell Valley. Turn right toward Rutherford, once again past Nichelini Winery.

Carneros District vineyards.

CARNEROS DISTRICT

Sonoma Mount Veeder
Valley
        Oak Knoll
Sonoma   Napa

Sonoma   Carneros
Coast   Wild Horse
                   Valley

Los Carneros American Viticultural Area, established in 1983, stretches across the cool lower reaches of Sonoma and Napa Counties. It overlaps the Napa and Sonoma AVAs, so a winery using grapes from this region may list its place of origin as Napa, Sonoma, Carneros/Napa, Carneros/Sonoma, Los Carneros, or, more commonly, Carneros District. The word *carneros* means "sheep" in Spanish, and the slopes now covered with vines were once thought to be good only for sheep pasture. (Locals now claim their region was not named after mere sheep but after a ram.) The soils here are shallow, and water drains off quickly to marsh and slough. During summer and autumn, strong west winds blow in from the ocean each afternoon, tempering the hot days of these seasons.

To understand how different the Carneros is from the other lands bordering San Francisco Bay, you must approach it from the roads that border the water. From San Francisco travel north on U.S. 101 to Novato and take the Highway 37 turnoff to the east, which will take you along the northern reaches of San Francisco Bay, at this point called San Pablo Bay. On a cold, gray day, the flat marshes and low hills near the bay look bleak indeed, more like Scottish moor than a California shore. Even where the hills rise to meet the Sonoma and Mayacamas Mountains, they look desolate, their grassy expanses interrupted only here and there by a copse of somber live oaks or the bright green of a vineyard.

Vines grow slowly in the Carneros and yield few grapes, but the wine made from these grapes is very special. Grapegrowers in the mid-19th century recognized this and planted vast tracts here. Because of the low yields, some of the land was allowed to revert to sheep pasture after phylloxera destroyed the vines in the 1890s; however, the reputation of the grapes survived, and shortly after the repeal of Prohibition, vines once again began to spread across the land. Most of the vineyards were owned by individual growers, who raised other crops to minimize their economic risks, but the Napa Valley's Louis M. Martini bought vineyards here in the 1940s. Sonoma wineries also expanded their plantings to the Carneros in the 1980s and 1990s: Sebastiani at first, followed by Buena Vista and others.

Carneros grapes have better acids and more subtle fruit flavors than grapes grown in the Wine Country's hot valleys. Even warm-climate grapes such as caber-

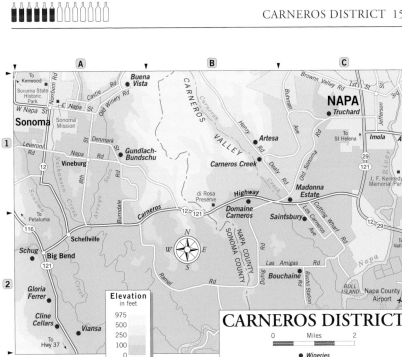

CARNEROS DISTRICT

Elevation
in feet

975
500
250
100
0

0   Miles   2

● Wineries

net sauvignon and merlot ripen well in favored Carneros locations. Zinfandel grapes, however, may not ripen at all, and chardonnay need shelter. Surprisingly, the fickle pinot noir grapes ripen well on exposed, windy slopes, making excellent wine of great complexity and depth. These and the chardonnay grapes grown here also make superb sparkling wine.

■ SONOMA COUNTY WINERIES

Viansa Winery & Italian Marketplace   *map page 155, A-2*

If you enter the Carneros by turning north off Highway 37 onto Highway 121, Viansa will be the first winery you encounter. It was established in 1989 by Sam Sebastiani, a scion of Sonoma's Sebastiani Vineyards, and his wife, Vicki, after the former left the family enterprise. (The name Viansa is derived from "Vicki and Sam.") The winery building resembles a Tuscan country house and overlooks the lowlands and marshes of lower Sonoma Creek; it is protected from the winds by a low ridge.

This plaque and sculpture celebrate the wetlands surrounding Viansa Winery.

Sam Sebastiani had gained experience at the family winery with traditional California grape varieties such as barbera, cabernet sauvignon, zinfandel, and chardonnay, but Viansa came into its own only after it started exploring such Italian varietals as nebbiolo, sangiovese, and muscat canelli. In addition, it has experimental plantings of vernaccia and malvasia.

The Sebastianis believe in the marriage of food and wine, so they have created the Italian Marketplace, an on-site store that sells a wide variety of Italian-style food products as well as tasty dishes ranging from focaccia sandwiches to pasta salads to *torta rustica* (a sort of Italian quiche). Visitors are encouraged to use the picnic area, which is shaded by olive trees and overlooks a restored wetland where turtles, river otters, and more than 60 species of birds—including herons, egrets, ducks, and golden eagles—have been spotted. Tours and tastings are offered at the winery, but if you can't make it there, try Cucina Viansa, a restaurant with deli and tasting room in Sonoma. *25200 Arnold Drive/Highway 121; 707-935-4700. Cucina Viansa: 400 First Street East, Sonoma; 707-935-5656.*

Cline Cellars *map page 155, A-2*

Farther along on Highway 121 is Cline Cellars, where you can really feel the famous Carneros winds. Although Cline has planted vineyards here, most of the grapes it uses come from the Oakley area of Contra Costa County, where the winery started and where the Cline family still raises old vines in very sandy soil at the edge of the Sacramento River Delta. Since the phylloxera root louse does not like sand, the vineyards in Oakley have never been devastated by it. Zinfandel and heat-loving Rhône varieties such as marsanne, mourvèdre, and carignane thrive in the Oakley climate. As you taste the wines you will encounter some unusual but very pleasing flavors. The marsanne tastes quite unlike any other California white, and the mourvèdre is different from the more familiar cabernet sauvignon. Be sure to taste the Cotes d'Oakley, a blend of red Rhône grapes, as well as the vin gris white, which is made with red mourvèdre grapes. There are also sémillon and zinfandel for more traditional palates.

Cline Cellars is located in a place of historical significance. On July 4, 1823, Father Altimira founded Sonoma Mission in this very spot by planting a cross. When he returned a month later, he moved the mission to present-day Sonoma. If you wonder why the venerable padre had a change of heart, just stand still for a while and feel the wind. Then drive to Sonoma and feel the lack of wind. The fact that this farm was an ancient Indian village site has been commemorated by the construction of two willow-frame huts, which need only a covering of tule reeds to become habitable. An old bathhouse with graffiti dating back to 1877 shows that white settlers were just as fond of the warm springs as the native inhabitants were. Tastings are offered daily; tours are by appointment. *24737 Arnold Drive/Highway 121; 707-935-4310.*

Gloria Ferrer Champagne Caves *map page 155, A-2*

As you drive north from Cline, look for a winery to your left up against the gentle slopes of the hills, a winery that looks sunny even on a gray Carneros day. This is Gloria Ferrer Champagne Caves, built in 1982 by the Spanish sparkling-wine maker Freixenet. The winery is named for the wife of José Ferrer, the company president. The sparkling wines made here under the direction of winemaker Bob Iantosca are truly superb, but be sure to taste his chardonnay and pinot noir as well. Both have that elusive Burgundian quality California winemakers strive for but don't always achieve.

Tours here include the caves and are offered daily. Sitting on the deck at Gloria Ferrer on a warm, sunny afternoon, sipping sparkling wine as you look out over the vineyards and listen to the birds sing, is a wonderful Wine Country experience. *23555 Highway 121; 707-996-7256.*

Schug Carneros Estate Winery   *map page 155, A-2*

After leaving Gloria Ferrer, turn north on Highway 121, and then left on Bonneau Road, at Big Bend, to reach Schug Carneros. Walter Schug comes from a family that has made wine on the Rhine for a long time. He studied wine making at the German Wine Institute in Geisenheim before coming to northern California in 1959. He gained acclaim as the winemaker for Joseph Phelps Vineyards, and in 1980, while still at Phelps, he launched his Schug brand. In 1983 he broke away to start a winery of his own. He was best known at Phelps for cabernet sauvignon and Riesling, but Schug now concentrates on chardonnay and pinot noir (though his cabernets remain superior). If you have a question about which wine to match to a certain food, call the winery's toll-free number. Tastings are offered, but tours for groups are by appointment. *602 Bonneau Road; 707-939-9363 or 800-966-9365.*

■ NAPA COUNTY WINERIES

Domaine Carneros   *map page 155, B-1*

Crossing into Napa County on Highway 121, you will see a large French château to the right side of the highway. It is a copy of the Château de la Marquetterie, an 18th-century mansion owned by the Taittinger family in Champagne, France. This is home to Domaine Carneros, established in 1987 by the Taittinger Champagne house along with a few American partners. The creation of Domaine Carneros was a direct response to the success achieved by Domaine Chandon, another French vintner making California sparklers. The sparkling wines made here are austere, the perfect accompaniment for fresh oysters. There is a visitors center that's open daily, and tours are offered. *1240 Duhig Road; 707-257-0101.*

Gloria Ferrer Champagne Caves, where the sun always seems to shine.

Madonna Estate   *map page 155, B/C-1*

At Highway 121 and Old Sonoma Road, Madonna Estate produces estate-grown chardonnay, muscat di canelli, gewürztraminer, Johannisberg Riesling, and pinot noir from the Madonna Vineyard, which straddles the border of Napa and Sonoma Counties along the west bank of Huichica Creek. Louis Bartolucci, whose family had farmed vineyards in the lower Napa Valley since the 1920s, opened this winery in 1977 under the name Mont St. John's Cellar. Tastings are offered daily; tours are by appointment. *5400 Old Sonoma Road; 707-255-8864.*

Saintsbury   *map page 155, C-1/2*

Continue east on Highway 121 and turn right on Los Carneros Avenue to reach Saintsbury, a small winery that has gained renown for its pinot noir. Named for the English author George Saintsbury, the winery was started in 1981 by David Graves and Richard Ward and also makes chardonnay from estate-grown grapes. The quality of the wine makes Saintsbury well worth a visit, but you must make an appointment to do so. *1500 Los Carneros Avenue; 707-252-0592.*

Carneros Creek Winery   *map page 155, B-1*

Backtrack to Highway 121 and Old Sonoma Road, which you should take north, turning left on Dealy Lane to visit Francis Mahoney's Carneros Creek, a truly pioneering winery, opened in 1972. Other wineries—most notably Louis M. Martini—established earlier Carneros vineyards, but it was Carneros Creek that proved cool-climate pinot noir can be very complex indeed. This winery also makes some chardonnay, but it is best known for its pinot noir. Tastings are offered. *1285 Dealy Lane; 707-253-9463.*

Artesa Winery   *map page 155, B-1*

From Dealy Lane, turn west onto Henry Road to reach the ultra-modern hilltop winery now known as Artesa. Built in 1991 and opened as Codorniu Napa, the winery made sparkling wine but failed to find its stride. So its owners changed its name and its product; Artesa released its first "still" wines in 1999. Now very successful, the winery consistently turns out some of the Napa Valley's best wines, including cabernet sauvignon, sauvignon blanc, chardonnay, and pinot noir. Artesa has a small wine museum and art exhibits in its visitors center. Tours and tastings are offered. *1345 Henry Road; 707-224-1668.*

Domaine Carneros is a copy of the 18th-century Château de la Marquetterie.

Dramatic Artesa Winery has a small wine museum.

Truchard Vineyards   *map page 155, C-1*
Backtrack to Old Sonoma Road and travel north to Truchard Vineyards, which has demonstrated that merlot reaches surprising complexity in the Carneros. The Truchard family immigrated from France to Texas in 1887. They planted a vineyard and built a winery, but neither survived Prohibition. Grandson Tony Truchard, a medical doctor who had moved to California, planted a vineyard in 1974; he sold grapes exclusively to other wineries until 1989, when he decided to start his own winery. Truchard uses only estate-grown grapes, and in keeping with the times, it now also grows roussanne, cabernet franc, cabernet sauvignon, tempranillo, and zinfandel. This small winery's pinot noir is in a class by itself. Call ahead for an appointment. *3234 Old Sonoma Road; 707-253-7153.*

Bouchaine Vineyards   *map page 155, C-2*
Somewhat off the Highway 121 trail of wineries is Bouchaine Vineyards, which you will find by traveling from Highway 121 south on Duhig Road, east on Las Amigas Road to Buchli Station Road. Bouchaine is rather close to tidewater, lying between Carneros and Huichica Creeks and the tidal sloughs of San Pablo Bay.

The alternately breezy and foggy weather has a special effect on the fermenting wine. Make an appointment to taste the chardonnay and pinot noir, which are made from Carneros grapes and are surprisingly Burgundian, as well as the gewürztraminer, which is made from Russian River Valley grapes and has a definite Alsatian character.

This is the oldest continuously operating winery in the Carneros. The old winery was built by the Garetto family, who made wine here until 1951. The winery was then bought by the Beringer Brothers, who used it as their primary production facility for 20 years. After Nestlé of Switzerland acquired Beringer in 1971, it continued using this location for racking, blending, and wine storage until Gerret and Tatiana Copeland and other investors bought the property in 1981. The facility was upgraded to a fully integrated wine-making operation and renamed Chateau Bouchaine. The Copelands became sole owners in 1991. They renovated and modernized the winery in 1995, but retained the traditional open-top concrete fermenters for their pinot noir production. Tastings are offered daily; tours are by appointment. *1075 Buchli Station Road; 707-252-9065.*

■ AWAY FROM THE WINERIES

Should you feel the need to take a break from wine tasting, grab a picnic lunch and take Cuttings Wharf Road south to the Napa River, stop at the public boat ramp, and dangle your feet in the river. If you have remembered to bring your fishing pole (and license), you might even catch a carp or two. Keep a lookout for white egrets, great blue herons, wood ducks, and other waterfowl. But beware: these waters are tricky and rise and fall with the tide. If the bleak marshes to the south look familiar, there's a reason: Francis Ford Coppola shot some of the Mekong Delta scenes for *Apocalypse Now* here.

You can also relax by the river and hike through wildflower meadows and marshes in **J. F. Kennedy Park,** just south of Napa on Highway 29. For a more rugged hike, climb the wooded knoll in **Westwood Hills Wilderness Park** (Browns Valley Road, west from First Street, Napa), a city-owned tract that is truly wild—mountain lions were spotted here in the late 1990s. **Skyline Park** (Imola Avenue east from Highway 121) is more bucolic, with open meadows garlanded with blue and white lupines, California poppies, and godetia in the spring. Wild

Is it art or is it nature? Veronica di Rosa's Endless Summer *(1989) at the di Rosa Preserve.*

turkeys strut their stuff uphill, where the meadows merge into the oak woods. Farther up, the banks are densely covered with small golden-backed and maidenhair ferns, and giant chain ferns grow from the stone walls of long-abandoned buildings. The trail ends above woodsy Lake Marie, whose placid waters are shielded by the oak and madrone woods of 1,630-foot Sugarloaf Mountain.

■ DI ROSA PRESERVE *map page 155, B-1*

The 20th century's last three decades were as productive for northern California artists as they were for the region's vintners. One man who participated in both realms was Rene di Rosa, vineyard owner, art collector, and, as was his late wife, Veronica, an artist himself. When di Rosa sold his Winery Lake Vineyard to Seagram in 1986, he withheld some of the acreage to create what he called an art and nature preserve. One of the Wine Country's best-kept secrets, this brilliant resource exhibits more than 2,000 works by more than 750 artists in a 100-year-old stone building and several barnlike galleries, under oak trees, in the rolling hills surrounding the lake, and in the lake itself.

Some of the works—such as Paul Kos's meditative *Chartres Bleu,* a video installation in a chapel-like setting that replicates a stained-glass window of the cathedral in Chartres, France—were commissioned for the preserve. Other highlights include Mark di Suvero's sculpture *For Veronica* (di Rosa), Veronica di Rosa's *Endless Summer,* and numerous works by San Francisco Bay Area stalwarts Robert Arneson, William T. Wiley, Viola Frey, Roy De Forest, Beth Hird, David Best, and Nathan Oliveira. One gallery contains two of Best's ornately decorated Cadillacs, and another has a corridor lined with superlative photography. Admission is by reservation only, and tours are limited to 25 people at a time. *5200 Carneros Highway; 707-226-5991.*

Olive trees grow on a ridge above a Sonoma Valley vineyard.

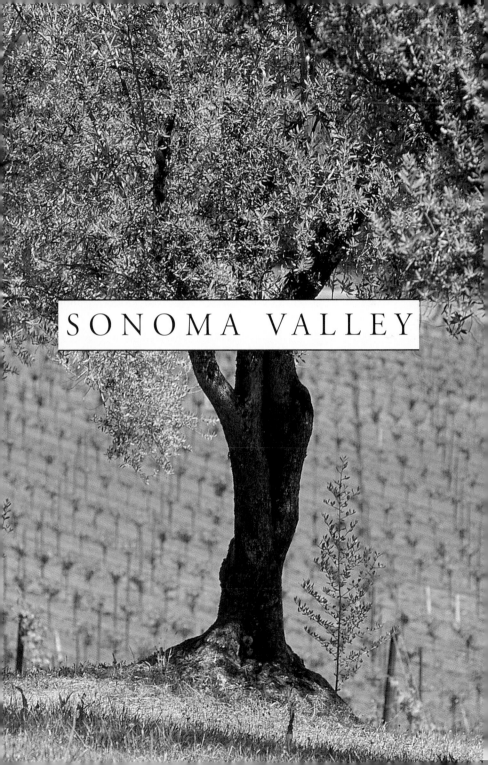

SONOMA VALLEY

The Sonoma Valley starts, like the Napa Valley, on the cool, windswept, and fogbound shores of the Carneros, but, unlike the latter, it is open to the north as well, allowing cool marine air to funnel south from the Russian River Valley via the Santa Rosa Plain. Vines growing high up in the mountains get more sun and thus have more sugar in their grapes, but they become stressed from growing in poor rocky soils. Water runs off quickly, making for deep-rooted vines and intensely flavored grapes. One district of the Sonoma Valley AVA, Sonoma Mountain, produces such unique and complex reds that it has itself been designated an AVA. The small towns of the Sonoma Valley share the same spirit, but they differ widely in appearance.

■ **Town of Sonoma**   *map page 169*

The town of Sonoma, the valley's cultural center, is the oldest town in the Wine Country and the place where the first wine north of San Francisco was made. Founded in the early 1800s, when California was still part of Mexico, it is built around a large, tree-filled plaza that is surrounded by historic buildings, hotels, restaurants, and shops. Plan on spending a fair amount of time here before you head out to tour wineries.

If you enter town from the south, on wide Broadway (Highway 12), you'll be retracing the last stretch of what was once California's most important road—El Camino Real, or "the king's highway," the only overland route through the state. During California's Spanish and Mexican periods, this road ran past all of the state's missions: beginning at San Diego de Alcala (1769), the first, and ending at San Francisco Solano de Sonoma (1823), the 21st and last. North of San Rafael, it traversed vast grasslands and ran through tule marshes and groves and groves of massive valley and live oaks. Farms and vineyards now cover these once-wild hills and valleys, where deer, elk, and grizzly bears roamed, but you can still spot tall oaks here and there on the hills and in draws, and even along the highway.

From the end of Broadway, turn right on Napa Street and left on First Street East to Spain Street, the site of the Mission San Francisco Solano de Sonoma, or **Sonoma Mission,** most of which has been restored. Gone are the large mission church and its plaza, but you will find the mission chapel on your right and the adobe barracks of Mariano Vallejo's Sonoma Fortress on your left. Continue on First Street for half a block and turn left behind the barracks to reach the municipal parking lot, which has unlimited free parking—there's a two-hour limit on the plaza. On the lot's north side are *petanque* courts (for playing the French version of bocce) in **Depot Park,** and the **Depot Park Museum** (270 West First Street; 707-938-1762), worth a quick stop for its local history exhibits.

Return on foot to **Sonoma Plaza,** where most of the historical sites are clustered, as are the best restaurants and some interesting shops. American rebels proclaimed California's independence from Mexico here on June 14, 1846. (The "Californios," as the Spanish settlers were called, had themselves declared independence in 1831 and 1836.) The rebels' Bear Flag flew over the plaza until July 9, when the U.S. flag was raised and Sonoma became an American garrison town.

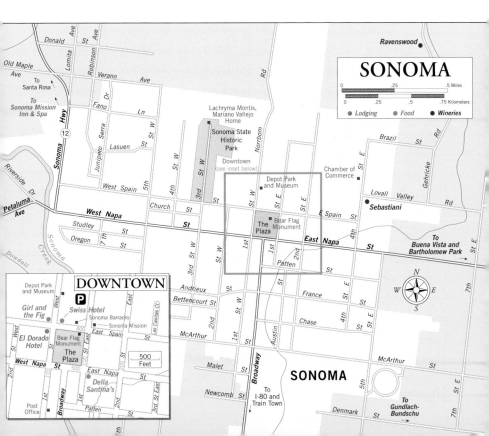

The adobe barracks of General Vallejo's Sonoma Fortress.

Among the surviving historic buildings, all of which can be found along Spain Street, on the north side of the plaza, are the whitewashed adobe padres' quarters (after 1823) of Sonoma Mission; the servants' quarters of General Vallejo's mansion (circa 1836); the barracks (built between 1836 and 1840); and the mission chapel (built by Vallejo in 1840). The **Blue Wing Inn,** built by Vallejo as a guesthouse, became a notorious saloon during gold rush days, with such diverse visitors as the scout Kit Carson, the bandit Joaquin Murietta, and the army officer Ulysses S. Grant. The **Toscano Hotel** dates from the 1850s, as does the nearby **Vasquez House,** which was built in 1855 by "Fighting" Joe Hooker, before he became a Union hero during the Civil War. It is now the home of the Sonoma League for Historic Preservation.

The **Sonoma Hotel** dates from the 1880s, but the third story was added and the building refurbished by Samuele Sebastiani in the 1920s. Sebastiani, the founder of his family's wine dynasty, believed in sharing his wealth: he deserves credit for the elaborate **Sebastiani Theatre** on the plaza's east side. He also built homes for his

A view looking north up Sonoma Valley. In the foreground is Sonoma's town plaza.

workers, donated a parochial school, built streets for the town, and contributed to many other civic projects. **Sebastiani Vineyards** is only four blocks east of the plaza. Besides taking a tour, tasting, and buying wine, you can picnic there.

The Salvador Vallejo Adobe on the west side of the plaza (home of Mariano's brother) dates from 1846. It has been the **El Dorado Hotel** on and off for nearly 160 years. The building has seen a variety of other uses, including brothel and boardinghouse, but in late 1989 it opened again as a hotel—and a very comfortable one. The rooms of choice are behind the courtyard in back, where the hotel serves breakfast—one of the highlights of a stay in Sonoma.

Sonoma is a town of courtyards. Some of the restaurants on or near the plaza are built around courtyards, as are several shops, most notably those of **El Paseo** and the **Mercato.** You can spend a whole day enjoying the plaza and nearby streets: browse the excellent selection of old tomes at **Plaza Books**; taste local wines at the **Wine Exchange of Sonoma**; and pick up picnic fixings at the **Sonoma French Bakery** or the **Sonoma Cheese Factory** (which in addition to great cheeses has a fine selection of wines, breads, and pickled olives). A block east of the plaza on Second Street are two more shops of note, **Vella Cheese Company,** the home of the superb dry jack, and the **Sonoma Sausage Company,** which sells great bratwurst and other sausages as well as ham and pâté. If you're planning to have a picnic barbecue, be sure to stop here.

Sonoma has more than its share of historic adobes from the city's Mexican period, but this is not at all a musty museum town, nor is the plaza a museum piece. The plaza is a place where people hang out, have lunchtime picnics, feed the ducks in the pond, and listen to musical performances at the small amphitheater. It has come a long way since being a dusty square where Vallejo drilled his troops and where locals butchered cattle.

Today Sonoma Plaza is a grassy park, shaded by trees and brightened by roses. After being briefly banished during a town brouhaha a few years back, ducks again swim in the pond near **City Hall,** a stone edifice erected in 1906. Its four sides were made identical so none of the merchants on the plaza would feel that city hall had turned its back to them. The plaza is the setting for some folksy events, most notably the **Ox Roast** and the **Valley of the Moon Wine Festival.** At the staffed visitors center, on the plaza's east side, you'll find all the information you need to plan your tour of the area.

The Sebastiani Building, with its mission-style facade, houses the Sebastiani Theatre.

■ **Wineries in Town**

Sonoma vineyards were planted by the mission padres in the 1820s, almost as soon as the first adobe walls went up. These vines came into the possession of General Vallejo and were later sold to Samuele Sebastiani, an enterprising Italian immigrant.

Sebastiani Vineyards *map page 180, C-7*

Although Samuele Sebastiani established a vineyard in Sonoma in 1904, he made only bulk wine until 1944, when his son, August, decided the wines were good enough to carry the family name on the label. With name recognition came increased sales, and Sebastiani was soon by far the largest winery in Sonoma County. Sebastiani was among the pioneers planting grapes in the Carneros (in the Schellville area). Lately, traditional varieties such as barbera, cabernet sauvignon, and zinfandel have been joined by cabernet franc, mourvèdre, syrah, and other intriguing varietals. Although the winery is known for its hearty reds, it also produces a full range of white wines. To reach Sebastiani from Sonoma Plaza, head east on Napa or Spain Street and turn left on Fourth Street. *389 Fourth Street East; 707-938-5532.*

Ravenswood *map page 180, C-6/7*

The Ravenswood winery building looks like a hillside bunker. You almost get the feeling these Sonomans are digging in to ward off a threatened invasion from Napa, on the other side of the ridge. Ravenswood was established in 1976 in the Russian River Valley, where winemaker Joel Peterson worked with the late Joseph Swan. The winery later moved to a shack at the edge of the Sangiacomo vineyard in the Carneros, and moved uphill into the former premises of the Haywood Winery in 1991, after the latter was bought by Buena Vista and shut down (though the Haywood name survives on a Buena Vista label). Ravenswood first went public, and then, in 2001, was sold to the Franciscan Estates Fine Wine Division of Constellation Brands.

Ravenswood is north of Sebastiani Vineyards. Continue up Fourth Street to Lovall Valley Road and turn right; turn left on Gehricke Road, and wind your way up into the mountains. Chances are you'll be following zinfandel pilgrims en route to their mecca, for Ravenswood is adored by many for its zinfandel. But try the other wines as well, especially the merlot. To complement them, there's a barbecue—chicken and ribs—in the vineyards every weekend from May through September. *18701 Gehricke Road; 707-938-1960.*

The 1871 harvest at Buena Vista was one of many wine-related images in the Napa and Sonoma Valleys captured on film in the 19th century by Eadweard Muybridge. The artist was most famous for his "body in motion" photography.

Buena Vista Carneros Estate   *map page 180, D-7*

The old Buena Vista winery, founded by Agoston Haraszthy in 1857, suffered heavy losses in the late 19th century when phylloxera devastated its vineyards, and then experienced a second blow when the great 1906 earthquake collapsed its cellars and destroyed the stored wine. The winery lay idle until the 1940s, when Frank Bartholomew, a war correspondent for United Press International, bought the old edifice, reopened the tunnels, and replanted the vineyards. When Bartholomew sold the winery to Young's Market of Los Angeles in 1968, he kept the vineyards, forcing the new owners to look for vineyard land elsewhere. They found it in the budding Carneros District of southern Sonoma and Napa Counties—hence the winery's new name.

Buena Vista is now owned by the international mega-spirits corporation Allied Domecq. The wines are well made and pleasant to drink, although they rarely achieve greatness, except perhaps the Carneros cabernet sauvignon. The winery has also produced some noteworthy ports in recent years. Its production facility in the Carneros is closed to the public, but the old Sonoma winery has a tasting room and a shaded courtyard perfect for picnicking or watching performances of Shakespeare plays. To reach the winery from Ravenswood, return to Lovall Valley Road, turn left, and follow the signs. *18000 Old Winery Road; 707-252-7117*

Bartholomew Park Winery   *map page 180, D-7*

Although this winery was founded only a decade ago by Jim Bundschu, grapes were grown in some of its vineyards as early as the 1830s, and some of the land it encompasses was part of Agoston Haraszthy's original Buena Vista winery. The emphasis at Bartholomew Park is on small lots of hand-crafted wines whose grapes—cabernet, merlot, pinot noir, and chardonnay—are all harvested from the same vineyard (though not always from a vineyard the winery owns). Organic farming methods are used whenever possible, and because terroir is such an important consideration, as little manipulation as possible occurs during the wine-making process. The wines themselves make Bartholomew Park worth a stop, but two other reasons to visit are its museum, whose exhibits include captivating photographs of the region taken by Eadweard Muybridge in the early 1870s, and the woodsy picnic area. The winery is west of Buena Vista off Castle Road. *1000 Vineyard Lane; 707-935-9511.*

Gundlach-Bundschu   *map page 180, C-8*

Like many wineries in northern California, Gundlach-Bundschu, established in 1858 as California Bonded Winery No. 64, closed its doors during Prohibition, but the property did not change hands. Great-great-grandson Jim Bundschu replanted the family's Rhinefarm Vineyard, one of California's oldest vineyards, and reopened the winery in 1973. Although in the 1800s Jacob Gundlach had gained fame for high-quality whites, the winery is now lauded for its red wines.

Gundlach-Bundschu, like Ravenswood, looks a bit like a large gun bunker, but don't let that scare you away. By the time Bundschu got around to rebuilding the winery, only three walls of the original building still stood, and, thanks to earthquakes and neglect, the aging tunnels had to be redug almost from scratch. Although the rebuilt winery isn't pretty, everything works again—splendidly—and Bundschu has imbued the winery with a sense of fun. Jazz, pop, or rock-and-roll play over the sound system as you walk into the tasting room, instead of the classical "muzak" permeating the air at more staid establishments.

Be sure to taste the Rhinefarm Vineyards merlot, the cabernet sauvignon, and the zinfandel. There's also a Rhinefarm Riesling made from the Kleinberger clone introduced by Jacob Gundlach. A short, breathtaking hike up the hill takes you to a viewpoint from which you'll be treated to a panorama of the lower valley and the

Attendees sample the goods at a Sonoma Valley olive oil festival.

Carneros. You'll likely see a lot of Sonomans picnicking here: this spot is a favorite local hangout. Gundlach-Bundschu can be reached by heading south from the Plaza, then east on Napa Road. *2000 Denmark Street; 707-938-5277.*

■ **GLEN ELLEN** *map page 180, C-3/4*

The Sonoma Valley Highway, Highway 12, runs north from Sonoma through strip malls, tract homes, and small towns with a hangdog look. After the valley opens up, oaks and stone fences dominate the landscape, as the road heads toward Glen Ellen, 9 miles up Sonoma Creek from Sonoma.

Tucked among the trees of a narrow canyon, Glen Ellen looks more like a town of the Sierra Foothills gold country than a Wine Country village. Its main street, narrow and crooked, runs past houses climbing a steep mountainside, the abandoned brick Chauvet Hotel, and the wood-balconied Poppe Store, as well as several old buildings housing up-to-date shops and restaurants. Two tree-lined creeks, the Sonoma and the Calabazas, merge in the center of town, just above the point where the main road turns sharply to cross the bridge.

Sonoma Mountain rises west of town, much of its eastern flank covered by the forests of **Jack London State Park,** once the author's Beauty Ranch, where he lived, wrote, and died in a small white farm cottage. Following his death, London's wife, Charmian, operated it as a dude ranch. After she died, in 1955, she willed the ranch to the state parks system.

Highly recommended is the 2-mile hike to the writer's grave and to the ruins of Wolf House, which burned under mysterious circumstances in 1913, a month before the couple were to move into it. Shaded by huge redwood trees, the remains of London's house look like an ancient castle from a European fairy tale. The author's grave, though, is a simple affair: a small picket fence and a plaque mark the spot where his ashes rest. This walk takes you through oak woods that, except for the vineyards that border the area, look much like they did when the native Coast Miwoks gathered acorns here. The setting is about as perfectly 19th century as you can experience anywhere in the Wine Country. *2400 London Ranch Road, off Arnold Drive; 707-938-5216.*

You can also hike a 3-mile trail to the top of Sonoma Mountain, or you can sign up with the **Sonoma Cattle Company** (707-996-8566) for a guided trail ride.

Wine has been part of Glen Ellen since the 1840s, when Joshua Chauvet's sawmill, built by Mariano Vallejo, and flour mill both proved to be unprofitable.

On the trail at Jack London State Park.

After carrying his millstones all the way from France, Chauvet first tried starting a flour mill in Oakland, then in the gold country, and then here. He ran his Glen Ellen mill for only 18 months before he ran out of grain, but he must have liked the place. Instead of moving on, he abandoned his millstones, planted grapes, and built a winery and the valley's first distillery. The winery machinery was powered by steam, and the boilers were fueled with wood from local oak trees.

In 1881, Chauvet built a stone winery, which the Pagani family bought in 1913. The Paganis tore down the building and replaced it with a concrete structure, where they produced about 50,000 gallons of wine each year, sold in four-packs of gallon bottles. When a customer finished the wine, he or she washed out the bottles and returned to the winery for a refill. The winery was shut down in 1954, when Charles Pagani died. The Paganis hung on farther north in the Sonoma Valley, where they operated the winery now known as Kenwood Vineyards.

Other valley farmers followed Chauvet's example, and soon many raised grapes besides the more traditional cattle. Wine was even made during Prohibition, when the locals took a liberal view of the 200 gallons each family was allowed to produce for personal consumption. Henry Garric, a local resort owner, quipped:

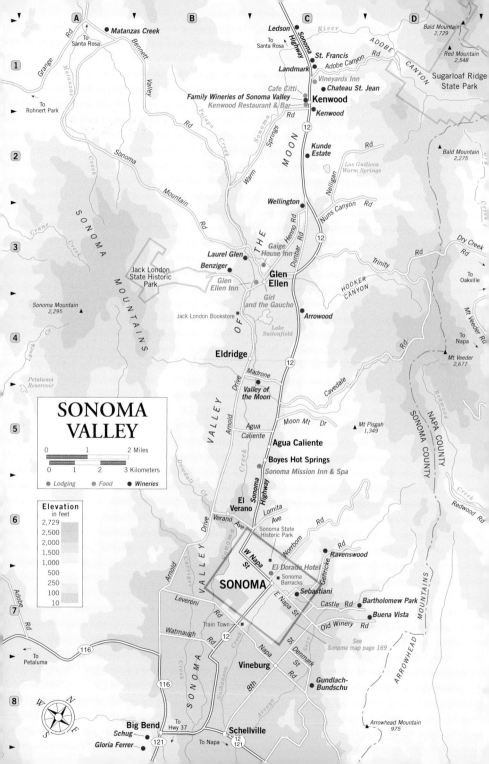

If you ran a resort or restaurant, you had to serve wine. So you probably made a little more wine than if you were making it for your own use. . . . It was common to have a little fermentation tank that I estimate held almost 200 gallons, and people had about 10 or 12 fifty-gallon barrels that they put the wine into after it got through fermenting. As I recall, law enforcement people didn't bother anybody; they knew it was mostly for family use.

Glen Ellen and neighboring Kenwood have several excellent resorts and restaurants. When you check into one of the utterly comfortable local lodging places such as the Gaige House, you're following in the footsteps of the countless visitors who have traveled to this sunny region to give their congested lungs a much deserved rest from San Francisco's foggy air. Dine at the Glen Ellen Inn or the Kenwood Restaurant. But whatever you do, be sure to stop at the Jack London Bookstore at the southern edge of Glen Ellen. Owner Jack Kingman knows a lot about Jack London, and the bookstore has several works hard to find elsewhere. Best of all, it has an excellent selection of books on local history and wine, as well as rare volumes on a variety of subjects. Stock up on picnic fare and wine at the Village Market, across the street from the Chauvet Hotel.

■ GLEN ELLEN WINERIES

At Glen Ellen, the Valley of the Moon narrows, and the grass-and-oak–clad slopes of Sonoma Mountain and the Mayacamas encroach on the valley floor. The wineries of this hilly region make excellent wines, albeit no longer from local grapes alone. The Glen Ellen brand name has been sold and resold several times since the 1990s and is no longer considered a premium product.

Valley of the Moon Winery   *map page 180, C-4/5*
Head north 3 miles from Sonoma Plaza on Highway 12 (the Sonoma Highway), turning left onto Madrone Road to reach the Valley of the Moon Winery. The first winery on this site was built by George Whitman, who acquired the property in 1863. In the late 1800s it was owned by Sen. George Hearst, the father of the newspaper magnate William Randolph Hearst. After Hearst's death, the winery changed owners several times, and it closed from the 1930s until 1941, when new owners, Enrico Parducci and Peter Domenici, gave the winery its current name.

A tram takes visitors to Benziger through the vineyards.

The owners of nearby Kenwood Vineyards purchased the property in 1997, tore down the old winery, and built a new, state-of-the-art winery, which opened in 1998. Bottlings include splendid zinfandel, deeply rich syrah, a lighter sangiovese, and the very drinkable Cuvee de la Luna. Tours and tastings take place daily. *777 Madrone Road; 707-996-6941.*

Arrowood Vineyards & Winery *map page 180, C-4*

Right on Highway 12, just outside Glen Ellen, is Arrowood, a small winery with a big reputation. Dick Arrowood made great wine when, until 1985, he was the winemaker at Chateau St. Jean, and he continues making great wine at Arrowood, once his own place but now owned by Robert Mondavi. Try the cabernet sauvignon and the zinfandel. The tasting room is open daily. Tours are by appointment only. *14347 Sonoma Highway; 707-938-5170.*

Benziger Family Winery *map page 180, B-3*

A mile or so outside Glen Ellen is Benziger, which since it sold off its Glen Ellen label to a bulk wine producer in the 1990s has been making serious wine from its surrounding estate vineyards. Opened in 1981, this winery in the Sonoma

Mountain AVA is known for cabernet sauvignon, merlot, sauvignon blanc, and chardonnay and is a fun and educational place to visit. A tram takes visitors through the vineyards, and signs point out grape varieties and explain what's happening in the vineyards. Seats on the tram can be hard to come by during summer and early fall, but near the tasting room is a demonstration vineyard in which various grape types are grown and explained. Bring a picnic—the grounds here are splendid. *1883 London Ranch Road; 707-935-3000.*

Laurel Glen Winery   *map page 180, B/C-3*

Production is small at Laurel Glen, but the wines made here are rich and supple. Since he opened in 1980, owner and self-taught winemaker Patrick Campbell has made only red wines—particularly cabernet sauvignon but also a generic red called Terra Rosa—from estate-grown grapes. In addition to cabernet sauvignon, Laurel Glen grows a little merlot and cabernet franc. This winery is not open to the public, but you can call to put your name on the mailing list. *6611 Sonoma Mountain Road; 707-526-3914.*

Wellington Vineyards   *map page 180, C-2/3*

Two generations of Wellingtons—father John and son Peter, the winemaker—run this small operation just off the Sonoma Highway. Merlot and cabernet sauvignon dominate the annual production of about 8,000 cases, but if you drop by for a tasting don't pass up the intense Noir de Noirs, an old-vine alicante bouschet wine with a blackberry kick (and then some). The sauvignon blanc from grapes grown on Sonoma Mountain's eastern slope is worth a taste too. If you've been traveling south on the Sonoma Highway and have found some of the showplace wine centers intimidating, the homey setup here will provide the perfect antidote. *11600 Dunbar Road; 707-933-0708.*

Matanzas Creek Winery   *map page 180, A-1*

Just 10 to 15 minutes from Glen Ellen via curvy Bennett Valley Road, Matanzas Creek, in the Sonoma Valley AVA's northwestern corner, is a lovely spot to visit. The building juts dramatically from the hillside, and the gardens are planted with more varieties of lavender than ever you've met. When the lavender's in bloom, in summer and autumn, it's truly a feast for the senses. Sandra McIver opened Matanzas Creek in 1978 with the intention of producing "the finest wine in California." Her winery is known for merlot and sauvignon blanc, although it does produce some chardonnay. *6097 Bennett Valley Road; 707-528-6464.*

■ KENWOOD WINERIES

The Sonoma Highway winds north from Glen Ellen to the small town of Kenwood, whose vineyards and wineries occupy the flat bottom and slopes of the Valley of the Moon's northern section. The wines from this area aren't really all that distinct from those of other Sonoma Valley regions, but the landscape is very pretty, with meadows and woods bordering the highway.

Several wineries in the Kenwood area are small operations, some of them started within the last decade or so, that do not have tasting rooms of their own. At **Family Wineries of Sonoma** (9200 Sonoma Highway; 707-833-5504), you can sample the output of a half-dozen or so wineries, including Sable Ridge Vineyards, which produces some special petite sirahs and old-vine zinfandels. This cooperative tasting room, which is open daily, is north of our first two stops, Kunde Estate and Kenwood Vineyards.

Kunde Estate Winery   *map page 180, C-2*

The first thing you will notice about Kunde is its rustic purity. Everything is almost uncannily tidy, from the square barn that serves as winery to the crush pad and the stainless steel tanks out back. A rock-walled road leads to a wooden door built into the side of the hill. The door opens to tunnels dug into the hillside—the caves where the wine ages in small oak barrels at a perfect and even temperature. You can take a tour of those cool caves and absorb their timelessness through the aromas of aging wine and oak.

As growers, the Kundes go back five generations, starting with Louis Kunde, who bought Wildwood Vineyards in 1904. The family continued making wine during Prohibition (no one says whether this was sacramental or under-the-counter wine) but stopped making wine in 1942, when the eldest son went off to war. The family returned to wine making in 1990, but they use only 50 percent of the grapes they grow; the remainder is sold to other wineries—who prize them highly. The Kunde wines are estate grown and well worth tasting, even the generic blend of cabernet sauvignon and zinfandel sold as Bob's Red. Considering how long it took the Kundes to get back into the business of wine making, their achievements are astounding. This winery is definitely worth a journey. *10155 Sonoma Highway; 707-833-5501.*

The welcome sign is out at Kenwood Vineyards.

The red soils of the Kunde Estate Winery produce some of the finest zinfandel in the region.

Kenwood Vineyards   *map page 180, C-1/2*

Back in California's Tortilla Flat days, when wine was sold by the barrel instead of the bottle, and when you could bring your gallon jugs to a winery to have them filled with rustic quaffing wine, this winery was owned by the Pagani brothers. When the Martin Lee family and friends bought out the Paganis in 1970, the wines were upgraded to the sipping variety, but even now Kenwood makes some good basic red wine, as well as its more showy cabernet sauvignons and zinfandels. The best of these come from Jack London's old vineyard, in the Sonoma Mountain appellation, above the fog belt of the Sonoma Valley (Kenwood has an exclusive lease). But what the wine connoisseurs keep coming back for is Kenwood's crisp sauvignon blanc. Tours and tastings are available daily. *9592 Sonoma Highway; 707-833-5891.*

Chateau St. Jean   *map page 180, C-1*

Off to the right of the highway, at the foot of the Mayacamas Mountains, are the grandiose grounds of Chateau St. Jean, an old country estate once owned by a family of midwestern industrialists and expanded when it was turned into a

Filling oak barrels at Kenwood Vineyards.

winery in 1973. A couple of ponds in the shape of Lakes Michigan and Huron reflect the estate's previous ownership. One of this winery's nicest features is the view over the vineyards you get from the tower. The wines are good, but they lost some of their sparkle after winemaker Dick Arrowood left in the 1980s to open his own winery. Chateau St. Jean is now owned by Blass Wine Estates, the winery division of the Australian beverage conglomerate Foster's Group. Taste the chardonnay and fumé blanc. There is a picnic area, garden, and daily tastings, but tours are not offered. *8555 Sonoma Highway; 707-833-4134.*

Landmark Vineyards   *map page 180, C-1*
Turn into Adobe Canyon Road and then left at the first driveway to reach Landmark Vineyards, founded in 1974 in Windsor, north of Santa Rosa. The winery moved to its present location in 1990 to escape encroaching subdivisions. Stop here to taste the wines, but also take a close look at the building, which is a faithful reconstruction of a mission-period rancho—right on up to the shingle roof. Landmark is best known for its chardonnay and pinot noir. *101 Adobe Canyon Road; 707-833-0053.*

The Spanish mission–style St. Francis bell tower appears on the winery's labels.

St. Francis Winery   *map page 180, C-1*

St. Francis recently expanded into a smart-looking Spanish mission–style facility about a mile or so north of Landmark. The winery produces excellent cabernet sauvignons, but it is best known for the quality of its merlots, which far predate the current merlot craze. There is a visitors center and tasting room. *100 Pythian Road; 800-543-7713.*

Ledson Winery and Vineyards   *map page 180, C-1*

About a half mile farther north on Highway 12, the strange purple-brick château of Ledson Winery sits incongruously amid vineyards, looking like a Victorian railway station in search of its town. Ledson has gained a local reputation for its merlot—it also makes a fine late-harvest zinfandel and fruity pinot noirs—and for its incredible deli. There are oak-shaded picnic grounds out back, and tastings are offered daily. *7335 Sonoma Highway; 707-833-2330.*

Well-tended gardens surround the Dry Creek Valley's opulent Ferrari-Carano winery.

From Glen Ellen and Kenwood, Highway 12 heads northwest to Santa Rosa, where you can pick up U.S. 101 to Healdsburg, the center of a vast, rapidly expanding agricultural region. Northern Sonoma AVA covers a large area and overlaps much of the three AVAs that meet at Healdsburg: the **Russian River AVA,** which runs southwest along the lower course of the river; the **Dry Creek Valley AVA,** which heads northwest from town; and the **Alexander Valley AVA,** which runs east and north of Healdsburg. Also in this area are the Knights Valley, Chalk Hill, Green Valley, and Sonoma Coast AVAs. Dozens of wineries dot the countryside. Add fine picnic sites and delis where the bread is freshly baked and the olives and cheeses are local, and you have the makings of a wine tourist's day in Eden.

To visit the Russian River region first, take Highway 12 west through Santa Rosa and turn northwest, in Sebastopol, onto Highway 116, the Gravenstein Highway (named for the apple, which is the region's most famous product). This will take you to the lower end of River Road. If you're coming directly from San Francisco on U.S. 101, take the west exit of Highway 116 (which comes 9 miles after the east exit). You might be tempted to take U.S. 101 directly to River Road, but be aware that the eastern portion of River Road is often crowded with cars. To reach the Dry Creek or Alexander Valley appellations, head straight north to Healdsburg.

■ RUSSIAN RIVER APPELLATION

The Russian River AVA has a unique climate, ideally suited to the growing of premium grapes. Because of its low elevation, sea fogs push far inland to cool the land, yet they dissipate often enough during summer to give the grapes enough sun to ripen properly. Also important is the fact that over the years the river has cut its way downward through strata of rocks and deposited a deep layer of gravel that in parts of the valley goes down 60 or 70 feet. The presence of this gravel forces the roots of grapevines to grow farther down in search of water and nutrients. In the process, the plants are nourished with a multitude of trace minerals that add complexity to the flavor of the grapes. In California as in France, such gravelly soils produce some of the world's greatest wines.

Iron Horse, best known for its sparkling wine, also produces an excellent chardonnay, above.

Iron Horse Vineyards *map page 193, A-3*

The first winery of note along Highway 116 is Iron Horse, whose sparkling wines smoothed the way of glasnost. Ronald Reagan served them at his summit meetings with Mikhail Gorbachev; George Herbert Walker Bush took some to Moscow for the signing of the START Treaty. Iron Horse also makes excellent chardonnay and, from time to time, pinot noir. Winemaker Forrest Tancer is the son-in-law of winery owners Barry and Audrey Sterling, and grapes from Tancer's Alexander Valley vineyards are used to make the winery's cabernet sauvignon.

Despite its fame, Iron Horse, founded in 1979, has avoided pretense and grandeur. The winery buildings are of the simple Sonoma redwood-barn style, but an access road lined with palms, olive trees, and vast flower beds, and acres of fruit orchards and vegetable gardens make this a beautiful place. In 1995, Tancer released his first "late disgorged" sparkling wine, a deeply flavored sparkler with a long, rich finish. Tancer also added to the complexity of his sauvignon blanc by blending in a little viognier, and he made sangiovese in the "Super Tuscan" style, by rounding it out with a touch of cabernet sauvignon. Iron Horse is open by appointment only. *9786 Ross Station Road, off the Gravenstein Highway; 707-887-1507.*

Korbel Champagne Cellars *map page 193, A-2*

From Iron Horse, drive west on the Gravenstein Highway to Guerneville, then a few miles east on River Road to Korbel Champagne Cellars. When the Korbel brothers, who had left their native Bohemia to escape political repression, logged the redwood forests of the Russian River, they began planting crops among the stumps. After trying tobacco and other crops first, they found that grapes grew best. So in 1882 they established a winery and began making "champagne." In 1954 Korbel passed into the hands of the Heck family, which originally came from the Alsace region.

Technically, Champagne is made only in the French region of that name; all other bubbly is "sparkling wine." The Champenois have tried to stop English-speakers from misusing their name for more than 100 years, but the fight goes on. Whatever you choose to call it, Korbel's wine is quite good and reasonably priced. The Natural is best. And the winery is a delight to visit, with its 19th-century buildings (including a tower in which brandy was made), a deli and microbrewery, and extensive rose gardens on the beautifully landscaped grounds. The tour—considered by many the best in Sonoma County—will give you a good idea of how sparkling wine is made. It includes a display of wine memorabilia and old photographs. *13250 River Road; 707-824-7000.*

■ WESTSIDE ROAD WINERIES

From Korbel turn left (east) on River Road. Look for the turnoff to Westside Road on the left—if you cross the Russian River, you've gone too far; the turnoff is just before the river. Slow down and enjoy the scenery of vineyards alternating with woods and meadows as you follow this meandering road into Healdsburg. There are more wineries along this road than we have space to mention. Stop at as many as you can—they all make good wine.

Gary Farrell Winery *map page 193, A-2*

The westernmost Westside Road winery is the high-tech and highly lauded Gary Farrell Winery. Farrell made his mark with a 1985 pinot noir from grapes grown at nearby vineyards, including Rochioli. In the 1990s, he turned his attention to zinfandel, garnering high praise for his work with that varietal—his full-bodied zin from the Maple Vineyard in the Dry Creek Valley is a triumph. Farrell also makes chardonnay wines and a red Bordeaux blend. *10701 Westside Road; 707-473-2900.*

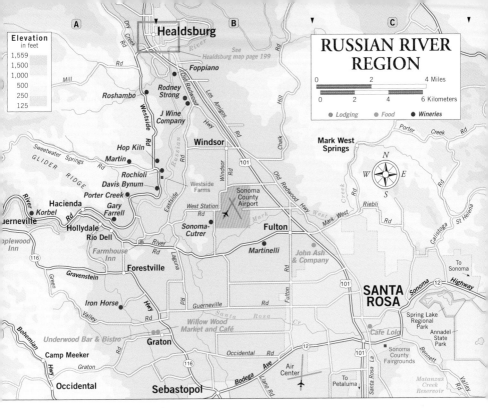

Porter Creek Vineyards   *map page 193, A-2*

Look closely for Porter Creek's sign; the driveway is just after a sharp bend in the road. Opened in 1982, Porter Creek hardly resembles a winery. It is a small family farm that happens to make good wine with estate-grown grapes. Compare the hillside pinot noir with the creekside pinot noir to taste which one you prefer. The chardonnay is made from hillside grapes only and has a very Burgundian character. Tastings are available here. *8735 Westside Road; 707-433-6321.*

Davis Bynum Winery   *map page 193, A/B-2*

From the road, Davis Bynum looks more like a summer retreat than a serious winery, but once you have made it past the white entrance cottages and tasted the wines, you'll agree that this winery's reputation is well deserved. Founded by Davis Bynum in 1965 in an Albany, California, storefront, the winery moved to its present location in 1973. Bynum was the first to make pinot noir exclusively from Russian River grapes and has championed local grapes ever since. Quality has kept up with the expansion of production. In addition to the pinot noir, be sure to taste the merlot, the zinfandel, the fumé blanc, and the gewürztraminer. There are no tours here, but you can taste the wines. *8075 Westside Road; 707-433-5852.*

Rochioli Vineyards & Winery   *map page 193, A/B-2*

Farther along Westside Road, look for the small parking lot of Rochioli Vineyards & Winery on your right. The Rochioli family started growing grapes in 1933. They began by tending vineyards planted in the 19th century and planting new vines on gravelly bench lands above the Russian River. After decades of selling grapes to local wineries, the Rochiolis started making their own wine in 1982. Production is small, but the wines are worth stopping for. Joe and Tom Rochioli believe in letting the vineyard determine the quality of the wine, and they have just the right vineyard to do this. Because of the cool growing conditions, the flavors of their pinot noir, cabernet sauvignon, chardonnay, and sauvignon blanc (from old vines) are intense and complex. The tasting room patio, shaded by roses, is a great place for sipping wine and enjoying the view across the Russian River vineyards. *6192 Westside Road; 707-433-2305.*

Martin Family Vineyards   *map page 193, A-2*

It's a long and winding 3-mile drive on Sweetwater Springs Road (the last 1.5 miles on gravel) from Westside Road to Martin Family Vineyards, which perches high on a ridge overlooking the Russian River Valley. The tiny winery, open only since 1996, made an instant splash with intense reds made from grapes grown in both Napa and Sonoma Counties. Its tasting area, at the entrance to an old barn filled with French oak barrels containing aging wine, is decidedly low-tech, but sample the zinfandel or petite sirah—Martin also makes cabernet, syrah, and pinot noir—and you'll quickly realize that something special is going on here. *2347 Sweetwater Springs Road; 707-433-9545.*

Hop Kiln Winery   *map page 193, A/B-2*

The first driveway after Rochioli leads to Hop Kiln, which was created in the mid-1970s in and around a historic hop kiln dating from 1905. None of the kiln's equipment was destroyed, so you'll find strange pipes and railcar tracks running through the building, and some of the wine is stored in the old ovens, kept cool by their thick stone walls. The wines of note here include zinfandel (particularly from the Old Windmill Vineyard), gewürztraminer, and Riesling. Most of the wines are from estate-grown grapes, including rare varietals such as valdiguié. Your best bet for a picnic on the winery's beautiful and sunny grounds is a wine appropriately called Marty Griffin's Big Red. Tastings are offered daily. *6050 Westside Road; 707-433-6491.*

The view from the starkly modern tasting room of Roshambo looks east over Russian River vineyards toward the Sonoma Valley.

Roshambo   *map page 193, A-1*

Spunky and new, Roshambo is a modern winery with a touch of Bauhaus in its design. The winery's story begins in 1970, when Frank Johnson planted a 55-acre vineyard and became a major Dry Creek and Russian River grower. When Johnson passed away in 1993, he left the vineyard to his family, and thirtysomething granddaughter Naomi Johnson Brilliant, and her husband, Tod, decided to make wine. They teamed up with Paul Brasset, one of Sonoma County's most gifted winemakers, to create a very exciting wine-making team. Roshambo won the Best of Show white wine sweepstakes at the 2002 Sonoma County Harvest Fair with a chardonnay and took home several more medals, including a gold medal for its Dry Creek syrah.

Roshambo's tasting room doubles as a gallery for avant-garde art, and the winery sponsors art events, such as an origami competition. Current wines include chardonnay, sauvignon blanc, syrah, zinfandel, and an incredible late-harvest traminer. *3000 Westside Road; 707-431-2051.*

■ EAST OF THE RIVER

Westside Road turns east into Healdsburg. Turn right onto Healdsburg Avenue, which becomes Old Redwood Highway and runs along the east side of the river. (Or you can go south on U.S. 101 and exit at the Old Redwood Highway.) Foppiano, one of Sonoma's oldest wineries, is a pleasant stop along this road, but two other wineries deserve attention: Rodney Strong and J Wine Company. Also worth visiting are Sonoma-Cutrer and Martinelli, which you can reach by taking U.S. 101 south to Fulton Road south, and then River Road west. From Martinelli, return to River Road west and then turn right on Slusser Road; Sonoma-Cutrer will be on your left. Sonoma-Cutrer and Martinelli could be visited first on this tour, before you make your way to Guerneville, but beware of heavy traffic on River Road, especially on weekends.

Foppiano Vineyards *map page 193, B-1*

Established in 1896, Foppiano made primarily bulk wine until 1970, but in recent years its varietal wines, most notably petite sirah and cabernet sauvignon, have shown that it can produce quality wines. The zinfandel is a good everyday wine in the Italian country-wine tradition. Tastings are available daily, and there is a self-guided vineyard tour. *12707 Old Redwood Highway; 707-433-7272.*

Rodney Strong Vineyards *map page 193, B-1*

This winery, founded by Rodney Strong in 1959, has awakened from its sleeping beauty snooze and has made great strides in recent years with intensely flavored reds. The tasting room, perched high above the high-tech cellars, is a must-see. The winery sponsors free outdoor concerts on the grounds during summer. Tours and tastings are offered. *11455 Old Redwood Highway; 707-431-1533.*

J Wine Company *map page 193, B-1*

The sparkling wines produced by Judy Jordan of J Wine Company are a lot more interesting than the "restaurant wines" produced at Jordan winery by her father, Tom. The tasting bar here is brightened up by a delightful metal, glass, and fiber-optic light sculpture giving a splendid impression of bubbly spurting from a bottle. The tasting fee includes such foods as foie gras, caviar, and cheese to complement each wine. J now also makes some still wines, including excellent chardonnay, pinot gris, and pinot noir. *11447 Old Redwood Highway; 707-431-5400.*

Harvest time at J Wine.

Martinelli Vineyards & Winery   *map page 193, B-2*

The Martinelli family has been growing grapes and other fruits in the Russian River Valley since the late 1800s—its Jackass Hill Vineyard, planted in 1899, still produces grapes—but it did not start making wine until 1986. The winery, in a 100-year-old hop barn, is rustic, but the wines are big, complex, well balanced, and often high in alcohol content. Martinelli currently makes sauvignon blanc, chardonnay, gewürztraminer, muscat Alexandria, pinot noir, syrah, and incredibly rich zinfandel. It is open daily, and there's a picnic area at the edge of the vineyard, overlooking the tasting room and winery. *3360 River Road; 707-525-0570.*

Sonoma-Cutrer   *map page 193, B-2*

Founded in 1973 by Brice Cutrer Jones, a former Vietnam War fighter pilot, this winery makes chardonnay. The grapes come from three renowned Sonoma County vineyards: Les Pierres, Russian River Ranches, and Cutrer Vineyard. The ultra-modern winery's other attraction comes as a bit of a surprise: professional croquet grounds. The winery hosts two annual events, the World Croquet Championship held in May and the ACA-US open in September. Chardonnay and croquet! *Quel mariage!* The winery is open to the public by appointment only, but it's well worth your time to call and plan for a tour. *4401 Slusser Road; 707-528-1181.*

■ HEALDSBURG   *map page 199*

The heady aroma of southern magnolias drifts through the open windows as you park your car on the Healdsburg plaza. The magnolias grow next to tall Canary Island date palms that are dwarfed by towering California redwoods—making the plaza a shady haven on a hot summer afternoon. There are no grapevines growing among the roses here. If the nearby vineyards are a hurricane of activity, the plaza is the eye of the storm, a center of repose, the poetic heart of a hard-working farm town. It's almost otherworldly. A sign in the window of a plaza bookstore sets the tone: "SHOPLIFTING IS BAD FOR YOUR KARMA."

Some of California's older towns were laid out with Hispanic-style plazas by their Mexican founders, but Healdsburg was founded in 1852 as a trading post by an American, Harmon Heald, who donated the plaza to the city with the catch that it be used for recreational activities only. Although a municipal water slide might meet that criteria, the city fathers wisely chose to keep the plaza as a tree-shaded park.

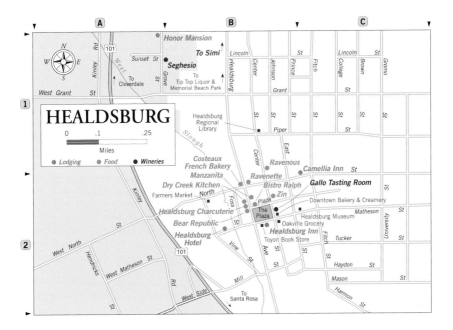

HEALDSBURG

Former Healdsburg resident Millie Howie describes the town as "straight out of a Norman Rockwell painting," and she's right. The flower beds are free of weeds, the bandstand always looks freshly painted, and the businesses are dressed up in style. Although the plaza attracts its share of visitors, it is mainly a local hangout, where Healdsburg residents enjoy free summer concerts, eat at the restaurants, and go to the movies. The multitude of stores along the plaza—selling baked goods, clothing, antiques, books, and toys—can keep the most discriminating visitor happy, but these are also establishments at which locals shop.

One place that's very popular with area winemakers is the **Oakville Grocery** (124 Matheson Street) inside the renovated former city hall. This luxury deli with patio dining is owned by the same folks who run the Oakville Grocery in Napa. It has a fine selection of local wines, breads, cheeses, olive oils, and other gourmet items, and there's a take-out counter that dispenses huge sandwiches, hearty soups, and other fare. This is a great place to grab a quick lunch or to stock up on fixings for a winery picnic.

To catch the Healdsburg spirit, go to the plaza early in the morning, before the sun bears down, and order a pastry and a cup of coffee at the **Downtown Bakery & Creamery** (308A Center Street). Sit in the plaza—in the shade in summer, on a

The small town of Healdsburg features a number of antiques stores around its charming central square. Nearby are bakeries and wine stores, a bookstore, and a farmers' market.

sunny bench during the rest of the year—and listen to the rustling of the palm fronds and the chattering of birds as they perform their morning chores. On Sunday, you might hang out in the plaza and listen to one of the popular concerts, which might be jazz, Cajun music, bluegrass, Gaelic folk songs, Broadway melodies, or even Sousa marches.

You could also go window shopping at galleries in the area or spend the morning browsing at **Toyon Book Store** (104 Matheson Street). If it happens to be Saturday morning, head to the open-air **Farmers' Market** (northwest of the plaza, west of Healdsburg Avenue), where local producers of cheese, olives, and olive oils, along with growers of the freshest of vegetables, gather to sell their wares. Not to be missed is **Bear Republic,** a brewpub on the square whose Racer 5 India Pale Ale won the gold medal at the Great American Beer Festival and where the food will not disappoint you.

Healdsburg is a very active community, with, it seems, a different public event every weekend. One of the best of these is the **Russian River Wine Festival,** held in the plaza in late May. You can browse artists' booths, taste local foods, sip wines

Canoeing on the Russian River.

from numerous wineries, and generally have a good time. In summer, head for **Memorial Beach Park,** on the Russian River, where you can swim in the pool created behind a seasonal dam (from Memorial Day to Labor Day) or rent a canoe and drift downstream.

The **Healdsburg Museum** (221 Matheson Street; 707-431-3325) displays a collection of local historical objects, including baskets and artifacts from native tribes, and contains exhibits about the Mexican Rancho period, the founding and growth of Healdsburg, and the history of local agriculture (grapes, hops, prunes). Or you might learn more about local wines at the superb Wine Library at the **Healdsburg Regional Library** (Piper and Center Streets).

You don't even have to leave town to sample local wines. Outlets for **Gallo** and **Windsor Vineyards** are on the plaza on Center Street, and **Kendall-Jackson** has a tasting room just north of the plaza on Healdsburg Avenue. From Kendall-Jackson, you can continue north on Healdsburg Avenue to **Tip Top Liquor Warehouse** (Healdsburg Avenue and Dry Creek Road), a nondescript looking establishment that stocks an impressive selection of Sonoma County wines.

At work in the vineyards of Seghesio.

◼ WINERIES IN HEALDSBURG

Seghesio Vineyards & Winery   *map page 199, tk-tk*

Italian immigrant Edoardo Seghesio and his wife, Angela, planted vineyards here in 1895 and added a winery in 1902. For years they and their descendants sold wine in bulk to other wineries, including Paul Masson and Gallo, but the winery began bottling wines under its own name in 1980. The majority of the grapes used by Seghesio are estate grown, in vineyards in the Alexander, Dry Creek, and Russian River Valleys. Even though winemaker Ted Seghesio prefers his wines to be immediately drinkable, they have surprising depth and aging potential. Be sure to try the reserve zinfandel and the sangiovese. It's a long walk from the plaza to Seghesio; the tasting room is open daily. *14730 Grove Street; 707-433-3579.*

Simi Winery   *map page 204, B-3*

The Simi brothers, two Italian émigrés, founded a winery at the northern edge of Healdsburg in 1876 and named it Montepulciano. When this proved too difficult for non-Italian locals to pronounce, the brothers changed the name to

Simi Winery. The winery had its ups and downs until 1981, when it was bought by French investors Möet-Hennessy–Louis Vuitton. Zelma Long, who became winemaker in 1979, helped turn Simi into a financial and critical success.

This winery looks mostly to the Alexander and Russian River Valleys for its grapes. About half the production has been chardonnay, but sauvignon blanc has shown well lately, as has Simi's Alexander Valley cabernet sauvignon. The Simi tour is informative, and the tasting room staff is knowledgeable. The winery has been a key player in the matching of food and wine through educational brochures, programs, and dinners. *16275 Healdsburg Avenue; 707-433-6981.*

Gallo Tasting Room   *map page 199, B-2*

The Gallo family has opened a tasting room, on the Healdsburg Plaza, for the first time in the 70-year history of its wineries. Tastings are offered of not only Gallo of Sonoma wines but also of other wines from the Gallo repertoire. Be sure to taste the Rancho Zabaco Dancing Bull zinfandel and the Gallo of Sonoma cabernet sauvignon. *320 Center Street; 707-433-2458.*

■ DRY CREEK VALLEY APPELLATION

From downtown Healdsburg, take Healdsburg Avenue to Dry Creek Road and turn west. Almost as soon as you pass under the U.S. 101 freeway bridge, you'll feel like you've slipped back in time. The area is rural, unspoiled, devoid of urban sprawl. Although the Dry Creek Valley has become renowned for its wines, it has preserved a rustic simplicity rarely found in California today.

The road, brightened by wildflower-strewn shoulders in spring and early summer, offers tantalizing vineyard views as it skirts a steep hillside on the east side of the narrow valley. The valley's well-drained, gravelly floor is planted with chardonnay grapes to the south, where an occasional sea fog creeping in from the Russian River cools the vineyards, and with sauvignon blanc to the north, where the vineyards are warmer. The red decomposed soils of the benchlands bring out the best in zinfandel—the grape for which Dry Creek has become famous—but they also produce great cabernet sauvignon. And these soils seem well suited to Rhône varieties such as cinsault, mourvèdre, and marsanne, which need heat to ripen properly.

Grapes like this valley so much that they grow wild in roadside thickets, the way blackberries cluster elsewhere in the West. These are not just native slip-skin grapes, but also vinifera grapes that have spread beyond the vineyards.

Frei Brothers Winery *map page 204, B-2*

On Dry Creek Road, shortly after the intersection with Lytton Springs Road, the E.&J. Gallo Winery makes wine from local grapes at the Frei Brothers Winery, purchased in 1976. This winery, not open to the public, is a culmination of a program started in the 1950s, when the Gallos began steering Napa and Sonoma County growers away from cheap bulk grapes, encouraging them to plant premium varietals by paying top price for them. This, more than anything else, prepared the way for the great winery boom that was to come. Had no premium grapes been available, no premium wine could have been made. The Dry Creek venture is an attempt to go beyond the pop wines that made the Gallos rich and to instead make serious wine. The Sonoma County cabernet is especially fine, and even the Hearty Burgundy has improved tremendously since being made from North Coast grapes. *3387 Dry Creek Road; 707-431-5500.*

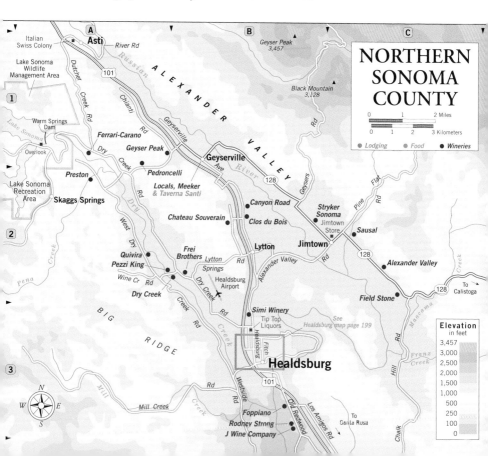

The Dry Creek Valley's gravelly soil has become renowned for producing quality zinfandel.

Dry Creek Vineyard   *map page 204, A/B-2*

A left turn at Lambert Bridge Road brings you to the Dry Creek Vineyard, often touted as the first local winery opened since Prohibition. The historical record shows that this is not exactly true, but Dry Creek's founder David Stare played a key role in putting the valley's wines onto the enological map. Opened in 1972, his winery offers the usual assortment of wines, from big reds to light and fruity whites, but it stands out for its fumé blanc and zinfandel. Dry Creek has a delightful picnic area brightened by flowers and is a perfect place to hang out on a hot summer's day. There are no tours given, but it is open for tastings. *3770 Lambert Bridge Road; 707-433-1000.*

Pezzi-King Vineyards   *map page 204, A/B-2*

Across Lambert Bridge Road from Dry Creek is Pezzi-King, a small winery with great views of the Dry Creek Valley. Founded in 1993 by Jim Rowe Sr., it pours excellent sauvignon blanc, cabernet sauvignon, and zinfandel (from estate-grown grapes) in its tasting room. The ambience is very friendly, making this a fun place to visit, but tours are not offered. *3805 Lambert Bridge Road; 707-431-9388.*

Quivira Vineyards *map page 204, A-2*

Continue west on Lambert Bridge Road and then turn right (to the north) when you get to West Dry Creek Road, a narrow lane that is the quintessential Wine Country road. It hugs the western slopes of the valley, forcing you to slow down—a good thing for the many bicyclists who navigate this route. Enjoy the flowers, look for quail crossing the road, and watch the hawks and ravens soar high overhead. After passing several vineyards on your right, you'll come to the attractive wood-and-cinder-block barn that is the Quivira Vineyards winery, founded in 1981.

The winery building here looks rustic, but this is a state-of-the-art facility that was erected in 1987. Quivira is best known for its sauvignon blanc and zinfandel, but it also produces an excellent blend of red varietals called Dry Creek Cuvée. If the weather's warm, the sauvignon blanc or the chardonnay are great to sip in the picnic area. Tastings are offered daily, but tours are by appointment. *4900 West Dry Creek Road; 707-431-8333.*

(opposite) Vines frame the tasting rooms at Quivira Vineyards. (above) The view from the terrace of Villa Fiore, the hospitality center at Ferrari-Carano.

During the Russian River Wine Road Barrel Tasting, you can "preview" wine before it's bottled.

Preston Vineyards   *map page 204, A-2*

Return to West Dry Creek Road and head north. Follow the lane past its junction with Yoakim Bridge Road (ignore the "dead end road" sign) and look for the Preston Vineyards sign. Take the even narrower lane along the bank of Peña Creek to the winery. The tasting room is on the west side of the large fruit-drying barn that's been converted into the winery.

All Preston wines are estate grown. There are two interesting Rhône-style blends: Faux, a red, and Le Petit Faux, a rosé. As with other Dry Creek wineries, the zinfandel and sauvignon blanc are standouts. The Cuvée de Fumé blend is tops. Preston is a worthy stop for its charm, beautiful surroundings, and homespun feel. Stroll in the gardens or sit on the back porch sipping wine and listening to the birds. *9282 West Dry Creek Road; 707-433-3372.*

Ferrari-Carano *map page 204, A-1*

Backtrack to cross Yoakim Bridge Road, then turn left on Dry Creek Road to reach Ferrari-Carano. Founded in 1981 by Don and Rhonda Carano, this winery added a hospitality center in 1994. Called Villa Fiore, it is a pink confection that's visible for quite a distance across the valley. The wines here are a bit less opulent than the winery, although the chardonnay and fumé blanc are as big as they come.

In addition to their Dry Creek vineyards, the Caranos own vineyards in the Alexander and Knights Valleys, as well as in the Napa part of the Carneros. Winemaker George Bursick believes in blending, so it's tough to figure out where exactly the grapes for a wine labeled "Sonoma County" come from. A zinfandel made from Dry Creek grapes is excellent; a cabernet-sangiovese blend named Siena shows promise. The wineshop in the villa carries an assortment of goods, from wines to specialty foods and garden tools to clothing. You must call ahead to reserve a spot on the single daily tour, but the tasting room and gardens are open all day. *8761 Dry Creek Road; 707-433-6700.*

Pedroncelli Winery *map page 204, A-1/2*

From Ferrari-Carano turn right on Dry Creek Road and left onto Canyon Road. The eclectic mix of farm buildings on the left is Pedroncelli Winery, founded in 1927, when John Pedroncelli bought 90 acres of grapes with an existing winery. Pedroncelli sold grapes until Prohibition ended; then he started making wine. The operation was very simple, as Jack Florence Sr. tells in *A Noble Heritage: The Wines and Vineyards of Dry Creek Valley:*

> By about 1935 Pedroncelli had a label and customers were coming
> by to fill their gallon jugs. The winery kept a spigot on one barrel to
> facilitate their customers' request for a fill-up. The wines of all oper-
> ating wineries were basically the same, a red and a white.

In 1963, sons James and John took over the business and began increasing production. They also started a varietal program. The wines have steadily improved in quality while prices have remained low. The Pedroncelli pinot noir is surprisingly good; the cabernet and zinfandel are among the best in the region. There's a picnic area and bocce court outside the tasting room—the perfect place for sipping the winery's refreshing chenin blanc. *1220 Canyon Road; 707-857-3531.*

■ ALEXANDER VALLEY APPELLATION

The Alexander Valley AVA covers both sides of the upper Russian River Valley from east of Healdsburg to the Mendocino County line north of Cloverdale. Its landscape varies from flat bottomlands—the drop in elevation at river level is only 50 feet from the upper to the lower part of the valley—to hills more than 1,500 feet high. It is warmer than the Russian River appellation, and its small side valleys become very hot in summer. Sea fogs only occasionally drift in from the Santa Rosa Plain, and though they cool the land, they burn off more quickly than they do on the lower river.

Climatically and geologically, the Alexander Valley is diverse. Soils include loam, gravelly loam, and gravelly sandy loam, as well as well-drained gravel flats near the river. But because a mere dozen years ago the valley was mostly planted to walnuts, pears, prunes, and bulk grapes—except for the sections left in scrub and pasture—one might argue that experimentation here has hardly begun. So far, chardonnay, sauvignon blanc, and cabernet sauvignon seem to do well in places; zinfandel may actually get too ripe. Italian grapes such as sangiovese or the Rhône varieties, which do so well in the Dry Creek Valley, may make great wines in the warmer parts of the Alexander Valley. Stay posted for a decade or two. This is a valley full of surprises.

■ GEYSERVILLE *map page 204, B-1/2*

Not too long ago Geyserville was a dusty little farm town with little to offer wine tourists besides a somewhat dim grocery store and a large mural depicting regional roadside attractions. Recently, however, an influx of young entrepreneurs has put the town on the wine-touring bandwagon. The centerpiece of this movement is a small and pleasant storefront tasting room named **Locals** (Geyserville Avenue and Highway 128; 707-857-4900), which pours wines from six wineries that do not have tasting rooms of their own: Camellia Cellars, Crane Canyon Cellars, Eric Ross Winery, Hawley Wines, Kosta Browne Winery, and Russian Hill Winery. Locals is open Friday through Monday. There is no tasting fee. **Meeker Vineyards** (21035 Geyserville Avenue; 707-857-1795) has a storefront tasting room next door to Locals that is open daily.

Harvesting the bounty of Sonoma County: red-hot chili peppers (above) and Alexander Valley grapes (below).

■ UPPER ALEXANDER VALLEY

From Pedroncelli, Canyon Road east leads to U.S. 101. The west side of U.S. 101 south contains a stretch where wineries of the Dry Creek and Alexander Valley appellations mingle. That's because the dividing line runs along Dry Creek Ridge, and wineries in the canyons are closer to the Russian River than to Dry Creek. Pedroncelli is in the Dry Creek AVA, whereas nearby Geyser Peak is in the Alexander Valley AVA.

Geyser Peak Winery   *map page 204, A/B-1*

Traveling east on Canyon Road toward U.S. 101, turn left on Chianti Road, just before the freeway. Geyser Peak, built in 1882, has had its ups and downs. Under the corporate ownership of Jos. Schlitz Brewing Co. the buildings were upgraded and garden terraces were added, but the corporation also brought us wine in a box.

Just before the old place slipped into bulk wine oblivion, Geyser Peak was rescued by the Santa Rosa developer Henry Trione and his sons in 1982. Since then, the wines have improved steadily and can once again be considered premium wines. More recently, the winery was bought by Jim Beam Brands, but Daryl Groom remains as one of four winemakers. He learned his trade in Australia, so it should come as no surprise to find a "shiraz" (syrah) among Geyser Peak's offerings. Still, the zinfandel, merlot, and cabernet are excellent too. A Meritage called Reserve Alexandre is a wine of great depth and beauty. It is a blend of the five Bordeaux varieties: cabernet sauvignon, cabernet franc, merlot, malbec, and petit verdot. Geyser Peak is open for tastings daily. *22281 Chianti Road; 707-857-9463.*

Canyon Road Cellars   *map page 204, B-2*

To reach Canyon Road Cellars, on the floor of the Alexander Valley, take U.S. 101 south to Independence Lane. Turn left, then left again onto Geyserville Avenue. The winery is on the right, after Clos de Bois. This was once the Nervo Winery, founded in 1896 by Frank Nervo. The stone-and-redwood winery building was finished in 1908. Nervo Winery held out as a small niche winery, making Italian-style country wines until the construction of the U.S. 101 freeway gobbled up a large chunk of its vineyard. Geyser Peak took over the winery in 1971 and renamed it Canyon Road. Like Geyser Peak, it is now owned by Jim Beam Brands. Canyon Road Cellars is a popular place for picking up inexpensive quaffing wines. Tastings are offered daily. *19550 Geyserville Avenue; 707-857-3417.*

Clos du Bois   *map page 204, B-2*

Backtrack south on Geyserville Avenue to visit the tasting room of Clos du Bois, founded in 1974, by Frank M. Woods, who planted the first vineyards in 1964. This winery is now owned by Allied Domecq, but its wines are still good. The top-of-the-line Marlstone Bordeaux blend has been superb in past years. Tastings are given daily. *19410 Geyserville Avenue; 707-857-1651.*

Chateau Souverain   *map page 204, B-2*

When it was built in 1972, Chateau Souverain was intended to be Pillsbury's Sonoma County winery under that conglomerate's short and ill-fated foray into the wine business. No expenses were spared in putting up an imposing structure that looks like a very elegant cross between a French château and a Sonoma County hop kiln. While under construction, the winery was called Ville Fontaine, but Pillsbury changed its name to Chateau Souverain before the 1973 vintage, and shortly after the 1974 crush it was renamed Souverain of Alexander Valley. By 1976, Pillsbury had sold both this winery and its sister winery in Napa.

Wine World Estates, which owned the winery until 1995, changed its name

Chateau Souverain, a well-known winery and restaurant in the Alexander Valley.

back to Chateau Souverain. It is now owned by Blass Wine Estates, the winery division of the Australian beverage conglomerate Foster's Group, and the wines are better than ever. The Alexander Valley cabernet sauvignon, the Dry Creek Valley zinfandel, and the Alexander Valley sauvignon blanc are worth searching out. To reach Chateau Souverain, take Geyserville Avenue south and turn right on Independence Lane. You can't miss the château. Tastings are offered daily; you need reservations to dine at the full-service restaurant. *400 Souverain Road, off Independence Lane; 707-433-8281.*

■ LOWER ALEXANDER VALLEY

To reach the lower Alexander Valley from Chateau Souverain, take U.S. 101 south to the Lytton Springs Road exit. Turn left and cross the freeway. Turn right at the stop sign onto Healdsburg Avenue and travel south for about half a mile, then turn left at the sign for "Alexander Valley Road/Calistoga" toward Jimtown. If you're coming from Healdsburg, drive north on Healdsburg Avenue and stay to the right when it splits into Lytton Station Road and Alexander Valley Road. At Jimtown, Highway 128, or Alexander Valley Avenue, comes in from the left. The **Jimtown Store** (6706 Highway 128; 707-433-1212), on your left, has great espresso and a good selection of deli items, including gourmet sandwiches.

Stryker Sonoma Winery and Vineyards   *map page 204, B-2*
Turn left on Highway 128, to reach Stryker Sonoma, perched high above the Alexander Valley. The dramatic tasting room, atop a tall stone wall, offers splendid views across the vineyards to the Coast Range hills. Stryker was founded in 2002, but it has already made a name for itself, both for its wines and for innovative architecture. It currently produces chardonnay, gewürztraminer, sangiovese, zinfandel, and Two Moon Cuvée, a splendid Bordeaux blend from Alexander Valley, Dry Creek, and Russian River grapes. It is open from Thursday through Sunday for tastings. *5110 Highway 128; 707-433-1944.*

Sausal Winery   *map page 204, C-2*
Backtrack to Jimtown and turn left to follow Highway 128 a couple of miles up the road to Sausal Winery, a beautiful place shaded by ancient oaks. It was founded in 1956 by Leo and Rose (Ferrari) Demostene, who had worked at Rose's

The Jimtown Store in Alexander Valley sells gourmet sandwiches and espresso.

father's winery for 20 years. With the help of their four children, the Demostenes turned the Sausal Ranch—which was planted to apples, plums, and old zinfandel vines—into a winery while still helping grandfather Abele Ferrari with his Soda Rock Winery. Although Leo passed away in 1973, the Demostene children have carried on. Sausal makes an excellent cabernet and truly outstanding zinfandel, the best of which comes from vines more than 100 years old. Buy a bottle, grab a table on the patio, and enjoy a picnic lunch and the view of vines stretching all the way to the hills. Watch ravens and turkey vultures and an occasional hawk soar overhead. Sniff the air. If the wind is right, the breeze carries a heady aroma of grapes and wild laurel. Tastings are offered daily. *7370 Highway 128; 707-433-2285.*

Alexander Valley Vineyards *map page 204, C-2*

Farther along Highway 128, off a long driveway on the left, is the 1841 homestead of Cyrus Alexander, for whom the valley is named. The Wetzel family bought part of the land homesteaded by Cyrus Alexander from his heirs in 1963 and restored the historic Cyrus Alexander Adobe to serve as their family home. But the Wetzels also planted vineyards, and in 1975 they built a winery with adobe blocks and weathered wood. You can wander up a grassy hill behind the winery to the cemetery of Cyrus Alexander and his family or grab a bottle of the splendid proprietary zinfandel, called Sin Zin, and head for the picnic tables. The cabernet is also good. Alexander Valley is open for tastings daily; you will need an appointment to tour the wine caves. *8644 Highway 128; 707-433-7209.*

Field Stone Winery & Vineyards *map page 204, C-2*

A few miles southeast on Highway 128 look for Field Stone Winery on the right. Founded in 1977 by Wallace Johnson, this winery takes its name from the fieldstones that cover its facade. These came from the trench that was dug across the crown of a hill to create aging cellars. (The cellars were built, and the excavated soil, minus the stones, was put back on top.) Johnson, who invented a mechanical grape harvester, passed away in 1979, but his family continues operating the winery. You should stop here and taste the cabernet sauvignon and petite sirah, as well as the sauvignon blanc. Tours at Field Stone are by appointment only. *10075 Highway 128; 707-433-7266.*

Poppies and grapes at Madroña Vineyards, in the Sierra Foothills.

BEYOND NAPA AND SONOMA

To many a visitor, "California Wine Country" is synonymous with the grape-growing areas of the Napa Valley and Sonoma County, but within the state lie several other regions with splendid wineries. In this chapter we slip north of Napa and Sonoma to Mendocino County's Anderson Valley and head east of the Wine Country to the Clarksburg, Lodi, and Sierra Foothills AVAs. In the next chapter we visit the best of California's Central Coast.

■ ANDERSON VALLEY APPELLATION

Navarro

Anderson Valley

Boonville

Mendocino
Ridge

After joining U.S. 101 at Geyserville, Highway 128 departs to the west just north of Cloverdale. This is the main route to Mendocino and the coast. Along the way, it traverses one of the less visited, but more important of northern California's wine-making regions, the Anderson Valley AVA, which is east of the higher-elevation Mendocino Ridge AVA. At first, Highway 128 climbs steeply in serried switchbacks through a mixture of chaparral and oak forest. As the road rises, it follows a creek bed. This is Dry Creek, which runs south from here through the renowned grape-growing valley that has taken its name. West of the mountain crest, you'll wind through seemingly endless stretches of blue oak savannah and sheep pasture, finally descending into the broad Anderson Valley, green with pastures, apple orchards, and an increasing number of vineyards.

■ BOONVILLE   *map page 220, A-4*

At the center of the valley is Boonville, a small farming town once so isolated its residents invented a lingo all their own, known as Boontling, or Boont, for short. Few traces of this unique language survive, except in the names of a coffee shop known as Horn of Zeese ("cup of coffee"), and a phone booth called Buckey Walter. Boonville, whose other regional claims to fame are the annual Apple Show and the Sheep Dog Trials held in October, is a less lonely place these days, thanks largely to the stream of Bay Area weekenders passing through town en route to the Mendocino Coast.

Anderson Valley grapegrowers have played a big role in ending the valley's isolation, but despite wineries moving into the valley and fancy restaurants popping up, Boonville retains a rustic look. Still, you can have a truly great dining experience

Boonville's brewing company opened in the 1980s, before many local wineries.

on a visit here. The **Boonville Hotel** (Highway 128 and Lambert Lane; 707-895-2210) serves marvelous roadhouse food and rents plain but comfortable rooms. Delectable dinners are prepared across the street at unpretentious **Lauren's Cafe** (14211 Highway 128; 707-895-3869).

For a change of pace from winery touring, you can visit the **Anderson Valley Brewing Company** (Route 253 and Highway 128; 707-895-2769) or bring the fixings for a picnic and enjoy the coolness of the redwoods at nearby **Hendy Woods State Park,** which borders the Navarro River.

Grapes were first planted in the Anderson Valley about 100 years ago, the ridges for the most part by Italians and the valley floor by farmers making wine for home use. Zinfandel found a unique home here. Some growers, such as Ukiah's Parducci family, slowly expanded their Anderson Valley holdings over the years, but the valley's wine boom dates from only the early 1970s, when Tony Husch of Husch Vineyards and Ted Bennett of Navarro Vineyards planted gewürztraminer vines in what they considered to be the perfect climate for this finicky Alsatian grape—the cool part of the Anderson Valley. But Husch found that chardonnay and pinot noir

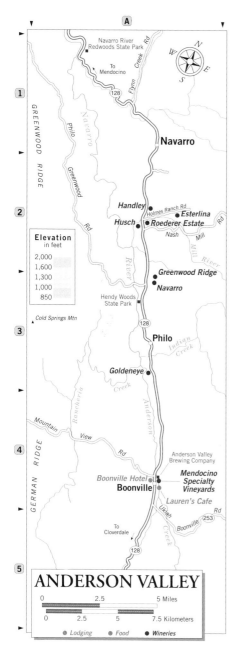

ANDERSON VALLEY

grew even better here—and sold better. He also believed that these two make a great sparkling wine.

It was John Scharffenberger who, in 1981, firmly placed the Anderson Valley among America's top producers. The French were so impressed with his bubbly that, in 1982, the champagne producer Roederer moved in next door instead of settling in the Napa Valley as other French wine entrepreneurs had done. Today, the sparklers of these neighboring wineries consistently rank among the top half dozen produced in North America.

In 1989, Scharffenberger sold a controlling interest in his winery to another French champagne maker, the house of Pommery, and his current endeavor, Eaglepoint Ranch Winery (888-686-9463), isn't open to the public. But you can sample his sangiovese, syrah, petite sirah, and grenache wines at **Mendocino Specialty Vineyards** (17810 Farrer Lane, at Highway 128; 707-895-3993), the Boonville tasting room that also serves wines by Claudia Springs, a family-run operation specializing in pinot noir and chardonnay, and Raye's Hills Vineyards.

Navarro Vineyards sits amid rolling hills of redwoods and other trees.

■ **PHILO**   *map page 220, A-3*

Northwest of Boonville, the highway cuts through a low ridge, which is just high enough to impede the sea fogs creeping up the Navarro River. North of here the land is much cooler than in the southern valley—making it perfect for redwoods, apples, and grapes. The area around the town of Philo, where the Rancheria, Anderson, and Indian Creeks merge to form the Navarro River, has long been an apple-growing center—primarily for Gravensteins and Sierra Beauties, which prefer cool climates. If you're visiting in summer or fall, stock up at one of the many fruit stands along the highway. Gowan's Oak Tree is the best.

From east to west, below are some of Anderson Valley's best wineries to visit.

Goldeneye Winery   *map page 220, A-1*

The owners of the Napa Valley's well-respected Duckhorn Vineyards bought the old Obester Winery in the mid-1990s and have been making pinot noir from local grapes with very satisfying results. The winery, which takes its name from the Goldeneye duck, whose migratory flyway is nearby, is only open for tastings from March through October and even then only on the first Friday and Saturday of the month. *9200 Highway 128, 707 895 3202.*

Navarro Vineyards *map page 220, A-3*

You can pick up the fixings for a picnic—wine, cheese, and smoked salmon—at the deli case at pioneering Navarro Vineyards, whose tasting room is open daily. The winery, started in 1974 by Ted Bennett, who's still involved, puts out luscious chardonnay and gewürztraminer and a much-heralded pinot gris. *5601 Highway 128; 707-895-3686.*

Greenwood Ridge *map page 220, A-3*

At an elevation of 1,200 feet, this winery in the Mendocino Ridge AVA has some of the region's coolest vineyards. Zinfandel and pinot noir are the stars at Greenwood, but the sauvignon blanc and chardonnay have also won multiple gold medals. The late-harvest Riesling has a full and fruity yet remarkably clean taste. Allen Green, one of the valley's acknowledged masters, opened this winery in 1980. He is also a graphic artist and designs his own labels. *5501 Highway 128; 707-877-3267.*

Roederer Estate *map page 220, A-2*

The French champagne maker opened its American operation in 1982, and the tasting room is one of Mendocino's swankest. For a small fee you can taste the brut, the brut rosé, and an extra-dry brut. The brut rosé consistently impresses. The top sparkler, a chardonnay–pinot noir blend, is called L'Ermitage. *4501 Highway 128; 707-895-2288.*

Husch Vineyards *map page 220, A-2*

You don't want to pass up a chance to visit Husch Vineyards, owned by the Oswald family, who bought the winery from Tony Husch in 1979. The estate-grown gewürztraminer is about as good as it gets, and the pinot noir has a distinctly Burgundian structure—as well as that elusive aroma and flavor characteristic of the best wines made from this varietal. But don't neglect the chardonnay, which is also excellent. *4400 Highway 128; 707-895-3216.*

Handley Cellars *map page 220, A-2*

Milla Handley, a former artist, caught the wine bug while studying at the University of California at Davis, and she and her husband, Rex McClellan, opened Handley Cellars in 1982. The winery produces a splendid chardonnay from Anderson Valley grapes, a delightful sauvignon blanc, and some very good sparkling wines. This is a perfect place to relax in the shade on a hot summer day, a cool glass of wine in hand. *3151 Highway 128; 707-895-3876.*

Turn north off Highway 128 on Holmes Ranch Road to reach Esterlina Vineyards and Winery.

Esterlina Vineyards and Winery   *map page 220, A-2*
One of the few African-American–owned wineries in California, the former Pepperwood Springs was bought by the Sterling family in 2000. It has made a name for itself by creating first-rate pinot noir with grapes grown in the Russian River Valley and chardonnay using traditional, labor-intensive Burgundian wine-making methods. Esterlina has also become well known for its deeply flavored, complex zinfandel. The winery makes a cabernet sauvignon from Alexander Valley grapes, merlot, and white Riesling. *1200 Holmes Ranch Road; 707-895-2920.*

There are no wineries west of the town of Navarro, but the **Floodgate Store & Deli** is a great luncheon stop serving a splendid chili. By now, you're quite close to the magnificent giants of **Navarro River Redwoods State Park.** Its cool glades are perfect for a postprandial stroll that will put you in the mood for an afternoon of wine tasting. You can return to Napa or Sonoma by backtracking on Highway 128, but for a dramatic alternative, continue west on Highway 128 and head south on Highway 1, which hugs the coast—sometimes precariously so. You can head back east at Jenner (Highway 116) or Bodega Bay (Highway 12).

■ CLARKSBURG AND LODI APPELLATIONS

Credit for calling attention to the excellent grapes produced in the Clarksburg and Lodi wine regions east of Napa and Sonoma belongs to Robert Mondavi, whose parents had been Lodi growers before moving to the Napa Valley. After establishing his now-famous Napa Valley winery in 1966, Mondavi returned to the Lodi area in 1979, bought an old wine company in Woodbridge, and opened a premium winery. At about the same time, Bogle, a Clarksburg grower, opened its winery. Others followed suit, and the two areas now have about four dozen wineries, many of which have tasting rooms open to the public.

The two official growing regions are the Clarksburg AVA, on the Sacramento River Delta, and the Lodi AVA, on the Mokelumne River, to the south. The delta lies along Highway 160 (take Highway 12 east from Napa). Lodi wineries can be

found on or near Highway 99 and are accessible from I-5. The soils of the two regions are similar—centuries ago, gravelly well-drained loam washed down from the Sierra to the east—with local variations. Like all the Central Valley, this land was an arm of the ocean until alluvial debris from the mountains filled it up. Vineyards were planted in the Lodi area before the end of the 19th century, and many pre-Prohibition vines, mainly zinfandel, survive.

■ CLARKSBURG APPELLATION

The Clarksburg AVA is surrounded by the canals and sloughs of the Sacramento River Delta, and travel is mainly over levee roads. Here egrets and great blue herons stalk through shallow marshes in search of prey, bitterns boom in the reeds, and gulls beg for handouts from picnickers dining along the grassy banks of the levees. In late summer, look for ripe black figs on "wild" trees growing below the levee crests. Farm stands sell pears and other local fruits in season. Several river hamlets, most notably the well-preserved ghost town of **Locke,** settled by Chinese immigrants more than a century ago, and the old-town area of **Walnut Grove,** are pleasant to stroll.

This appellation is bordered by I-5 to the east, by the Sacramento Deep Water Channel to the west, by the town of Freeport to the north, and by Twin Cities Road to the south (an area 16 miles long and 8 miles wide). Nearly 10,000 acres of vineyards, tucked among orchards and field crops, produce an average of 40,000 tons of wine grapes a year. There are more than 20 varieties of wine grapes, including chardonnay, merlot, sauvignon blanc, petite sirah, syrah, zinfandel, viognier, cabernet sauvignon, pinot noir, pinot gris, and, most notably, chenin blanc, a French grape that does so well here that the region has been called the "Vouvray of California," after the chenin blanc grape's place of origin. Chenin blanc loves the well-drained loamy soils and the warm-to-hot summer days and cool nights of the long, dry growing season.

Most of the grapes grown in the Clarksburg AVA are raised under long-term contract to Napa and Sonoma wineries such as Beringer, Domaine Chandon, Gallo of Sonoma, Dry Creek, and Landmark, but one well-established local winery, Bogle, makes wine from local grapes. To reach Bogle, take I-5's Jefferson Boulevard Exit and head south for 13 miles. Make a left on Clarksburg Road, a right on Riverview, a right on Road 141 and continue left when Road 141 becomes Road 144.

(previous pages) Coastal fog creates perfect conditions for Roederer's sparkling-wine grapes.

Bogle Winery *map page 227, A-2*

The Bogle family planted its first 20 acres of wine grapes in Clarksburg in 1968 and added a winery in the 1970s. Today Bogle Vineyards stretches over 1,200 acres in the Delta. The chardonnay, merlot, and petite sirah have attracted favorable notices in recent years; other wines include sauvignon blanc, old-vine zinfandel, and petite-sirah port. Bogle is the only Delta winery whose wines are widely distributed throughout the United States. Its tasting room overlooks a lawn that stretches to the vineyards and makes for a perfect picnicking spot. *37783 Road 144; 916-744-1139.*

Two small Clarksburg wineries worth checking out are **River Grove Winery** (52183 Clarksburg Road, Clarksburg; 916-744-9000) and **Six Hands Winery** (13783 Isleton Road, Walnut Grove; 916-776-2053). You'll need to call before visiting these wineries.

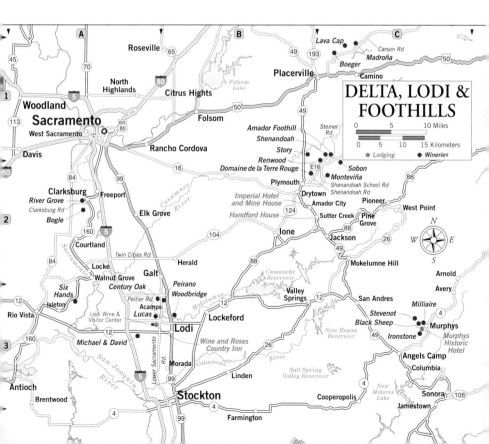

DELTA, LODI & FOOTHILLS

■ LODI APPELLATION

The Lodi AVA, 35 miles south of Sacramento off I-5 or Highway 99 and 75 miles east of Sonoma on Highway 12, produces about 18 percent of California's wine grapes. About 40 percent of the state's zinfandel grapes are grown here, along with cabernet sauvignon, chardonnay, and several Italian and Rhône varieties.

An important initial stop before exploring this region is the **Lodi Wine & Visitor Center,** which has exhibits on grape growing and wine making, a gift shop that sells handcrafted products, and a tasting room with a wide selection of area wines. The staff here includes a "community concierge," who assists visitors trying to choose a tasting room, a lodging, or a restaurant. *2545 West Turner Road (east off I-5 and west off Highway 99); 209-367-4727.*

Tucked into large gardens behind the center is the **Wine and Roses Country Inn.** A 1902 mansion set on 5 acres, the inn has 40 guest rooms and a spa. Popular with celebrities visiting Lodi—Margaret Thatcher, Robert Mondavi, Colin Powell, and Martha Stewart have stayed here—this is the locals' choice for weddings and special-occasion dinners. *2545 West Turner Road; 209-334-6988.*

Among the Lodi area wineries west of Highway 99 with tasting rooms, the Lucas Winery is one of the best. Head west about 1.7 miles from the visitor center and turn right (north) on North Davis Road.

Lucas Winery   *map page 227, A-3*

Lucas was one of the first local producers to start making "serious" wine, back in 1978. A new winery, completed in 2000 and dedicated to zinfandel, incorporates an aboveground storage room with a single layer of oak barrels, to provide ready access without disturbing or moving the barrels. This prevents the mixing of sediment back into the wines as they age. Crushed gravel under the barrels helps to maintain the proper temperature and humidity. In addition to zinfandel, Lucas makes a light chardonnay with subtle oaky flavors. The tasting room here is open from Thursday through Sunday. *18196 North Davis Road; 209-368-2006.*

Backtrack south on Davis Road to Kettleman Lane (Highway 12) and turn right (west) to reach Michael & David Vineyards.

Michael & David Vineyards   *map page 227, A-3*

Fifth-generation grapegrowers and produce farmers Michael and David Philips operate a fruit stand and tasting room where they pour their wines and purvey heirloom vegetables, gourmet provisions, picnic lunches, and bakery goodies. Founded in 1984, Michael & David Vineyards uses only 10 percent of the total harvest for its own wines; the rest is sold to other wineries. Varietals include syrah, merlot, zinfandel, cabernet sauvignon, viognier, roussanne, and chardonnay. *4580 West Highway 12; 209-368-7384.*

Peirano, the Robert Mondavi Company's Woodbridge winery, and several boutique wineries do business just north of Lodi in Acampo. To reach them, head east on West Turner Road and north on Lower Sacramento Road.

Century Oak Winery   *map page 227, A/B-3*

In 2001, the Housley family built this winery on the front 40 acres of a cabernet vineyard to better showcase grapes grown in Acampo, Lodi, and Woodbridge. The winery, at which tastings are by appointment only, takes its name from a 100-year-old valley oak in the main vineyard. As growers, the Housleys have access to some of the best locally grown grapes, and their chardonnay and estate-grown cabernet sauvignon have a local following, but it is the old-vine zinfandel—supple, complex, and pleasing on the palate—that has been their best wine. *22211 North Lower Sacramento Road; 209-334-3482.*

Peirano Estate, one of the area's oldest vineyards, can be reached by continuing north on North Lower Sacramento Road, turning right on East Peltier Street, and then right (south) again on Highway 99.

Peirano Estate Vineyards   *map page 227, A/B-3*

Italian immigrant Giacomo Peirano established his Lodi vineyards in 1885, and they have been in continuous production since then. Today, the 300-acre estate is owned by his great-grandson, Lance Randolph, who is also the winemaker. The winery makes chardonnay, sauvignon blanc, viognier, merlot, cabernet sauvignon, shiraz, petite sirah, barbera, and zinfandel from old, head-trained vines and newer stock. The wines are rich and full-flavored, as one would expect from this growing region, but they also have a good complexity and a crisp acid backbone. The tasting room is open on Fridays and weekends, and there is a picnic area among the vines. *21831 North Highway 99; 209-369-9463.*

To reach Woodbridge Winery, head south from Peirano Estate on Highway 99 to the Woodbridge Road exit and head east.

Oak-barrel aging takes place on a grand scale at Woodbridge.

Woodbridge Winery *map page 227, B-3*

When Robert Mondavi returned to his native Lodi in 1979 he acquired the old co-op facility known as the Cherokee Wine Association to augment production at his Napa Valley winery, and his company has been adding buildings and wine-making facilities ever since. The architecture of Woodbridge Winery is a curious blend of 1930s industrial, surviving from the co-op days, and Mondavi's signature mission style. The thermal-mass cellar, housing 60,000 barrels, is one of the largest and most modern wine-aging facilities in the world.

In 1979, Woodbridge became the first in the region to abandon jug wines in favor of single-label red and white wines, and in 1986, Woodbridge became the first area winery in the "premium" category to produce and vintage-date varietally labeled wines, thus leading the way for other local wineries away from bulk wines to higher-quality ones. Woodbridge is currently the number-one varietal wine brand in the United States, with a production of about 7 million cases annually. At the tasting room, which is open daily except Monday, you can sample hard-to-find Woodbridge wines such as the Lodi Old Vine Zinfandel. *5950 East Woodbridge Road; 209-365-2839.*

■ SIERRA FOOTHILLS APPELLATION

As the rays of the setting sun touch the hillsides, they tinge rows of vines with streaks of gold, while the deep creek and river canyons below the vineyards already lie in deep shade. Vines were planted in these hills shortly after the gold rush of 1849, and vineyards were well established by 1872, when the travel writer Charles Nordhoff passed through the town of Columbia. As he recalled in his book *California,* published the next year, a winemaker's family poured "a red wine which they call claret here, but which is thin, and to my taste too strong for claret, and a very sweet angelica, almost like sirup."

The naturalist John Muir, exploring the mountains later in the 19th century, also commented on local vines, noting "secluded flats" that were "settled mostly by Italians and Germans, who plant a few vegetables and grape-vines at odd times, while their main business is mining and prospecting." There were wineries in the foothills by the 1890s, and though most of them fell victim to Prohibition, their vines did not. According to local vintners, some of the vines John Muir saw are still in the foothills. You can tell old zinfandel vines by their knobby heads. The vines are commonly "head-pruned," that is, pruned as freestanding vines, instead of being strung out along trellis wires.

More vines were planted in the 1970s, when the California wine boom spilled over into the Sierras, leading to the establishment of wineries in the central Sierra counties of El Dorado, Amador, and Calaveras. The Sierra Foothills AVA overlaps the El Dorado and Shenandoah Valley AVAs. Most wineries here are very small, producing only a few thousand cases, but there are a couple of "giants," Monteviña in Amador County and Ironstone in Calaveras County.

Spring is a great time to visit. The hills are green with velvety grass, and wild turkeys strut their new feathers beneath golden-tasseled oaks that succeeded the native oaks cleared away by 19th-century miners, the better to extract gold. But the hills survived the environmental havoc and are again picture-pretty. Suburban sprawl has begun to encroach, but in the historic districts of former mining towns like Jackson and Sutter Creek, buildings with white-railing porches and balconies that shade sidewalks from the summer sun have been preserved. As in the Napa and Sonoma Valleys, old stone buildings now serve as hotels, shops, and residences.

John Muir strolls a Sierra Foothills vineyard he planted.

As industrious as the miners were, they did not remove all the gold from the canyons. Even now, there's some to be found in the foothills, and hordes of weekend prospectors scour the bottoms of creeks and rivers for nuggets. But the area has also attracted grapegrowers. The main vineyard region stretches for about 70 miles along Highway 49 from Placerville in the north to Murphys in the south, with a few wineries above and below these cities.

The microclimates of local vineyards depend largely on the elevation at which they are planted. El Dorado County vineyards are the coolest, not because this is the northernmost of the three foothill wine counties, but because the vineyards here are the highest—as much as 3,000 feet above sea level, with one vineyard at 3,600 feet. Amador County, in the middle, has the lowest—from 1,200 to 1,600 feet above sea level—and thus the warmest vineyards; Calaveras County vineyards are planted at elevations of 1,550 to 2,400 feet above sea level.

El Dorado vintners claim that their cool growing conditions lend their wines a special elegance—something winemakers from the other two counties dispute. In any case, El Dorado grows excellent chardonnay and Riesling; Amador produces heavy, alcoholic, and multifaceted zinfandels; and Calaveras has a slight edge with recently introduced Mediterranean grape varieties such as barbera, dolcetto, marsanne, mourvèdre, nebbiolo, syrah, and tempranillo.

Historic hotels in the foothills include Amador City's **Imperial Hotel** (14202 Highway 49; 209-267-9172), which first opened as a hotel in 1879, closed in 1927, but was restored and reopened in the late 1980s. The **Mine House Inn** (14125 Highway 49; 209-267-5900), at the southern end of Amador City, was built in the 1860s but its rooms have been thoroughly modernized. The **Hanford House** (64 Hanford Street; 209-267-0747), on Highway 49 in Sutter Creek, was remodeled in 1995. **Murphys Historic Hotel** (457 Main Street; 209-728-3444) is within walking distance of the Murphys tasting rooms. Except for the Hanford House, all these hotels have restaurants.

Though the Sierra Nevada range itself is rugged, the wineries in the foothills are relatively easy to visit: El Dorado County wineries can be accessed off U.S. 50 from I-5 at Sacramento, and those of Amador and Calaveras Counties can be reached from Sacramento via Highway 16 and Highway 49.

■ EL DORADO COUNTY

Several wineries in **Placerville**, 45 miles east of Sacramento, are just off U.S. 50, one of the major cross-Sierra highways. To reach the first stop, Boeger Winery, exit at Schnell School Road and turn left. When you get to Carson Road, turn right.

Boeger Winery   *map page 227, C-1*

Greg Boeger, a scion of the Napa Valley's Nichelini family, resurrected a gold rush–era vineyard in the 1970s and turned it into one of El Dorado County's leading wineries. Planted on steep hills, the estate vineyards supply most of the grapes—zinfandel, cabernet sauvignon, and sauvignon blanc, as well as some muscat canelli, sangiovese, nebbiolo, and refosco. Boeger also grows syrah and grenache, graciano, tempranillo, cabernet franc, merlot, and petit verdot, but he is best known for his barbera. An old wine-storage building now serves as tasting room. Boeger's zinfandel is also excellent. Hangtown Red, a blend of leftover reds, has a loyal local following. *1709 Carson Road; 530-622-8094.*

To reach the next winery, Lava Cap, continue north about a mile and a half on Carson Road, turn left on Union Ridge Road, and then make a right on Hassler Road. Turn left when you get to Fruitridge Road.

Lava Cap Winery *map page 227, C-1*

In the Apple Hills area, northeast of Placerville, Lava Cap's vineyards range in elevation from 1,500 feet to 2,900 feet. Founded in 1981, the winery produces chardonnay, fumé blanc, and a superb zinfandel that is full-bodied yet surprisingly elegant and complex. *2221 Fruitridge Road; 530-621-0175.*

Follow Fruitridge Road east and turn right (south) on North Canyon Road and left (east) on Carson Road. Turn left again when you get to High Hill Road, where amid the rolling hills west of the village of Camino lies Madroña Vineyards.

Madroña Vineyards *map page 227, C-1*

At an elevation of 3,000 feet, Madroña ranks with Lava as one of the highest California wineries and can claim to offer truly mountain-grown wines. The hot days and cooler nights at this elevation produce fruit with excellent balance and intense character. Carved from the local woods by Richard and Leslie Bush, the vineyard was planted around a giant madrona tree, which gave the winery its name. The first crush was held in the rustic winery building in 1980. The wines include zinfandel, merlot, chardonnay, and gewürztraminer, as well as a mourvèdre rosé, a cabernet port, a late-harvest Riesling, a late-harvest zinfandel, and other dessert wines. *High Hill Road, Camino; 530-644-5948.*

■ AMADOR COUNTY

The Shenandoah Valley AVA, Amador County's prime vineyard region, is not a valley at all but rather a mesa of gently rolling hills high above the deep canyons of the Cosumnes River and Dry Creek. Most of the vineyards are off of Highway 49, 20-plus miles south of Placerville. To reach Story Winery, whose vineyards hold some of the Shenandoah Valley's oldest zinfandel and mission vines, take Highway 49 south to Bell Road east. The winery is a few miles east of Plymouth.

Story Winery *map page 227, B/C-1*

Founded in 1973, Story is one of the few wineries to still make wine from mission grapes, the *criollo* variety originally brought to California by Spanish missionaries more than 200 years ago. Besides the mission-zinfandel blend and a very powerful zinfandel, the winery makes barbera, merlot, chardonnay, chenin blanc, and white zinfandel. You can picnic here under huge oak trees that survived the gold rush. *10525 Bell Road; 209-245-6208.*

Boeger is one of El Dorado County's largest wineries.

Other Shenandoah Valley wineries can be reached by continuing south on Highway 49 and then heading east on Fiddletown Road. Turn left almost immediately onto Plymouth-Shenandoah Road. Signposts mark the wineries, most of which are on Shenandoah School Road or Steiner Road. Make a right turn on Shenandoah School Road to reach Monteviña Wines, a major contributor to the foothills wine renaissance.

Monteviña Wines   *map page 227, C-2*

In 1968, Bob Trinchero, the winemaker at his family's Sutter Home Winery in the Napa Valley tasted a zinfandel produced from Deaver Ranch grapes in the Shenandoah Valley. Trinchero liked what he tasted and began to make some zinfandel from Deaver's almost 100-year-old vines. In 1988, the Trinchero family bought Monteviña, which had been founded in 1970, as the Sierra Foothills' first post-Prohibition winery.

A decade later, a 64,000-square-foot facility was built, and though this is by far the region's largest winery, it has managed to maintain the spirit of a boutique operation. Its 400 acres of vineyards are planted (at elevations from 1,300 to 1,600 feet) with proven varieties such as zinfandel and barbera. Monteviña also is well known for its pioneer experiments in developing Italian grape varieties in Amador County, among them aglianico, freisa, nebbiolo, refosco, and sangiovese. With its covered picnic patios, the winery is a favorite picnic spot. *20680 Shenandoah School Road; 209-245-6942.*

About a mile from Monteviña on Steiner Road are three wineries of note. To reach them, head north on Shenandoah School Road and follow the signs.

Renwood Winery   *map page 227, C-2*

In 1992, Renwood bought the Santino winery, which had prospered from the white-zinfandel craze of the 1980s and early 1990s and became known for its zinfandel port. Renwood now produces zinfandel, syrah, barbera, viognier, fumé blanc, muscat, and two dessert wines: Amador Ice and a port. One of the largest wineries in Amador County and one of the few here that is not a family operation, Renwood also produces a Rhône-style blend called Satyricon. *12225 Steiner Road; 209-245-6979.*

Sierra Foothills towns like Amador City attract many weekenders with cafés, country stores, and bed-and-breakfast inns.

Shenandoah Vineyards *map page 227, C-1/2*

In 1977, Leon Sobon—a research scientist from Los Altos—and his wife, Shirley, came to Amador County and planted vineyards at the former Steiner Ranch. They then built a winery on the site of an old garage and made 1,200 cases of wine during their first year of production, 1977. Today, Shenandoah, several times its original size, produces two zinfandels, a barbera, a cabernet sauvignon, a sauvignon blanc, and a black muscat, as well as a sangiovese, a sangiovese-zinfandel blend, and a cabernet-syrah blend. The Sobons also own Sobon Estate, a little less than 5 miles to the east. *12300 Steiner Road; 209-245-4456.*

Amador Foothill Winery *map page 227, C-1/2*

Amador Foothill, established in the 1970s, produces vineyard-designated zin-fandel, sangiovese, sémillon, and fumé blanc. The oldest of the zinfandel vine-yards, the Murril Vineyard, was first planted 80 years ago, and a portion of the vines, which were overgrown and neglected for a long period, have been brought back to life. Another of the zinfandel wines comes from Frank Alviso's notable Clockspring Vineyard. Amador Foothill is open only on weekends and holidays. *12500 Steiner Road; 209-245-6307.*

Backtrack west on Steiner Road and turn right on Dickson Road to reach Domaine de la Terre Rouge, whose slogan is "where the Rhône Valley meets the Sierra Nevada."

Domaine de la Terre Rouge *map page 227, B/C-2*

This winery has two labels—Terre Rouge, first made in 1985, and Easton, first made in 1991—with different wine-making styles. The Terre Rouge label focuses on Rhône varietals: syrah, grenache, mourvèdre, viognier, marsanne, rou-sanne, and dessert muscat. The Easton label is reserved for old-vine zinfandel and barbera. As a leader in the California Rhône wine movement, the winery has gained cult status among lovers of thick, powerful (if occasionally unbalanced) wines. The approach works better with syrah than with zinfandel. The winery is open only on Fridays and weekends. *10801 Dickson Road; 209-245-3117.*

Head east on Dickson back to Shenandoah Road and head east (left) on Shenandoah School Road to reach Sobon Estate Winery, California's third-oldest winery and the oldest one in the foothills.

Sobon Estate Winery

map page 227, C-1/2

The winery here was established in the 1800s by a Swiss immigrant, Adam Uhlinger, and run by the D'Agostini family from 1911 until the 1980s. Exhibits at the on-site Shenandoah Valley Museum, in the original D'Agostini winery building, include huge wine casks and early farming and wine-making implements. Sobon makes three zinfandels (each from a different vineyard), a syrah, an orange muscat, two Rhône-style varietals (viognier and rousanne), and two blends, Rhône Rouge and Rhône Rose. *14430 Shenandoah Road; 209-245-6554.*

Zinfandel grapes at Sobon Estate.

■ CALAVERAS COUNTY

Many of Calaveras County's small wineries are near the hamlet of **Murphys,** off Highway 4 a few miles east of Angels Camp and Highway 49, or have tasting rooms along Main Street in Murphys itself—very convenient, except that parking can be very hard to find, even midweek. John Muir described the town in *The Mountains of California* as a "curious old mining town . . . at an elevation of 2400 feet above the sea, situated like a nest in the center of a rough, gravelly region rich in gold."

Milliaire Winery *map page 227, C-3*

Founded in 1983, Milliaire is a down-home street-front winery occupying a former gas station at the southern end of Murphys, but it doesn't need any glitz—the wines speak for themselves. Two notable zinfandels are made from grapes grown in Calaveras County's Ghirardelli Vineyard and in Amador's Clockspring Vineyard. The Murphys Reserve White is a perfect picnic wine. The winery is open from Friday through Monday. *276 Main Street; 209-728-1658.*

Black Sheep Winery   *map page 227, C-3*

Black Sheep was named by its owners—Dave and Jan Olsen—to signify their bold style of wine making (black sheep standing out in the field of white ewes), which runs to small lots of premium varietals, including zinfandel, cabernet sauvignon, and sauvignon blanc. The winery, opened in 1986, also puts out a white blend, True Frogs Lily Pad White, and a red True Frogs counterpart. *Main Street and French Gulch Road; 209-728-2157.*

You can taste Stevenot wines at its downtown Murphys tasting room, but to view its unusual winery tasting room, head north from Main Street 2 miles on Sheep Ranch Road and turn left on San Domingo Road.

Stevenot Winery   *map page 227, C-3*

Established in 1973 by fifth-generation Calaveras resident Barden Stevenot, this winery produced ordinary table wines until Chuck Hovey came aboard as winemaker in 1983 and started making better wine from the estate grapes. One of the region's larger wineries, Stevenot makes chardonnay, sauvignon blanc, orange muscat, cabernet sauvignon, syrah, zinfandel, merlot, and tempranillo. The winery has a large picnic area next to its tasting room, the Alaska House, a sod-covered building dating from gold rush days. *Winery: 2690 San Domingo Road; 209-728-3436. Downtown Murphys tasting room: 458A Main Street; 209-728-0148.*

Backtrack to Main Street on Sheep Ranch Road, turn left and then quickly right (south) on Algiers, which after 2.6 miles becomes Six Mile Road. About 3.1 miles from Main Street you'll come to Ironstone Vineyards.

Ironstone Vineyards   *map page 227, C-3*

This odd place is Calaveras County's largest winery and quite an unusual experience. Modeled after a 19th-century gold-stamp mill (used to extract gold from ore and quartz), Ironstone has a tasting room but also houses the Ironstone Heritage Museum and Gallery, a display on the history of gold and viticulture in the Sierra Foothills. Also here are a lakeside park, an amphitheater, an antiques collection, and a culinary center. Well worth a stop, this is about as close to a Napa Valley–style wine theme park as you'll find in the foothills. Ironstone makes a very good cabernet franc from foothills grapes as well as good cabernet sauvignon and merlot from foothills and Lodi grapes. *1894 Six Mile Road, 209-728-1251.*

J. Lohr's hilltop vineyard at Paso Robles.

CENTRAL COAST WINERIES

The Central Coast grape-growing region covers a large territory, from the Santa Cruz Mountains to southern Santa Barbara County. The wineries in the Santa Cruz Mountains, less than 60 miles from San Francisco and about 100 miles south of the town of Sonoma, lie on twisting roads off Highway 17 or the coastal Highway 1. Many of the wineries south of the Santa Cruz Mountains are just east or west of U.S. 101, which runs north-south through the state. The ones in Santa Barbara County are just off U.S. 101 about 300 miles south of San Francisco and 100 miles north of Los Angeles. The drives to nearly all these wineries are highly scenic, especially in spring, when the hills are green after the winter rains and wildflowers frame the roads and spread beneath the oaks. There are many more wineries than we have space to cover in this chapter, so we have given the highlights of the area, which many believe will come to rival Napa and Sonoma for the quality of its grapes. Unless otherwise stated, the wineries listed here are open daily for tastings.

■ SANTA CRUZ MOUNTAINS

Palo Alto

Santa Cruz Mountains   San Jose

Santa Cruz   Santa Clara Valley

Perhaps the strangest semi-urban grape-growing region in the country, the Santa Cruz Mountains AVA, flanked by the Silicon Valley and the Santa Clara Valley AVA on one side and beach towns on the other, is one of California's oldest and most important wine areas. The rugged Santa Cruz range, 74 miles long and between 6 and 29 miles wide, is cut by steep, redwood-studded canyons amid which lie small vineyards and even smaller wineries. Because the mountains are tall enough (between 2,000 feet and just less than 4,000 feet) to intercept weather systems drifting in from the Pacific Ocean, the region has two distinctive growing climates: vineyards west of the ridge are subject to sea fogs and are thus cooler (and moister) than fields east of the ridge, which often bask in sunshine when the western slopes are chilled by fogs.

Wine grapes were first planted here in the 1800s, but most vineyards and wineries fell victim to Prohibition and competition from more prolific regions. Productivity has always been a problem, because the slopes are steep and rocky and Pacific Ocean fog slows the ripening of grapes. But the wineries hang on, despite periodic rumors of their demise, because they turn out world-class wines.

Even so, there are only about 800 acres of vineyards and 40 wineries in the Santa Cruz Mountains AVA, which stretches from Half Moon Bay almost to the

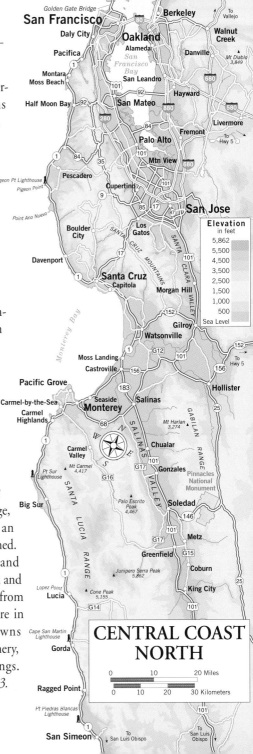

Salinas Valley. Most are tiny family operations, the most notable exceptions being Ridge, Bonny Doon, and David Bruce, all of which make wine from nonlocal as well as local grapes.

Wineries west of the ridge can be reached fairly easily from Highway 1. The ones east of the ridge call for some white-knuckle driving on twisting mountain roads, but the scenery is gorgeous and the views are splendid.

■ **CUPERTINO** *map this page*
To visit Ridge, the northernmost winery in this chapter, take I-280 south from San Francisco and exit south in Cupertino onto the Foothill Expressway. The expressway becomes Foothill Boulevard, which in turn becomes Stevens Canyon Road. Turn right after 3 miles onto Monte Bello Road and follow it 4.4 miles to the winery.

Ridge Vineyards *map page 247, A-1*
At 2,300 feet above sea level, Ridge, founded in 1962 on the site of an older, ramshackle winery, is aptly named. The winery is famed for its sturdy and intense Montebello cabernet sauvignon and vineyard-designated zinfandels made from local grapes and ones grown elsewhere in California. Ridge, which also owns Sonoma County's Lytton Springs Winery, is open only on weekends for tastings. *17100 Monte Bello Road; 408-867-3233.*

635' A VIEW OF FOOT hill ORCHARDS . LOS GATOS

IN DISTANCE. FROM SANTA CRUZ MTS. MRS HARE PHOTO

Alice Iola Hare took this early 1900s photo of Foothills Orchards, with Los Gatos in the distance.

A quiet moment at the often raucous Bonny Doon tasting room.

■ **LOS GATOS** *map page 247, A-1*

Two wineries of note can be found on Bear Creek Road in Los Gatos, about 28 miles south of Cupertino. Head south on Highway 85 and continue south on Highway 17. Take the Bear Creek Road exit and turn right.

David Bruce Winery *map page 247, A-1*

A participant in the 1976 Paris blind tastings of French and California wines that turned out so favorably for the stateside entrants, David Bruce Winery, founded by its namesake in the early 1960s, was well respected long before the current crop of premium wineries came onto the local scene. The winery still produces first-rate chardonnay, zinfandel, and petite sirah, and (most notably) pinot noir. *21439 Bear Creek Road; 408-354-4214.*

Byington Vineyard & Winery *map page 247, A-1*

The view from the manicured grounds of Byington's Italianate stone winery ranges across the slopes of the western Santa Cruz Mountains all the way to the distant Pacific Ocean—if there's no fog. Byington, founded in 1987, specializes in chardonnay and red Bordeaux-style wines. Some of the Bordeaux grapes are derived from local sources, and others come from Sonoma County. Byington's owners recently acquired 234 acres in the Paso Robles AVA to increase production and to experiment with Rhône varieties. *21850 Bear Creek Road; 408-354-1111.*

■ **SANTA CRUZ** *map page 247, A-1*

The iconoclastic Bonny Doon winery lies in northern Santa Cruz. From Byington, take Bear Creek Road to Highway 9, then go west on Western Avenue, west on Alba Road, and southwest on Empire Grade Road, which eventually runs into Pine Flat Road. If you're coming from Highway 1, head east on Bonny Doon Road, which becomes Pine Flat Road.

Bonny Doon Vineyard *map page 247, A-1*

This winery's founder, Randall Grahm, has described his outfit's role as the "court jester of the wine world," and with its fanciful label art and pun-filled

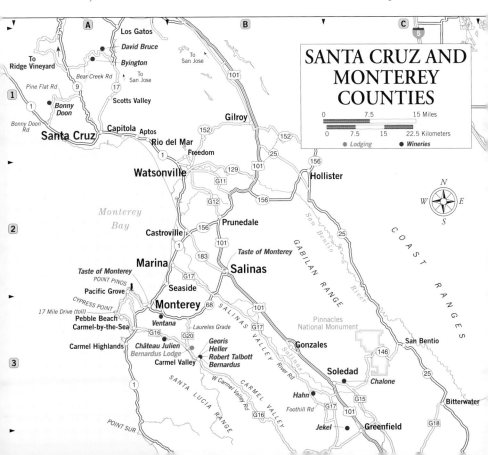

wine names—among them Critique of Pure Riesling, Cardinal Zin, and Le Cigare Volante—Bonny Doon epitomizes Santa Cruz's different-drummer reputation. The tasting room often has a party atmosphere, with one employee playing a tune on his didgeridoo each time a customer signs up for the wine club. Yet for all the frivolity, the appellation's largest winery takes its wines seriously. Founded in the early 1980s—its first vintage was released in 1986—Bonny Doon built its reputation on lesser-known French, German, and Italian varietals but now specializes in wines made from Rhône-Italian grapes and has been instrumental in popularizing them in California. *2 Pine Flat Road; 831-425-3625.*

■ MONTEREY COUNTY

Almost 85 miles long from Monterey Bay south to San Luis Obispo County, the Salinas Valley is, on the average, only 12 miles wide. Cut off from the Pacific Ocean by the Santa Lucia Mountains to the west and from the Central Valley by the Gabilan Mountains to the east, the valley is subject to cooling air and fog from Monterey Bay to the north and through the Templeton Gap to the south. Monterey AVA encompasses the entire valley. The smaller Carmel Valley, Chalone, and Santa Lucia Highlands AVAs touch its borders. Mary L. White, a travel writer passing through here in the early 1890s described the area's "perfect" climate and "soil in places well adapted to fruit and grapes."

But the region's first winery, Chalone, was established in 1962, on the slopes of the Gabilan Mountains, whose climate was far cooler and more changeable than that of the valley it overlooked. Vineyards also came to Salinas Valley itself in 1962, when San Jose's Mirassou winery began to feel the pressure of suburbia and decided to move its vines south, to the slopes of the lower Salinas Valley. Other wineries followed suit, but the plantings met with variable success because the region's soils and microclimates turned out to be more complex than the vintners thought. The rolling terrain, with its pockets of warm or cold air, causes grapes to ripen unevenly, and the variability of sun and fog has an impact.

Even today, after four decades of planting and experimenting, people here are still trying to figure out how best to grow their grapes and make wine from them. In spite of these challenges, plantings in the Salinas Valley increased dramatically

A travel writer touring Monterey County in the 1890s described the area's grape-friendly climate and soil, but wine making here did not take off for many decades.

during the 1990s, especially in southern Monterey County. But most of the area's grapes are bought by wineries from other regions, and there are just a handful of wineries, a few of which are open to the public.

The two **Taste of Monterey** tasting rooms are great starting places for a wine-tasting tour. One is near the coast in the city of Monterey's Cannery Row, and the other is inland, in Salinas, near the National Steinbeck Center, a great source of information about the region. Staff members pour wines from more than 100 wineries, some of which have no tasting rooms of their own. These include Lockwood Vineyard, whose noteworthy offerings include its chardonnay, cabernet sauvignon, and syrah; Morgan, which produces chardonnay and pinot noir from organically farmed Santa Lucia Highlands grapes; and Parsonage, a new winery, opened in 1998, whose wines include a syrah and a Bordeaux-style blend that bears watching. The tasting rooms are open daily from 11 to 6. *700 Cannery Row, Monterey; 831-646-5446. 127 Main Street, Salinas; 888-646-5446.*

This winery tour begins near the coast at Monterey and Carmel, and then moves southeast to Carmel Valley and then into the heart of the Salinas Valley.

Château Julien has the textbook winery look.

■ **MONTEREY** *map page 247, A-2/3*

Monterey lies about 40 miles south of Santa Cruz on Highway 1. From San Francisco, head south on I-280 to Highway 85 to Highway 17 to Highway 1. From Highway 1, head east on the Monterey-Salinas Highway (Highway 68) to reach Ventana Vineyards/Meador Estate.

Ventana Vineyards/Meador Estate *map page 247, A-3*

Doug Meador, who arrived in Monterey County in the early 1970s and planted 2,500 acres of grapevines, set out to master the art of cold-climate viti-culture. He succeeded. A leader in Monterey County's emergence as a wine region, Meador has always been as interested in the growing of grapes as in the vinification of them, and his experimentation has benefited all the Salinas Valley wineries. Ventana's most successful wines, made from locally grown grapes, include sauvignon blanc, pinot blanc, gewürztraminer, chenin blanc, cabernet sauvignon, merlot, cabernet franc, and syrah. The tasting room occupies an old stone house that's an easy five-minute drive from downtown Monterey. *2999 Monterey-Salinas Highway; 831-372-7415.*

■ **CARMEL** *map page 247, A-3*

Almost-too-pretty Carmel lies on the coast southwest of Monterey. To reach its most popular winery, head south on Highway 1, turning left onto Carmel Valley Road. (From Ventana Vineyards, drive east on Highway 68, south on Laureles Grade Road, and west on Carmel Valley Road.)

Château Julien Wine Estate *map page 247, A/B-3*

Built in the style of a small French château, this winery, established in 1982 by Bob and Patty Brower, looks the way many people think a winery should. But the effect is more than just show: the wines made here from Monterey County grapes—sauvignon blanc, pinot grigio, chardonnay, gewürztraminer, merlot, cabernet sauvignon, syrah, sangiovese, and zinfandel—are first-rate. If you have time to visit only a few wineries in the area, this is a fine choice: the wines are good, the views are captivating, and you can sip and snack at a cobblestoned picnic area. *8940 Carmel Valley Road; 831-624-2600.*

(following pages) The hills surrounding Carmel Valley turn a rich green each spring; by summer many are golden.

■ CARMEL VALLEY   *map page 247, B-3*

Though it is in Monterey County, the Carmel Valley AVA is not part of the
Monterey County AVA. The vineyards, flanking the upper Carmel River, are quite
cool and thus produce more intense fruit with higher acid levels than other
Monterey County vineyards. Because the wineries are high up in the rugged northern Santa Lucia Mountains and can be difficult to reach, most of the tasting rooms
are in the lower Carmel Valley, along Carmel Valley Road. To reach them from
Carmel, continue east and then south along West Carmel Valley Road.

Heller Estate Vineyards   *map page 247, B-3*

The original vineyard at the former Durney Vineyards was planted in 1968 by
the late William Durney and his wife, Dorothy. He died in 1989, and the vineyards were sold to a group of European investors in 1994. The winery is now
known as Heller Estate, but it still makes some wine under the Durney label. The
estate-grown wines include chenin blanc, chardonnay, pinot noir, cabernet sauvignon, and merlot. *69 West Carmel Valley Road; 831-659-6220.*

Robert Talbott Vineyards   *map page 247, B-3*

Robb and Cynthia Talbott started their winery in 1982 in the Carmel Valley
and still maintain a tasting room (open from Thursday through Monday)
there, but since 1990 their operations have been centered east of the Tularcitos
Range in the Santa Lucia Highlands, where they own several vineyards. Using old-
style Burgundian growing and producing methods, the Talbotts make only small
lots of chardonnay and pinot noir. The wines, sought after by connoisseurs, are
clean, crisp, and intense. *53 West Carmel Valley Road; 831-659-3500.*

Bernardus Vineyards & Winery   *map page 247, B-3*

Inspired by the vineyards of Bordeaux, Bernardus "Ben" Pon planted his grapes
high amid the rugged hills surrounding Carmel Valley, though his winery's tasting room is on the more accessible valley floor. Opened in the early 1970s,
Bernardus produces chardonnay, sauvignon blanc, merlot, pinot noir, cabernet
sauvignon, and a proprietary blend (mostly cabernet sauvignon and merlot) called
Marinus. The rustic-chic **Bernardus Lodge** (415 Carmel Valley Road; 831-658-
3400), which is associated with the winery, has 57 rooms and the very fine
Marinus restaurant, which serves California-French cuisine. *5 West Carmel Valley
Road; 831-659-1900.*

Georis Winery *map page 247, B-3*

This small winery makes cabernet sauvignon and merlot in small quantities plus a sauvignon blanc and three Bordeaux blends. The tasting room, in an old adobe, is surrounded by a lush garden and has a patio with tables. When the weather's cool, you can stay inside where there are comfortable chairs and a fireplace. The wines can also be tasted at the Georis family's Casanova restaurant, in the seaside town of Carmel, on 5th Street between Mission and San Carlos. *4 Pilot Road, at West Carmel Valley Road; 831-659-1050.*

■ SOLEDAD *map page 247, B/C-3*

In the heart of the Salinas Valley agricultural area, Soledad is more famous for produce and its state prison than for grapes, though two mainstays of the Monterey County wine scene can be found here. Because of the mountains, it is easiest to backtrack north on Carmel Valley Road to Laureles Grade Road and turn right; turn right again onto Highway 68 and right again onto River Road, also signed as County Road G17. Continue south for 24 miles, veering right onto Foothill Road.

Hahn Estates/Smith & Hook Winery *map page 247, B-3*

In 1974, Nicholas "Nicky" Hahn and his wife, Gaby, bought the former Smith & Hook ranches along the western slopes of the Santa Lucias—terrain with a climate they correctly thought perfect for growing cabernet sauvignon. Founded as Smith & Hook Winery, Hahn Estates first released a cabernet in 1979 and has over the years added viognier, chardonnay, cabernet franc, and merlot to its repertoire. *37700 Foothill Road; 831-678-2132.*

Chalone, the sole winery in the Chalone AVA, lies east of U.S. 101 on the road to the Pinnacles National Monument, the dramatic remains of a prehistoric volcano. Exit U.S. 101 east at Highway 146 and continue up into the hills, following the signs to the monument until you see the ones to the winery.

Chalone Vineyard *map page 247, C-3*

A Frenchman planted this vineyard with chenin blanc grapes in 1919—just in time for Prohibition—and other owners added chardonnay, pinot blanc, and pinot noir vines in the 1940s. By the early 1960s, the vines were barely alive, but Dick Graff resurrected them and began making some exceptionally fine wine. A winery was added in 1974, and the rest is history. Today the Chalone Group, now based in Napa and partly owned by the Rothschild wine-making family of France,

Harvesting grapes at Chalone.

controls several first-rate wineries in California and Washington State. In addition to chenin blanc, chardonnay, pinot blanc, and pinot noir, the flagship operation makes estate syrah and viognier. The tasting room is open only on weekend afternoons. *Stonewall Canyon Road off Highway 146; 831-678-1717.*

■ **GREENFIELD** *map page 247, C-3*
From Chalone, return to U.S. 101 and travel south to the Walnut Avenue exit and the town of Greenfield, whose jolly main drag is lined with Mexican grocery stores and other establishments that serve the many agricultural workers that live in this area. Head west on Walnut and follow the signs to Jekel Vineyards.

Jekel Vineyards *map page 247, C-3*
Bill Jekel planted his first vineyard back in 1972 and released his first wine in 1978. After getting the winery off to a strong start, Jekel sold it to a large corporation that still makes excellent wines—chardonnay, cabernet sauvignon, cabernet franc, merlot, petit verdot, malbec, Riesling, pinot noir, and syrah. *40155 Walnut Avenue; 831-674-5522.*

Oak-barrel aging at Chalone.

■ SAN LUIS OBISPO COUNTY

Wine making took hold in San Luis Obispo County soon after California became part of America. The county's oldest surviving winery, York Mountain, was established in 1882. By the end of the 19th century, the wine industry was thriving, but Prohibition ended that, and by the 1960s, when the most recent renaissance began, only three of the early wineries remained.

The adjacent Arroyo Grande Valley and Edna Valley AVAs, south of San Luis Obispo and east of Pismo Beach, have many similarities in their chalky soils and maritime climates. These valleys were first planted with grapevines in the 1880s, though most of the vines were uprooted during Prohibition. The vineyards were replanted in the 1970s, and the region soon gained fame for its excellent chardonnay and sauvignon blanc. Pinot noir grapes grown in the Edna Valley do not produce great wine, but those in the Arroyo Grande Valley do. Zinfandel thrives in the region's hot inland margins.

North of San Luis Obispo, the Paso Robles AVA is the heart of the Central Coast wine region, with the greatest number of vineyards and wineries, most of which are in the Santa Lucia foothills near the small towns of Templeton and Paso Robles. Though it might not seem so on a hot summer afternoon—when the temperature can rise to more than 100 degrees Fahrenheit—the region has two distinct climates: marine air, rushing inland through a cleft in the mountains known locally as the Templeton Gap, spreads out across the eastern slopes of the upper Salinas and Estrella River Valleys, making the vineyards in the gap and on the east side cooler than those tucked into the folds of the Santa Lucia Mountains northwest of Paso Robles. For this reason, zinfandel and Rhône varieties do better to the west, and chardonnay and pinot noir do better to the east.

■ SAN LUIS OBISPO   *map page 260, B-3*

Not all the wineries in San Luis Obispo County are open to the public, but it's worth stopping by the ones that are. Most are just a few miles east of U.S. 101 and south of San Luis Obispo. From U.S. 101, take Highway 227 (signed first as Broad Street and then as Edna Road) south to Biddle Ranch Road and turn left.

Edna Valley Vineyard has had success with its chardonnay.

Edna Valley Vineyard *map page 260, B-3*
This vineyard evolved out of the desire of Dick Graff, the highly respected winemaker of Monterey County's Chalone Vineyard, to diversify into other growing regions. Persuaded that the Edna Valley's singular soil—a haphazard mixture of gravels and alluvial sands and loams, with an admixture of limestone—was well suited for producing chardonnay and perhaps pinot noir, he experimented with both here. The vineyards produce fine chardonnay, but success has been less easily achieved with the pinot noir, though the winery has made a few nice wines from this difficult variety. *2585 Biddle Ranch Road; 805-544-5855.*

Continue east on Biddle Ranch Road and turn right (south) on Orcutt Road. Two miles after your turn you'll come to Domaine Alfred.

Domaine Alfred Winery
map page 260, B-3
This young Edna Valley winery established in the mid-1990s produces estate-bottled wines from its Chamisal Vineyard, which was the first vineyard in the Edna Valley. Originally planted in 1972, Chamisal was replanted by new owner Terry Speizer in 1996 with pinot noir, syrah, and chardonnay (some of which was grafted over to grenache and pinot gris). The pinot noir, first released in 1998, is the winery's strong suit. Domaine Alfred is open for tastings on Friday and weekends. *7525 Orcutt Road; 805-541-9463.*

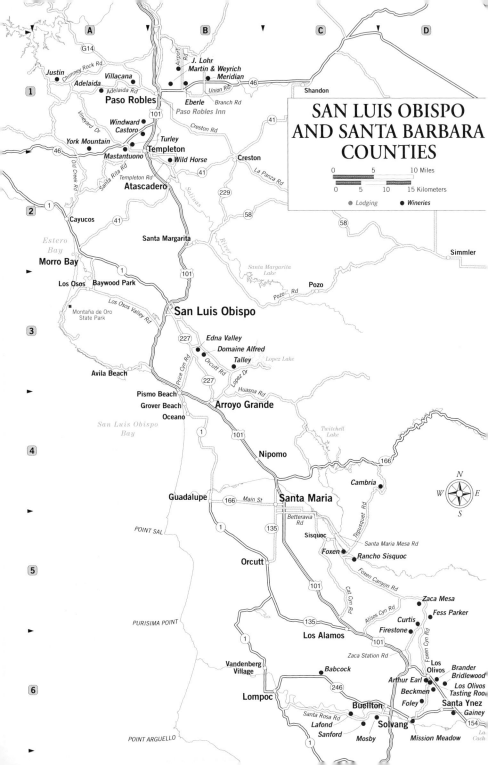

SAN LUIS OBISPO AND SANTA BARBARA COUNTIES

0   5   10 Miles

0   5   10   15 Kilometers

● Lodging   ● Wineries

A **B** **C** **D**

1

G14

Justin

Chimney Rock Rd

Adelaida

Villacana

Adelaida Rd

Paso Robles

Airport Rd

J. Lohr

Martin & Weyrich

Meridian

46

Union Rd

Eberle

Branch Rd

Paso Robles Inn

Shandon

Vineyard Dr

Windward

Castoro

101

Creston Rd

41

York Mountain

Turley

Templeton

Mastantuono

Wild Horse

46

Old Creek Rd

Santa Rita Rd

Templeton Rd

Creston

41

La Panza Rd

Atascadero

Salinas

229

2

1

Cayucos

41

Santa Margarita

58

River

58

Estero Bay

Santa Margarita Lake

Simmler

Morro Bay

1

Los Osos

Baywood Park

Pozo Rd

Pozo

Los Osos Valley Rd

Montaña de Oro State Park

San Luis Obispo

3

227

Edna Valley

Domaine Alfred

Talley

Lopez Lake

Avila Beach

Price Cyn Rd

Orcutt Rd

227

Lopez Dr

Huasna Rd

Pismo Beach

Grover Beach

Arroyo Grande

Oceano

San Luis Obispo Bay

1

101

Twitchell Lake

4

Nipomo

166

Guadalupe

166

Main St

Santa Maria

Cambria

POINT SAL

1

Betteravia Rd

135

Sisquoc

Santa Maria Mesa Rd

Tepusquet Rd

Foxen

Rancho Sisquoc

Orcutt

Foxen Canyon Rd

5

PURISIMA POINT

101

Cat Cyn Rd

Zaca Mesa

Fess Parker

135

Alisos Cyn Rd

Curtis

Firestone

Vandenberg Village

1

Los Alamos

101

Zaca Station Rd

Foxen Cyn Rd

Los Olivos

Brander

Bridlewood

6

Babcock

Arthur Earl

Beckmen

Los Olivos Tasting Room

Lompoc

246

Foley

Santa Ynez

154

Santa Rosa Rd

Buellton

Gainey

Lafond

Solvang

La Cach

Sanford

Mosby

Mission Meadow

POINT ARGUELLO

■ **ARROYO GRANDE** *map page 260, B-4*
From Domaine Alfred, continue south on Orcutt Road and head east (left) on Lopez Drive. Look for Talley Vineyards on the left after about a half mile.

Talley Vineyards *map page 260, C-3*
Talley Vineyards makes estate-bottled chardonnay and pinot noir from three vineyards in the Arroyo Grande Valley and has a second label, Bishop's Peak Wine. El Rincón Adobe, built in the early 1860s by Ramon Branch, son of Francisco Ziba Branch, the holder of the 16,955-acre Rancho Santa Manuela land grant and one of the valley's original settlers, has been pictured on the winery's labels since its first vintage, in 1986. The adobe was restored in 1988 to serve as the winery's first tasting room, though it no longer does so. A bonus of a visit to Talley is that you can taste the wines of the small, nearby Saucelito Canyon Winery, renowned for its powerful zinfandels, some of which come from 3 acres of vines planted in the early 1880s. *3031 Lopez Drive; 805-489-0446.*

■ **PASO ROBLES** *map page 260, A/B-1*
Paso Robles was once known as the Almond City because the surrounding region contained the largest number of almond orchards in the world. But grapes were grown here in the late 1800s, and the area became famous after the concert pianist Ignace Paderewski bought a ranch in the early 20th century and planted first almonds and then grapes. Paderewski first came here for a spa experience to cure an arthritic hand, at the Paso Robles Hot Springs, still in the center of town. The springs, whose waters pour from the earth at a temperature of 106 degrees Fahrenheit, precede the town, which got its start when the Paso Robles Hot Springs Hotel was built in 1864. (The hot springs had been popular with local Indians and grizzly bears long before that.) The hotel was replaced in 1906 by the **Paso Robles Inn** (11th and Spring Streets; 805-238-2660). Designed by W. H. Weeks, the inn became a world-class resort.

Paderewski acquired grapevines for his Rancho San Ygnacio, in the foothills of the Santa Lucia Mountains, from Frederick Bioletti, at the time the foremost authority on California wine. Bioletti recommended mainly petite sirah and zin-fandel—the latter with reservations, because the ranch was just below what was then considered to be the "quality line" for zinfandel. But, according to Idwal Jones in the 1949 book *Vines in the Sun,* zinfandel produced better wine than any of the other varieties and even won a prize at the California State Fair.

Dining al fresco at the popular Bistro Laurent in Paso Robles.

Paso Robles made headlines in late 2003 when an earthquake measuring 6.5 on the Richter scale struck the area. Many historic buildings along the main square were ravaged, though few of the wineries suffered major damage.

Most Paso Robles AVA wineries are close to U.S. 101, on or just off Highway 46. We'll start our tour east of town, swing back west of town, and then head south into Templeton. To reach our first stop, the birthplace of "Super Tuscan" wines, head east from Spring Street on 24th Street, which becomes Highway 46 East.

Martin & Weyrich   *map page 260, B-1*
It's hard to miss the elaborate, very Tuscan Martin & Weyrich tasting room. This winery, established in 1981, specializes in classic Italian grape varieties, though it also produces an Edna Valley chardonnay and zinfandel. Namesake owners David Martin and Mary Weyrich, who helped introduce California to nebbiolo, the noble and spicy red grape of the Piedmont region of Italy, also grow sangiovese, muscat canelli, pinot grigio, and malvasia bianca. But their winery's claim to fame is its "Super Tuscan" Cabernet Etrusco, a blend of 85 percent cabernet sauvignon and

The elegant courtyard of Martin & Weyrich.

15 percent sangiovese. (Villa Toscana, a winery-associated B&B northeast of Paso Robles, opened in early 2003.) *2610 Buena Vista Drive; 805-238-2520.*

Continue north and then east on Buena Vista Drive to Airport Road and turn left to reach the J. Lohr complex, then head back south on Airport Road to Highway 46, where a detailed bronze sculpture of a boar guards the entrance to Eberle Winery.

J. Lohr Paso Robles Wine Center   *map page 260, B-1*

In 1988, Jerry Lohr moved a portion of his winery operations from San Jose to Paso Robles to grow grapes for his reds, especially the deservedly acclaimed J. Lohr Estates Seven Oaks Cabernet, Los Osos Merlot, South Ridge Syrah, and Hilltop Cabernet. The grapes for the cabernet are grown across the street from the tasting room. *6169 Airport Road; 805-239-8900.*

Eberle Winery   *map page 260, B-1*

Gary Eberle, the owner of Eberle Winery and a founding father of the Paso Robles wine renaissance, knows his stuff, having grown grapes and made wines for the nearby Estrella River Winery in the 1970s before establishing his own operation in 1983. His barbera, cabernet sauvignon, chardonnay, viognier, zinfandel, sangiovese, syrah, and a "Côtes-du-Rôbles" blend are among the best the region has to offer, and his late-harvest muscat canelli is exquisite. You can bring your own food and picnic on a deck that has panoramic views of estate vineyards, or attend guest-chef dinners and private events held regularly in the cave dining room. *Highway 46 East and Airport Road; 805-238-9607.*

To reach the next stop, the formidable Meridian Vineyards, part of the Beringer Blass Wine Estates empire, head back east (left) on Highway 46 East.

Meridian Vineyards   *map page 260, B-1*

This local heavyweight, established in 1988 by winemaker Chuck Ortman and what is now Beringer Blass Wine Estates, has extensive vineyard holdings on the Central Coast. Grapes for chardonnay come from Santa Barbara County and the Edna Valley. The home vineyards, east of Paso Robles in a warm pocket of land surrounding Meridian's hilltop winery, provide cabernet sauvignon, syrah, and zinfandel. Limited release and reserve wines, sold only from the winery, can be sampled here. The picnic area, shaded by giant oaks, has sweeping vineyard views. *7000 Highway 46 East; 805-237-6000.*

From Meridian, loop back toward downtown Paso Robles by heading south on

Branch Road and west on Union Road, continuing west on Highway 46. In Paso Robles, the road's name changes to 24th Street, which shortly thereafter becomes Nacimiento Lake Drive. When the road forks, bear left on Adelaida Road and follow it to Villacana Winery.

Villacana Winery   *map page 260, A-1*

Drop by Villacana (open on weekends only), established in the mid-1990s, and you're likely to have your wine poured by Alex or Monica Villacana, the namesake owners of this small operation. The couple, who grow grapes on a 10-acre vineyard, produce about 1,000 cases per year of estate chardonnay, cabernet sauvignon, merlot, and zinfandel. The cabernet and zinfandel, both of them rich wines with a heavy berry flavor, are particularly successful. *2725 Adelaida Road; 805-239-9456.*

Adelaida Cellars   *map page 260, A-1*

Adelaida Cellars occupies a hilltop ranch with elevations of up to 2,300 feet. Founded in 1981 by John Munch and now owned by the Van Steenwyk family—though Munch remains a consultant—Adelaida produces estate-grown pinot noir (from the HMR Vineyard, planted in 1967); old-vine zinfandel, cabernet sauvignon, barbera, chardonnay, chenin blanc, sangiovese, syrah, and viognier. *5805 Adelaida Road; 805-239-8980.*

Continue west 4.5 miles on Adelaida Road, turning right on Klau Mine Road and left onto Chimney Rock Road to reach Justin, this area's (for now) westernmost winery.

Justin Vineyards & Winery   *map page 260, A-1*

Justin and Deborah Baldwin started their winery in 1981 on pastureland that had been homesteaded by Mennonites in the 19th century. The winery is best known for two Bordeaux blends, Isoceles (cabernet sauvignon, cabernet franc, merlot) and Justification (cabernet franc, merlot), but it also produces cabernet sauvignon and chardonnay, as well as wines from several Rhône varieties. You can sample the wines at the tasting room and also at the Deborah's Room restaurant. Lunch, served only on weekends (prix-fixe dinners are served during the week), is a delight—for the food and the vineyard views. The winery also operates an on-site B&B. *11680 Chimney Rock Road; 805-238-6932.*

■ **TEMPLETON** *map page 260, A/B-1/2*

You can reach Templeton and its many wineries from Justin by backtracking east on Adelaida Road to Vineyard Drive, which heads south into Templeton. When you arrive at Highway 46, you'll see the distinctive white château of Mastantuono Winery, but before stopping here swing west about 4 miles to York Mountain Road to reach the region's oldest winery. Turn right, following the road to York Mountain Winery through woods of gnarled madrone and ancient oaks draped with Spanish moss.

York Mountain Winery *map page 260, A-1/2*

San Luis Obispo County's most historic winery, whose vineyards are part of the exclusive York Mountain AVA, was founded in 1882 by Martin York as Ascension Winery. Pianist Ignace Paderewski brought zinfandel here to be made into wine, and plantings were expanded after Prohibition, but not much changed until the late 20th century, which saw a succession of owners. The current ones, David Martin and Mary Weyrich, make chardonnay, cabernet sauvignon, sauvignon blanc, pinot noir, and zinfandel. The winery's signature wine in years past was a delectable port-style black muscat that Martin and Weyrich still produce, but York Mountain has been gaining acclaim more recently for its zesty viognier. *7505 York Mountain Road; 805-238-3925.*

From York Mountain Road, head back east on Highway 46 to its intersection with Vineyard Drive, at which you'll see the Oak View Road entrance to Mastantuono Winery.

Mastantuono Winery *map page 260, A-1/2*

Pasquale Mastantuono, who started the winery that bears his name in 1976, makes a very complex barbera and sells cabernet sauvignon, chardonnay, chenin blanc, muscat canelli, nebbiolo, and pinot grigio. But the emphasis here is on the gutsy zinfandel, which he declares "the best wine in the world." Mastantuono designed the handsome château that serves as winery, tasting room, and family home. *2720 Oak View Road; 805-238-0676.*

Turley Wine Cellars *map page 260, A-1*

Farther south and east on Vineyard Drive lies an old-vine zinfandel vineyard that was planted in the 1920s on limestone soils with good drainage. From 1933 until 2000, when the Napa Valley's Larry Turley bought the property, this was the Pesenti Winery, known for decent if not spectacular table wines. Turley

Wild Horse is off the beaten path but worth a visit.

refurbished the winery and brought in his wine-making crew, who have already scored success with zinfandels (the ones not from the old vines are labeled as Juvenile) that are deep in color, intense in flavor, and full-bodied. Turley also makes a roussanne-viognier blend. *2900 Vineyard Drive; 805-434-1030.*

Continue east on Vineyard Drive until you get to Templeton Road and then head south, turning left at the sign for Wild Horse Winery. The last part of the road is unpaved gravel.

Wild Horse Winery & Vineyards   *map page 260, B-2*

Wild Horse, founded in 1983 by Ken Volk, is off the beaten path but well worth searching out for the extraordinary quality of its wines, which include cabernet sauvignon, chardonnay, merlot, mourvèdre, pinot blanc, viognier, zinfandel, pinot grigio, pinot noir, and syrah, as well as several lesser-known varieties (dolcetto, malvasia bianca, negrette). The winery's estate vineyard in Templeton is on the east bank of the Salinas River bordering the Carissa Plains. Its name was inspired by the wild mustangs, descendants of the original horses brought to California, that roam the plains to this day. The tasting room overlooks vineyards planted on gently rolling hills. *1437 Wild Horse Winery Court; 805-434-2541.*

Backtrack north on Templeton Road and then west on Vineyard Drive to Bethel Road and head north to Castoro Cellars.

Castoro Cellars   *map page 260, A/B-1*

Niels and Bimmer Udsen founded Castoro in 1983 while Niels—a.k.a. "Beaver" (*il castoro* is Italian for beaver)—was still learning about wine making at Estrella River Winery. Castoro makes heady zinfandel, cabernet sauvignon, chardonnay, merlot, pinot noir, fumé blanc, valdiguié, late-harvest zinfandel port, and muscat canelli from estate vineyards and locally bought grapes. The tasting room, just off Highway 46 West, is surrounded by a grape arbor, a zinfandel vineyard, and young cork trees. *1315 North Bethel Road; 805-238-0725.*

Continue north from Castoro on Bethel Road, turning right on Highway 46 and left (north) shortly thereafter on Arrow Road. Take another left at Live Oak Road to reach Windward Winery.

Windward Winery   *map page 260, A/B-1*

The Paso Robles AVA gained a reputation for superlative pinot noir starting in the early 1970s, after the Napa Valley wine master Andre Tchelistcheff advised a local grower. Continuing that tradition of complex, Burgundian-style pinot noir wines are Marc Goldberg and Maggie D'Ambrosia, who in 1989 purchased 15 acres just north of Templeton in Paso Robles. These pinot devotees—pinot noir is the only wine they make—introduced their first vintage in 1993 and have had great success in recent years, fine-tuning their process to produce increasingly sophisticated wines. *1380 Live Oak Road; 805-239-2565.*

Paso Robles

San Luis Obispo

Edna Valley

Arroyo Grande Valley

Santa Maria Valley

Lompoc

Santa Rita Hills   Santa Ynez Valley

Santa Barbara

■ SANTA BARBARA COUNTY

Of all of California's major grape-growing regions, only Santa Barbara County had no major vineyards until the 1960s. The Franciscan padres who colonized the region in the late 1700s had planted grapes, for sacramental wine, at their missions of Santa Barbara, Santa Inez, and La Purisima, but none of those vineyards survived. In 1964, a local farmer, Uriel Nielson, planted vines in the Santa Maria Valley. Santa Barbara County's first winery had arrived a little earlier, in 1962, when Pierre Lafond, a Quebecois architect and deli owner, opened the Santa Barbara Winery downtown, a few blocks from the beach. It was an unpretentious place, making fruit wines as well as grape wines in its first years—the sort you'd take to the beach to enjoy with a picnic of spiny lobster, rock crab, or seafood salad.

By the late 1970s, Santa Barbara County had joined the California wine boom. Vineyards were planted throughout the Santa Maria and Santa Ynez Valleys and in the Los Alamos region. Most grapes from these vineyards were (and still are) turned into wine elsewhere in California, though wineries sprouted up here as well. In the 1980s and 1990s, so many were established near the Danish-style town of Solvang that some locals feared the region might turn into another Napa Valley.

This winery tour begins in northern Santa Barbara County in the **Santa Maria Valley AVA,** which has a diverse climate. Fogs frequently drift in from the ocean, making the western portion too cool to grow grapes—though this area produces many winter vegetables as well as early-season strawberries. Cool-climate grapes like chardonnay and pinot noir thrive on the warmer slopes east of U.S. 101 and north of the Santa Maria River; grapes needing heat to ripen do better in the eastern valley and in Foxen Canyon. This growing region has more vineyards than wineries, and most of its grapes are shipped to wineries throughout the state.

■ SANTA MARIA *map page 260, C-4/5*

Two noteworthy operations, Cambria Winery and Byron Vineyard, occupy a benchland at the northern edge of the Santa Maria Valley. Their vineyards lie only about 15 miles from the Pacific Ocean but are high enough above the Santa Maria Valley floor to avoid its fogs. Byron, owned by Mondavi, recently closed its tasting room, but you can visit Cambria. On the city of Santa Maria's south side, follow Betteravia Road east from U.S. 101, continuing east after the name changes to Santa Maria Mesa Road. After 5 miles, the road forks left, at which point you'll see a sign pointing to the winery, which is 7 miles from here.

Cambria Winery & Vineyard *map page 260, C/D-4*

Some of the vines at Cambria are part of the original Tepusquet Vineyard, planted between 1970 and 1971 by Uriel Nielson. Barbara Banke and her husband, Jess Jackson, of Kendall-Jackson fame, bought Tepusquet's premium acres in 1987, renamed the winery Cambria, and over the years purchased more acreage. Tepusquet had earned a reputation for character-laden chardonnay and velvety-textured pinot noir, in addition to those wines, a viognier and a rich, spicy syrah, both from the Tepusquet vines, are produced here. The tasting room is open only on weekends. *5475 Chardonnay Lane; 805-937-8091.*

Cambria Winery has built its reputation on chardonnay and pinot noir.

The long **Foxen Canyon,** north of Los Olivos and east of Los Alamos, gets quite warm in summer, a boon to Bordeaux grapes. The canyon is split between two appellations. The Rancho Sisquoc and Foxen wineries are in the Santa Maria AVA; the ones farther south—including Zaca Mesa, Fess Parker, Curtis, and Firestone—are in the Santa Ynez Valley AVA.

From Cambria Winery, backtrack to Foxen Canyon Road and turn left (south). The white San Ramon Chapel, built in 1875 by a local landowner for his wife, marks the turnoff to Rancho Sisquoc Winery, the first of several wineries on or just off this road, The tasting room is at the end of a 2.5-mile-long driveway off Foxen Canyon Road.

Rancho Sisquoc Winery   *map page 260, C-5*

With its old ranch house and barn shaded by ancient trees, this is the region's most romantic winery. The vineyards here are warmer than those of the western Santa Maria Valley but cooler than those of the Santa Ynez Valley to the south. Grapes were first planted on this land in 1968, but it wasn't until 1977 that Rancho Sisquoc became a bonded winery and the rustic tasting room was built.

Foxen Canyon, ranchland for many years, is increasingly being planted to grapes.

The excellent, reasonably priced wines include cabernet sauvignon, merlot, malbec, sauvignon blanc, chardonnay, pinot noir, and Riesling. Rancho Sisquoc is the last winery in California to still make sylvaner each vintage. *6600 Foxen Canyon Road; 805-934-4332.*

Foxen Vineyard   *map page 260, C-5*

This small winery, established in the mid-1980s, produces big wines from grapes grown on the Tinaquaic Estate Vineyard and from several other Santa Barbara County vineyards. Be sure to taste the pinot noir, chardonnay, syrah, and cabernet franc. A house on this property was built by Benjamin Foxen, who settled in this area in the 1830s; Richard Dore, the winery's co-owner (with Bill Wathen), is a descendant. Foxen is open in the afternoon from Thursday to Monday. *7200 Foxen Canyon Road; 805-937-4251.*

Continue down Foxen Canyon Road to enter the **Santa Ynez Valley.** As small as it is, the Santa Ynez Valley AVA has several distinct climates. West of U.S. 101 in Buellton and east of Lompoc, the cool vineyards of the Santa Rita Hills AVA (an appellation within the Santa Ynez Valley AVA) are influenced by marine air from the nearby Pacific Ocean. Pinot noir thrives here. In the warmer vineyards east of U.S. 101, cabernet sauvignon, merlot, sauvignon blanc, and Rhône and Italian varietals do well. But there is no fixed rule to this. Grapes of the cabernet group ripen in warm pockets of the western hills, and Riesling and other cool-climate grapes do surprisingly well in cool niches east of this dividing line, which is somewhat arbitrary

Zaca Mesa Winery   *map page 260, D-5*

With its tall working metal windmill out front and its barnlike buildings tucked into a small side canyon, Zaca Mesa might be mistaken for a cattle ranch. Chances are you won't even see the vineyards here, which rest high above the winery on a 1,500-foot-high mesa, where warm sunny days and cool, breezy afternoons create ideal conditions for Rhône varietals. Among Zaca Mesa's signature wines are its syrah, viognier, and the much-lauded Z Gris, traditional rosé made from grenache, mourvèdre, cinsaut, and viognier. The winery, established in 1978, is a quiet place, where you can picnic under the oaks or play a game of lawn chess. The word *zaca* comes from the local Chumash language and means "peaceful"—an appropriate name. *6905 Foxen Canyon Road; 805-688-9339.*

Fess Parker Winery & Vineyard   *map page 260, D-5*

Wine Country meets the Alamo at Fess Parker Winery & Vineyard, whose namesake owner starred as Davy Crockett in three 1950s movies and as Daniel Boone on a 1960s TV series before establishing his winery in 1987. The wines poured at the region's hokiest tasting room—no one else sells coonskin caps and other mountain-man paraphernalia—include syrah, viognier, pinot noir, chardonnay, and white Riesling. *6200 Foxen Canyon Road; 805-688-1545.*

Curtis Winery   *map page 260, D-5*

Rhône-style wines— most notably syrah, viognier, roussanne, mourvèdre, and grenache—are the specialty at Curtis, founded in 1995. The lavender plantings on the grounds are part of the Santa Ynez Valley Lavender Company. Curtis is owned by Firestone, about a mile south, and a hiking trail connects the winery to the Firestone Vineyard. *5249 Foxen Canyon Road; 805-686-8999.*

Curtis is at the junction of Foxen Canyon and Zaca Station Road. To reach Firestone, continue south until just after Foxen Canyon Road turns into Zaca Station Road.

Syrah, viognier, and the Z Gris blend are the specialties of ranchlike Zaca Mesa.

Firestone Vineyard   *map page 260, D-5/6*

Firestone, Santa Barbara County's first estate winery (founded in 1975), is big and proud of it, spreading across a hilltop like an enological fortress. Firestone produces a wide variety of wines from its Santa Ynez Valley estate vineyards, most notably chardonnay, merlot, syrah, and late-harvest Riesling. The picnic area here has spectacular vineyard views. *5000 Zaca Station Road; 805-688-3940.*

■ Los Olivos

Continue south on Zaca Station Road to Highway 154 and head east (left). A right on Grand Avenue brings you into downtown Los Olivos, which in its several blocks has a few good restaurants and cafés.

One very good reason to stop here is the **Los Olivos Tasting Room and Wineshop,** whose knowledgeable staff members pour the wines of many local wineries, including some—Au Bon Climat, Hitching Post, Qupé among them— that aren't open to the public. *2905 Grand Avenue; 805-688-7406.*

Arthur Earl Winery *map page 260, D-6*

This small winery based in Buellton operates a tasting room in Los Olivos. Founded in 1993, it specializes in varieties traditional to France's Rhône region and Italy's Piemonte. Known for its nebbiolo and viognier, it also produces grenache, roussanne, syrah, mourvèdre, zinfandel, and pinot grigio. *2921 Grand Avenue; 805-693-1771.*

Head east from Grand Avenue on Alamo Pintado Road in the center of town, and turn south on Highway 154. When you get to Refugio Road, make a right, and when the road takes a sharp turn south, go straight instead onto Ontiveros Road to Beckmen Vineyards.

Beckmen Vineyards *map page 260, D-6*

Family-owned Beckmen makes Rhône-style wines from grapes grown on its 365-acre Purisima Mountain Vineyard, above Ballard Canyon. The neighboring Stolpman Vineyards were planted in 1992 to various grape varieties, including syrah. The winery currently makes marsanne, sauvignon blanc, cabernet sauvignon, grenache rosé, a southern Rhône blend called Cuvée Le Bec, and a proprietary wine called Atelier. Backtrack to Refugio Road, crossing Highway 154 and heading north briefly to reach Brander Vineyard. *2670 Ontiveros Road; 805-688-8664.*

Brander Vineyard *map page 260, D-6*

One of the Santa Ynez Valley's oldest wineries—it opened in 1981—Brander makes excellent sauvignon blanc, merlot, cabernet sauvignon, and a proprietary blend (cabernet sauvignon, cabernet franc, and merlot) called Bouchet. *2401 Refugio Road; 805-688-2455.*

■ **SANTA YNEZ** *map page 260, D-6*

Before going south to the town of Santa Ynez, backtrack on Refugio Road to Roblar Avenue and head east a little more than a mile to Bridlewood Winery.

Bridlewood Winery *map page 260, D-6*

This lushly landscaped mission-style winery began life as one of Santa Barbara County's premier facilities for equestrian rehabilitation. It was transformed into a premium winery in 1998. Bridlewood makes syrah, pinot noir, chardonnay,

(bottom) The mood is laid-back at the Los Olivos Tasting Room. (top and following pages) Fields of lavender amid oaks at Beckmen.

cabernet sauvignon, zinfandel, merlot, sauvignon blanc, and Arabesque, a proprietary Rhône-style blend. *3555 Roblar Avenue; 805-688-9000.*

From Bridlewood, head west on Roblar, turning south (left) on Edison Street. At Highway 154 make a left and continue south to Highway 246, where you'll make a right turn to reach Gainey Vineyard.

Gainey Vineyard   *map page 260, D-6*

The 1984 Spanish mission–style winery building here stands out among the more mundane ones in the town of Santa Ynez. Gainey's chardonnay, pinot noir, merlot, cabernet sauvignon, cabernet franc, and sauvignon blanc are consistently excellent, and in some years, there's also an exquisite late-harvest Riesling. People come to the winery in summer to enjoy concerts under the stars. At nearly any time of year, the well-groomed picnic area provides the perfect setting to have lunch or a snack and sip fine wine. *3950 East Highway 246; 805-688-0558.*

■ SOLVANG   *map page 260, D-6*

Visitors have flocked to the eastern Santa Ynez Valley ever since a local community of immigrant Danish farmers decided in the 1940s to turn their small town of Solvang, west of Santa Ynez on Highway 246, into a half-timbered, thatch-roofed tourist attraction. The overall effect is a bit much, but the town is worth a peek for its kitsch value and the chance to dine on authentic Danish dishes. Mission Meadow Winery/Plam Vineyards is right downtown. Heading west into town on Highway 246, make a left on First Street and a right onto Copenhagen Drive.

Mission Meadow Winery/Plam Vineyards   *map page 260, D-6*

Ken Plam started out with the Napa Valley's Plam Vineyards back in 1984, but later sold that winery, preferring to make limited-production wines at various facilities in the Napa Valley. Now he has relocated to Santa Barbara County, where he produces superb merlot, as well as chardonnay and viognier. While a new winery is being built on 93-acres of former pastureland, the Plam tasting room is in downtown Solvang. *1659 Copenhagen Drive; 805-693-1344.*

Backtrack east on Highway 246 and head north on Alamo Pintado Road to get to another Solvang winery of note, Foley Estates.

Foley Estates Vineyard & Winery   *map page 260, D-6*

You don't see any traces of the former dairy farm where Foley Estates Winery was established in 1997. Estate wines as well as wines from Santa Maria Valley vineyards include pinot noir, chardonnay, cabernet sauvignon, merlot, and sauvignon blanc. *1711 Alamo Pintado Road; 805-688-8554.*

■ **BUELLTON** *map page 260, C/D-6*
Buellton lies west of Solvang at Highway 246 and U.S. 101. Three wineries of note can be found just south of Buellton, west off U.S. 101 on Santa Rosa Road, which snakes parallel to the Santa Ynez River. The wineries are all just south of the river.

Mosby Winery *map page 260, C-6*
Locally famous for its twice-a-year wine dinners, Mosby makes sangiovese, pinot grigio, nebbiolo, dolcetto, cortese, teroldego, and an excellent Italian-style traminer. This winery, founded in the mid-1970s, is just west of U.S. 101; look for the driveway in the sharp bend Santa Rosa Road takes west from the freeway. *9496 Santa Rosa Road; 805-688-2415.*

Sanford Winery *map page 260, C-6*
The long driveway to Sanford Winery, founded in 1981, winds along a creek lined with ancient sycamores to the rustic tasting room. Sanford wines are very

The ambience of Sanford is decidedly rustic.

distinctive, with big flavors. Besides the trademark chardonnays and pinot noirs, Sanford makes an excellent pinot noir vin gris from Santa Rita Hills grapes. Picnic tables under sycamores overlook the creek. *7250 Santa Rosa Road; 805-688 3300.*

Lafond Winery and Vineyards *map page 260, C-6*
Pierre Lafond opened his new winery in early 2001, just before the establishment of the Santa Rita Hills AVA in the western Santa Ynez Valley. Lafond Winery makes its SRH wines—chardonnay, pinot noir, and syrah—exclusively from grapes grown in that appellation. Lafond also makes an excellent Northside Santa Ynez Valley red wine blend. *6855 Santa Rosa Road; 805-688-7921.*

■ LOMPOC *map page 260, B/C-6*
Continue west on Santa Rosa Road to Highway 1, where you'll head north (right). Turn right (east) in Lompoc at Highway 246 to reach our last winery, Babcock.

If you have the time, stop along the way to Babcock at **La Purisima Mission State Historic Park,** one of the 21 missions established by the Franciscans. Unlike the mission in bustling Sonoma, this one remains isolated to this day. A visit here provides a glimpse into just how lonely life could be in this region two-plus centuries ago. *2295 Purisima Road; 805-733-3713.*

Babcock Winery & Vineyards *map page 260, C-6*
A family-owned winery in the northern Santa Rita Hills about 9 miles west of U.S. 101, Babcock is known for chardonnay but also makes first-rate pinot noir, estate-grown pinot grigio, gewürztraminer, syrah, and a red Bordeaux blend called Fathom. The first vineyards here were planted in the early 1980s, and after a few years of selling to other winemakers, the first Babcock wine, an estate-grown sauvignon blanc, was released to acclaim that has continued throughout the years. The winery is open on Fridays and weekends. *5175 Highway 246; 805-736-1455.*

The chef at work at Yountville's French Laundry.
Reserve your table far in advance.

NAPA AND SONOMA
RESTAURANTS

Wine Country cuisine was influenced over the years by Spanish colonialists, Russian fur traders, and northern Italian immigrants, but it remained relatively staid until the 1960s, when the back-to-the-land movement permanently changed the way Californians looked at food. People who had been perfectly happy subsisting on hamburgers and fried chicken rediscovered local produce, which, because of California's unique climate, proved to be Mediterranean—and was often organic.

The movement found its high priestess in Alice Waters, who read the *Larousse Gastronomique* and decided that California food was Provençal by nature, if not outright Mediterranean. The cooking styles pioneered in Waters's Berkeley restaurant, Chez Panisse, were admired and replicated throughout the Wine Country, in part because so many chefs who had trained in her kitchens later opened restaurants of their own.

This new Wine Country cookery is more down to earth than the style the French call haute cuisine, yet it has too many fancy touches and complex flavors to be classified as bourgeois. Some consider the food Tuscan, since Tuscan cookery is based on simplicity as well as on fresh ingredients used at their peak of flavor.

At the same time that Wine Country food changed, so did the wines. They went from predominantly sweet styles that were hard to match to any food to the familiar dry wines of today. As Wine Country food became more hearty, in a Mediterranean fashion, so did the wines. Wineries increasingly produced Rhône blends instead of cabernet; marsanne and viognier instead of Riesling or chenin blanc; sangiovese instead of gamay.

Wine Country dining became a world-class experience in 1977, when Domaine Chandon opened a restaurant in its new sparkling-wine facility in Yountville. Auberge du Soleil followed, with the inspired cooking of the late Masa Kobayashi. In the wake of these came other restaurants, most notably Mustard's Grill, Trilogy, and the French Laundry. Sonoma County also participated in the culinary revolution, with early stalwarts John Ash & Co. and the restaurant at Chateau Souverain leading the way. Today, Wine Country cuisine is more exciting than ever, from the exquisite fare at the high-profile Tra Vigne and Dry Creek Kitchen to the subtly stunning offerings at the Applewood Inn and Taverna Santi.

Prices per person, without wine or tip

$ = less than $10 **$$** = $10–$20 **$$$** = $20–$30 **$$$$** = over $30

★ = Top Pick

Rustic French classics are served in a former boathouse at Angèle.

■ SOUTHERN NAPA VALLEY

■ **NAPA**   *map page 96*

★ **Alexis Baking Company.** You don't go to this downtown neighborhood café for the atmosphere, but for great hamburgers, sandwiches, tacos, and pasta salads. The "ABC" is popular with locals; one patron complains that she can never come here for lunch because she runs into so many friends she ends up talking instead of eating. *1517 Third Street; 707-258-1827.* **$**

★ **Angèle.** The Napa Valley's Rouas family (of Auberge du Soleil and Piatti fame) created this French restaurant in a former Napa River boathouse that dates back to the 1890s. In good weather, you can dine outside. The kitchen dishes up refined versions of rustic French classics such as steamed mussels with braised fennel; an onion and goat cheese tart with a frisée salad; shepherd's pie; striped bass with flageolet beans; veal stew with onions and mushrooms; and oxtail and lentil salad. The dessert list is short and very French (pot de crème, chocolate terrine, and apple tart). *540 Main Street; 707-252-8115.* **$$$**

Bistro Don Giovanni. This longtime favorite near La Residence serves some of the best California-Italian food in the valley, delights such as Mediterranean chicken salad (grilled chicken breast, spinach, romaine, avocado, and sweet pepper relish with Roquefort vinaigrette), warm calamari, and spaghetti and clams. Also on the menu are braised lamb shank with Tuscan white beans, house-made ravioli, pizza, and other pastas and specials. *4110 St. Helena Highway; 707-224-3300.* **$$**

Celadon. This restaurant moved from its location near Napa Creek to the newly restored Hatt Market, downtown, on the west bank of the Napa River. Although it now has a bigger space, the intimacy of the dining room has not been diminished. The flawless California dishes with Asian and Mediterranean touches might include Thai steak salad, flash-fried calamari, grilled portobello mushrooms, honey-glazed pork chops, tatake of tuna, and polenta-crusted halibut. Reservations are recommended. *500 Main Street; 707-254-9690.* **$$$**

Julia's Kitchen. The decor of this first-rate dining room in the American Center for Wine, Food and the Arts is a bit sterile—even the chairs are made of aluminum—but the food is delicious. Try the "market" salad, made with greens from the organic gardens out front. Also on the menu are chilled pea soup, pan-seared shrimp, poached chicken breast, softshell crabs, and a platter of California and French cheeses. Service is gracious but can be slow. The wine list is excellent, and there is an extensive list of wines by the glass. *500 First Street; 707-265-5700.* **$$$$**

★ **Pairs Bistro.** Run by two graduates of the Culinary Institute of America, this California-Asian restaurant has captured the hearts of locals because the food is very good and the dining room is rarely crowded. The eclectic menu includes such delicacies as vegetable spring rolls, fried calamari with fennel and lemon, and ahi tuna with soba noodles. The name "Pairs" reflects the fact that each dish is paired with a complementary wine. *4175 Solano Avenue; 707-224-8464.* **$$**

★ **Pearl.** Casual and upscale, this restaurant serves some of the best food in the southern Napa Valley, including fresh Tomales Bay oysters; a marvelous smoked-chicken and roasted-*pasilla* (a dried chili) quesadilla; and mouth-watering soft tacos filled with chopped ginger flank steak, chilies, cilantro, and onion, accompanied by a beautifully smooth and spicy guacamole. Fresh fish is cooked to perfection. Best of all, you can order food to be taken out for the perfect Wine Country picnic. *1339 Pearl Street; 707-224-9161.* **$$$**

Casual, upscale Pearl.

★ **River City.** Napa's version of a steak and seafood house—a basic place for the meat and potatoes crowd—overlooks the Napa River. Some visitors are surprised to discover the river running through town, and even more surprised that it is quite broad at this point. *505 Lincoln Avenue; 707-253-1111.* **$$**

★ **Wine Train of Napa Valley.** This restaurant won't hold still while you eat. During lunch or dinner it chugs from Napa to St. Helena and back, past industrial neighborhoods and wineries. Unfortunately, it doesn't stop to let you taste local bottlings. Black Angus tenderloin, grilled chicken, roasted salmon and crab salad, and other standard dishes are served. *1275 McKinstry Street; 707-253-2111.* **$$$$**

■ **YOUNTVILLE** *map page 72*

Bistro Jeanty. Philippe Jeanty, long the star chef at the upscale Domain Chandon restaurant, has proved that it is possible to cook simply and well. The fare at his quintessential bistro runs to French comfort dishes such as tomato soup, duck pâté, pigs' feet and green-bean salad, skate fillet with mashed potatoes, pike quenelles with lobster sauce, coq au vin, beef stew, and cassoulet. You'd be hard-pressed to find these dishes better prepared anywhere in France. The service is professional and friendly, and the wine list has a good percentage of French bottlings in addition to the mandatory local ones. *6510 Washington Street; 707-944-0103.* **$$–$$$**

Compadres Mexican Bar & Grill. This simple restaurant serves good Mexican food and great margaritas. Menu highlights include seafood tacos, green-corn tamales, and *carnitas* (a dish made with cooked, and often shredded, pork). A word of caution: If you're dining outside and the oranges on the trees in the garden are ripe, beware. Squirrels have been known to toss the fruit at unsuspecting diners. *6539 Washington Street; 707-944-2406.* **$$**

★ **Domaine Chandon.** It may seem impossible for a restaurant to start out perfect and maintain a high level of quality for more than two decades, but that's what has happened at Domaine Chandon. Robert Curry, who took over the kitchen in 1997, continues to keep standards high. Enjoy the food with L'Etoile, the winery's premium bubbly. In warm weather you can dine outside on the terrace while the birds sing in the oak trees. The restaurant's service is impeccable, and the wine list is among the region's best. *1 California Drive; 707-944-2892.* **$$$$**

French Laundry Restaurant. Chef-owner Thomas Keller serves French food to a valley increasingly dominated by sunnier fare. His restaurant, in an old stone house with a courtyard in the center, serves such dishes as sautéed shad roe wrapped in applewood-smoked bacon with English peas, and pan-seared breast of Liberty Valley duck with Belgian endive marmalade. It's wise to reserve a table two months ahead of your visit. *6640 Washington Street; 707-944-2380.* **$$$$**

Gordon's Cafe and Wine Bar. Relaxed and pleasant, this restaurant and gourmet food and wine shop occupies the 1876 Yountville General Store, a clapboard building that has aged gracefully. Breakfast and lunch are served daily; dinner, on Friday evenings only. The breakfast menu includes such delectable items as granola made on the premises and freshly baked muffins and scones. Dinner includes such fare as wild-mushroom ragout, roast pork loin, grilled swordfish, and fresh Dungeness crab. *6770 Washington Street; 707-944-8246.* **$–$$**

★ **Mustard's Grill.** Busy and often noisy, Mustard's serves American comfort food with a California twist: grilled rabbit, tender pork chops, mesquite-grilled seafood and duck, as well as very good salads and soups. The food is a form of mom's home cooking raised to the level of haute cuisine. Service is fast and efficient, and though the staff seems always to be rushing about, no one ever rushes you. Make a reservation or you may have a long wait. *7399 St. Helena Highway; 707-944-2424.* **$$$**

Home-style cooking is raised to the level of haute cuisine at Mustard's.

■ NORTHERN NAPA VALLEY

■ CALISTOGA   *map page 103*
All Seasons Cafe & Wine Shop. Visitors mingle with winemakers over tasty food and local wines at this near-perfect Wine Country café. The freshest of valley food products are used in the dishes, yet meals are inexpensive. You can accompany your soups, salads, pastas, pizzas, or sandwiches with wines from one of the region's most complete wine lists. If you're not sure about how to pair wine and food, this is the place for you: the menu is built around wine recommendations. You can also buy a bottle at the wineshop and, for a corkage fee, have it poured at your table. *1400 Lincoln Avenue; 707-942-9111.* **$$**

Catahoula Restaurant & Saloon. Chef Jan Birnbaum cooks unabashedly Louisiana-style food that tastes great but does not always go well with the local wines, unless you're willing to settle for generic red or white. The restaurant has been billed as a refuge from wine snobs. *1457 Lincoln Avenue; 707-942-2275.* **$$$**

★ Wappo Bar & Bistro. Rustic flavors are prominent at this comfortable restaurant whose menu includes fish tacos and a steak sandwich with aioli. Also served are osso buco; lemongrass prawns; chile rellenos; cracked-wheat and herb salad; grilled eggplant sandwich on focaccia with baked goat cheese, roasted sweet peppers, tapenade, and aioli; rosemary-scented rabbit served with potato gnocchi with mustard cream and baby spinach; and spiced chickpea fritters served with a green herb salad. Portions are more than ample—order one dish at a time. In warm weather, try to snag a table under the vine-covered patio trellis. *1226 Washington Street; 707-942-4712.* **$$**

■ RUTHERFORD   *map page 103*
Auberge du Soleil. This elegant restaurant in a spiffy hillside resort of the same name sometimes achieves the greatness for which it was once known. Dishes have recently ranged from cioppino to Dungeness crab toast, from shaved Smithfield ham with corn pudding to grilled New Zealand venison rack with sweet-potato rosti and Oregon huckleberries. But never mind the food; the view is as great as ever. *180 Rutherford Hill Road; 707-963-1211.* **$$$$**

Sublime views and food to match at Auberge du Soleil.

■ St. Helena *map page 112*

★ **Ana's Cantina.** Beer, rather than wine, is the beverage of choice at this Mexican cantina in downtown St. Helena. But it's a place where locals congregate on sweltering summer evenings, acting on the old saying that "it takes a lot of beer to make good wine." The food is simple Mexican *campesino* fare, but the burritos, tacos, and enchiladas are uncommonly tasty. *1205 Main Street; 707-963-4921.* **$**

Gillwoods. This plain storefront restaurant proves that you can eat well—and cheaply—even in the heart of St. Helena, which is perhaps why locals like to hang out here. The food is basic American fare: pancakes, scrambles, omelets, and other egg dishes for breakfast; burgers and sandwiches for lunch; and the same for dinner, except for specials. But it's all well prepared and proves that plain American cooking can hold its own even in the heart of the Wine Country. There's a limited wine list. *1313 Main Street; 707-963-1788.* **$**

The Grill at Meadowood. The decor of this bright café epitomizes the understated elegance of Meadowood Resort. The food has a vaguely California-French tenor, and dishes tend to be on the light side. A separate spa menu allows you to diet in style on lamb chops, potatoes, and green beans with mustard-herb juice or steamed clams and mussels with peppers, white wine, garlic, and herbs—both under 400 calories. Every afternoon, an English tea is served on the terrace with house-made scones and finger sandwiches. At night the Restaurant at Meadowood, above the grill, serves sumptuous four-course dinners. Service is about as good as it gets, and the bartenders pour great martinis. *900 Meadowood Lane; 707-963-3646.* **$–$$**

Martini House. Tucked into a side street of downtown St. Helena, this restaurant occupies the former home of the opera singer Walter Martini, a bootlegger during Prohibition. His 1923 Craftsman structure was redesigned by the noted restaurant architect and co-owner Pat Kuleto. Great food, exceptional service, and a knockout wine list have made Martini House so popular that you may be unable to get a reservation (it helps to know a friendly concierge). Expect such dishes as sautéed foie gras, pork chops with crimini mushrooms and garlic sauce, cream of sweet-turnip soup, polenta cake, Sonoma rabbit, poached prawns, carpaccio of salmon, and vegetarian tarts. The wine list includes many rare and extraordinary bottlings, including several Napa Valley cult wines. *1245 Spring Street; 707-963-2233.* **$$$$**

Miramonte. This homey dining room in a 19th-century hotel building serves very good food in a somewhat eclectic vein. The signature appetizers are stuffed *pasilla* (a dried chile) and house-smoked sturgeon. You might try the wild mushrooms in a pinot noir butter sauce. For the main course, choose from pork tenderloin, steak, lamb, duck, and fresh seafood. Breads are baked fresh twice daily. On warm nights you can dine under the fig tree in the courtyard, and, yes, there are fig dishes in season. *1327 Railroad Avenue; 707-963-1200.* **$$$**

★ **Terra Restaurant.** Comfortable, friendly Terra serves great food in the converted workroom of a stone-walled foundry. Chef Hiro Sone, formerly of Spago in Los Angeles, has created a vaguely southern French–northern Italian style of cookery with unexpected Asian twists that make his dishes truly delightful. He shows just the right touch with quail, which may come deep-fried with a golden glaze that makes the skin alone worthy of Lucullus. Sone manages an East-West harmony that other chefs vainly strive to achieve. Seasoned to perfection, the dishes go well with local wines. The list here has some older, hard-to-find Napa Valley bottlings. *1345 Railroad Avenue; 707-963-8931.* **$$$**

★ **Tra Vigne Restaurant.** It's hard to say whether this restaurant is most appealing in spring, when the wildflowers in the small vineyard out front are in full bloom, or on a rainy winter day, when the bright decor and friendly staff help mitigate the chill in your bones. The food has the good flavors and textures of California-Mediterranean cuisine. The menu changes frequently, but gnocchi, grilled swordfish, and lamb stew have been among recent offerings. The wine list is divided between California and Italy, with some obscure bottlings from small wineries. *1050 Charter Oak Avenue; 707-963-4444.* **$$$**

★ **Vitte.** This family restaurant, brought to you by the same folks who opened Mustard's and Tra Vigne, is popular with locals because the food is both good and inexpensive. Favorites include minestrone, tomato salad, thin-crust pizzas, and pasta dishes. Don't worry if there's a line out the door: things move quickly here. You order at the counter and pick a seat at small, private tables or long European-style communal tables. In sunny weather you can sit outside in the courtyard. *1016 Main Street; 707-967-9999.* **$**

(following pages) Tra Vigne is one of the Wine Country's culinary meccas—and rightfully so.

★ **Wine Spectator Greystone Restaurant.** When this restaurant opened at the Culinary Institute of America's St. Helena campus, there was talk that it might become the new culinary trendsetter for Napa Valley food. It didn't. Reviews have been somewhat mixed. But the restaurant seems to have hit its stride with broad-based Mediterranean cookery matched to local wines. The menu changes frequently, but you might find such dishes as sweet-white-corn soup, grilled quail, oven-roasted chicken breast, and wild king salmon with cucumber salad. *2555 Main Street; 707-967-1010.* **$$**

■ SONOMA VALLEY

■ GLEN ELLEN   *map page 180*
The Girl and the Gaucho. This storefront restaurant with orange and gold walls might be best described as an eclectic Latin cantina. The food here is inspired by the cuisine of various Latin countries, including Spain. Grilled or roasted fish, chicken and roasted-pepper empanadas, grilled steak with red mole sauce, and rabbit confit with crunchy jicama sticks are complemented by simpler dishes such as fried spiced almonds, taro chips and tomatillo guacamole, mini mushroom tamales, and chili-glazed winter squash. The wine list has some varieties unfamiliar to the average American diner (carmenere and tempranillo, for example). Dinner is served from Thursday through Monday. *13690 Arnold Drive; 707-938-2130.* **$$$–$$$$**

★ **Glen Ellen Inn.** This café in a creekside house is small enough that you can converse with the chef while you eat. The exceptionally tasty food is prepared simply from fresh local ingredients, so the menu changes often. You might find prawns margarita with tequila-flavored tomatillo gazpacho and guacamole, duck confit with crumbled goat cheese, roast venison with huckleberry cabernet sauce, or pork chops with syrah barbecue sauce. The wine list is short but well chosen. *13670 Arnold Drive; 707-996-6409.* **$$**

■ KENWOOD   *map page 180*
★ **Cafe Citti.** This Tuscan-style trattoria is popular with locals. Go for plain fare, such as the spaghetti with olive oil and garlic, the focaccia sandwiches, or the rotisserie chicken. *9049 Sonoma Highway; 707-833-2690.* **$**

★ **Kenwood Restaurant & Bar.** The menu changes constantly at Kenwood Restaurant, but you will always find a great variety, from perfectly sauced meat dishes to hearty hamburgers. The bird feeder at the end of the dining patio allows you to watch the birds' antics and compare them to the behavior of fellow diners. The wine list is very good, especially when it comes to local bottlings. *9900 Sonoma Highway; 707-833-6326.* **$$**

★ **Vineyards Inn.** A great place to refresh yourself if you've been hiking through too many wineries or woods, this restaurant at the turnoff to Sugarloaf Ridge State Park serves casual Mexican food and pasta. *8445 Sonoma Highway; 707-833-4500.* **$**

■ SONOMA   *map pages 169 and 180*

★ **The Cafe at Sonoma Mission Inn.** This place is less snooty than the resort's more formal restaurant, Sante, and the food is at least as good. Appetizers, such as beet salad and Maine scallops, are the best dishes and big enough to be a meal. The wine list is good, and so is the service. *18140 Sonoma Highway, Boyes Hot Springs; 707-938-9000.* **$$$**

★ **Della Santina's.** Owner-chef Robert della Santina, who is from Lucca, and his extended family run this truly Tuscan trattoria. All pastas are made in-house, and the meats are roasted on a rotisserie. Don't miss the lasagna Bolognese, or try the roasted rabbit, duck, or chicken. *133 East Napa Street; 707-935-0576.* **$$**

★ **The Girl and the Fig.** Maybe it's the down-to-earth bistro cuisine, or the quality of the service, or the excellent wine list focused on Rhône varietals from both France and California (many of which are available by the glass), but owner Sondra Bernstein's Girl and the Fig is succeeding in a space that had been a restaurant graveyard. The dishes vary but might include a selected charcuterie platter, a very flavorful white-bean and winter-kale soup, a fig salad (figs are included in many of the dishes), a hearty mushroom ragout, and simple fare such as hamburgers and pork chops. There's an admirable selection of local and imported cheeses. *110 West Spain Street; 707-938-3634.* **$$$–$$$$**

★ **Swiss Hotel.** Locals and good old boys like to hang out in the bar at this eatery inside Salvador Vallejo's 1840 adobe. The dishes include burgers, steaks, pizzas, and innovative salads such as greens with citrus vinaigrette and green olive tapenade crostini. *18 West Spain Street; 707-938-2884.* **$**

La Vita Rustica: Picnics

You don't have to cook a fancy meal or go to a restaurant to experience the joys of the Wine Country's foods and wines. Enjoying wine with a simple meal of bread, cheese, and dry sausage—under sunny skies—is an old tradition. M.F.K. Fisher recalled in "Wine Is Life," an introductory essay she wrote for *The Book of California Wine,* how as a child she drove to small wineries with her father:

> The ranchers always seemed glad when we drove up their roads in our open Model-T. The women would put tumblers and a long loaf of their last baking, and cheese or a dry sausage, on the kitchen table or under the grape arbor out back. When the men came with two or three bottles from the old barn or hillside cellar where the casks were stored, they would eat and try the wines and talk.

You can have a similar experience at wineries that have picnic areas. Stock up at a Wine Country delicatessen for your picnic, drive to a winery for a bottle of wine, settle in the shade of a tree, and enjoy your meal. (Etiquette requires that if you use a winery's picnic grounds, you must buy wine there.) Following are a few suggestions for al fresco dining.

Picnicking at Chateau St. Jean.

Zinfandel Lane Picnic
In the lower Napa Valley, the Oakville Grocery (7856 St. Helena Highway, Oakville) has the widest selection of foods. Drive to Raymond Winery, buy a bottle of wine and enjoy the picnic area.

Napa Valley Views Picnic
For picnic supplies like bread, cheese, dry salami, and great olives, drop in at the Napa Valley Olive Oil Mfg. Co., at Charter Oak and Allison Avenues in St. Helena, or try the splendid Dean & DeLuca store on St. Helena Highway, 1.5 miles south of downtown. Next, drive to Rutherford Hill Winery (take Allison to Pope Street, turn right on the Silverado Trail, left at Rutherford Hill) and enjoy the views across the Napa Valley from the shade of the olive grove while sipping a glass of merlot.

Trail or Mountain Picnic
In the northern Napa Valley, the Palisades Market in downtown Calistoga has the best selection of picnic supplies. Hike out of town on the Oat Hill Trail for a picnic in the hills or drive to the trailhead on Mount St. Helena.

Literary Picnic
Pick up your supplies in Glen Ellen Village Market and then head west of town to Jack London State Park.

Alexander Valley Picnic
Drive east on Route 128 to the Alexander Valley, buy a bottle of zinfandel at Sausal Winery, and picnic on the winery's vine-shaded patio.

Sonoma Picnic
In the town of Sonoma, stock up on everything at the Sonoma Cheese Factory on the north side of the plaza, then head for Gundlach-Bundschu Winery. Or drive up the valley to Chateau St. Jean to picnic on the lawn, accompanied by a bottle of chardonnay.

Russian River Picnic
On the east side of Healdsburg's plaza, buy all the fixings for a picnic at the Oakville Grocery, or pick up your picnic bread at the Downtown Bakery and Creamery and get the toppings a few steps away at the Center Street Cafe & Deli. Then drive on Westside Road into the Russian River Valley to picnic at Rochioli Vineyards with a bottle of sauvignon blanc or pinot noir. The Hop Kiln Winery next door also has a picnic ground, but the views across the Russian River Valley vineyards are a lot better at Rochioli.

◼ RUSSIAN RIVER REGION

◼ FORESTVILLE   *map page 193*

★ **Farmhouse Inn and Restaurant.** Giant California bay trees shade this secluded inn housing one of Sonoma County's best restaurants. The dining room feels like a down-home Italian café, and a mural frieze depicting scenes of the owners' family history encircles the room. The menu, however, is short and not Italian at all. The dishes are simple but prepared with consummate skill, and the flavors are sublime. You might find Jerusalem artichoke soup; passion-fruit and habañero chili–glazed Niman Ranch pork chop; honey-mustard braised lamb shank; and Chef Steve Litke's signature dish: Rabbit, Rabbit, Rabbit, which includes apple-wood-smoked, bacon-wrapped loin, roasted rack, and confit of leg with whole-grain mustard sauce. The homemade desserts alone are worth a drive into the countryside, and there's a splendid cheese plate. The wine list has some uncommon Sonoma County bottlings. Dinner is served from Thursday through Sunday only. *7871 River Road; 707-887-3300.* **$$$$**

◼ GRATON   *map page 193*

★ **Underwood Bar & Bistro.** The owners of the Willow Wood Market and Café took a major leap forward in the transformation of the formerly dusty backcountry town of Graton when they opened this upscale restaurant across the street. The rich dark wood of the bar contrasts with the stainless steel open kitchen in a place that might as well be in San Francisco. The tapas, or small plate, menu—with influences from Spain, Portugal, Italy, and France—suffices to still anything but the most ravenous appetites. The main menu lists fresh oysters and hamburgers, as well as Moroccan lamb stew and grilled fish or meat. The assortment of cheeses includes Point Reyes Blue, a tangy handmade raw cow's-milk cheese. The wait staff is very knowledgeable and helpful. Underwood is the only place in the West County where you can get fresh oysters and a glass of wine at 11:30 at night. *9113 Graton Road; 707-823-7023.* **$$$**

★ **Willow Wood Market and Café.** This simple store and café serves breakfast, lunch, and dinner six days a week (it's closed on Sundays). The homey fare—soups, salads, and sandwiches—is basic but very tasty. You can pick up the fixings

A serving of Rabbit, Rabbit, Rabbit, the Farmhouse Inn's signature dish.

for a picnic here, then head half a block west to Blackstone/Martin Ray Winery (707-824-2401), which has tables in the garden outside its Victorian tasting room. *9020 Graton Road; 707-823-0233.* **$**

■ GUERNEVILLE   *map page 193*
★ **Applewood Inn and Restaurant.** The restaurant in the Applewood Inn is without question one of the most elegant dining rooms on the Sonoma Coast and in all the Wine Country. A fireplace at one end separates the reception area and tiny bar from the dining area; a fireplace at the other end serves as a focal point and helps make the space intimate, and large windows frame views of the surrounding redwoods and vineyards. The kitchen turns out perfect meals. The menu includes such dishes as local king salmon roasted on its skin with potato–olive oil purée, mushrooms, and chive-caviar butter; seared northern halibut in herbed crust with littleneck clams, lemon noodles, and savory summer vegetables in saffron broth; and stuffed and roasted pork loin cured in spiced black tea with basmati rice, figs, apricots, and cashews. Sonoma, California, and European wines round out a memorable dining experience. *13555 Highway 116; 707-869-9093.* **$$$$**

■ SANTA ROSA   *map page 193*
★ **Cafe Lolo.** This downtown Santa Rosa restaurant with a simple bistro atmosphere serves delicious soups and salads, such as roasted beets with caramelized shallots, toasted walnuts, and a wash of sherry vinaigrette; and roasted duck with rhubarb chutney. *620 Fifth Street; 707-576-7822.* **$$**

John Ash & Co. John Ash was one of several trendsetting chefs who put Wine Country cooking on the culinary map. He no longer participates in the stylish restaurant he started, but under executive chef Jeffrey Madura the contemporary California dishes—which emphasize seasonal local meats, fish, and produce—are as good as ever. The wine list is large and reasonably priced. *4330 Barnes Road; 707-527-7687.* **$$$$**

■ NORTHERN SONOMA COUNTY

■ GEYSERVILLE   *map page 204*
★ **Chateau Souverain.** The quintessential Wine Country restaurant, this simple bistro has views across the vineyards. The menu changes often, but recent dishes include local greens with roasted pearl onion–zinfandel vinaigrette, dried pears, and warm salted cashews; Dungeness crab and shrimp risotto with grilled green garlic in a roasted-shrimp broth; crispy-skin bass over braised Swiss chard; and New York steak with a confit of shallots over roasted garlic cloves. The food is well matched to the splendid wines created by winemaker Ed Killian. Chateau Souverain is open for lunch daily but for dinner on weekends only. Reservations are recommended. *400 Souverain Road; 707-433-3141.* **$$$**

★ **Taverna Santi.** Close to the downtown tasting room of Meeker Vineyards is the northern Alexander Valley's most exciting restaurant, Taverna Santi, owned by two former winery chefs, Thomas Oden and Franco Dunn. Taverna Santi dishes up California-Italian fare made with the best seasonal local ingredients and complemented by wines from neighboring vineyards. You might try the *insalata alla pera e nocciole* (salad with grilled pears and hazelnuts), marinated rabbit, Ligurian fish stew, *fagioli all'uccelletto* (cannellini beans with sage and olive oil), or *bistecca alla brace agrumata* (rib-eye steak with garlic and rosemary potatoes, roasted asparagus, and citrus and olive oil salsina). *21047 Geyserville Avenue, at Highway 128; 707-857-1790.* **$$$$**

■ HEALDSBURG   *map page 199*
★ **Bear Republic.** This wide-open hall of a brewpub on the Healdsburg Plaza is one of the most fun places around. The beers are uncommonly tasty, the food is delicious, and the service is friendly and fast. In warm weather, there's outdoor seating with a view toward the creek. This pub for people who like to socialize and don't mind laughing in public can be a welcome relief from the serious demeanor of some local eateries and wineries. *345 Healdsburg Avenue; 707-433-2337.* **$**

★ **Bistro Ralph.** The fare served at this understatedly chic but very friendly place is simple, seasonal, and made primarily from fresh local ingredients. The kitchen does as spectacular a job with shoestring potatoes as it does with ahi tuna. In spring, the grilled marinated asparagus is an extraordinary treat. The menu changes regularly, but there's something for every palate: filet mignon with onion rings, lamb meatloaf, grilled Columbia River sturgeon, Dungeness crab ravioli, and, you should hope, Szechuan pepper calamari. The wine list is excellent, including such rarities as Preston viognier, Frick cinsault, and Seghesio sangiovese, but ask for the "Local Stash" as well. Try to get a table out front or in the front of the restaurant for the best people-watching. *109 Plaza Street; 707-433-1380.* **$$**

★ **Costeaux French Bakery & Cafe.** This upscale European-style pastry shop–café serves simple lunches and rich pastries. There's outdoor seating. *421 Healdsburg Avenue; 707-433-1913.* **$$**

★ **Dry Creek Kitchen.** Arched trusses and floor-to-ceiling windows add drama to this ultra-modern restaurant, the Sonoma Wine Country's most cosmopolitan dining room. Fresh local organic produce determines the menu choices, to which the executive chef, Charlie Palmer, applies American, French, and northern Italian touches. Recent offerings have included sweet-corn chowder, pan-seared Sonoma foie gras, pomegranate-molasses-glazed Liberty duck, and Delmonico steak paired with braised kale, *romanesco* broccoli, and Yukon Gold potato puree. The service is first rate, and the huge wine list includes several hundred local wines. A walk-up window purveys take-out sandwiches and picnic snacks, as well as gourmet products. *317 Healdsburg Avenue; 707-431-0330.* **$$$$**

★ **Healdsburg Restaurant Charcuterie.** This airy restaurant just off the Healdsburg Plaza serves not only great burgers and steak sandwiches but also superb pastas: fusilli with smoked chicken, rigatoni with roasted eggplant, and cheese ravioli with sun-dried tomatoes. A delectable smoked chicken breast salad and assorted sandwiches are also prepared, and, best of all, there's a take-out menu for picnickers. *335 Healdsburg Avenue; 707-431-7213.* **$**

Manzanita. This pretty little restaurant has no sign: its name is written in the bricks of its outside walls. Its New Continental cuisine includes lamb shank, cassoulet, roasted sea bass, gnocchi, and grilled rabbit—all prepared with a sure touch. Some favorites are a flavorful carrot soup, truffled beet salad, and, yes, pizza. *336 Healdsburg Avenue; 707-433-8111.* **$$$$**

Freshly baked bread at the St. Helena farmers' market, held on Friday mornings in Crane Park, behind the high school.

★ **Ravenette.** The site of the original Ravenous (see below) is a tiny space attached to an old movie theater that has been transformed into a performing arts center. Seven tables of lucky diners here enjoy the incredibly delicious food that comes out of the open kitchen. Chef Joy Pezzolo's menu changes daily, but there are always great sandwiches and pastas, as well as wine by the glass. Reservations are not taken, so arrive early or be prepared for a long wait—no one is ever rushed. Some locals consider this one of the best restaurants in Sonoma County. *117 North Street; 707-431-1770.* **$$**

Ravenous. This local favorite expanded to a bigger space around the corner from its original location, but the decor remains simple, and the cooking is as eclectic as ever, ranging from the best hamburger in town to Caesar salad, grilled flank steak with an avocado quesadilla, cannellini bean soup with corn and potato, steamed and roasted Liberty duck legs, and beef brisket braised in red wine. There are some uncommon local bottlings on the carefully chosen wine list. *420 Center Street; 707-431-1302.* **$$$**

Zin Restaurant & Wine Bar. The cooking is simple, the portions are large, and the service is quick at this local hangout, where diners often drop by their friends' tables to chat. Owners and childhood friends Jeff Mall and Scott Silva, the sons of farmers in California's Central Valley, have planted their own garden to supply their restaurant with heirloom tomatoes, herbs, and peppers, which they match with the finest local meats and seafood. Nightly Blue Plate Specials change with the season; you might see such dishes as buttermilk fried chicken with collard greens, mashed potatoes, and hot biscuits; maple roast turkey with drunken cranberry sauce, sage-sausage stuffing, and mashed potatoes and gravy; and spicy meatloaf with wild-mushroom and zinfandel gravy, garlic mashed potatoes, and fresh peas and carrots. Other possibilities are corn-husk grilled shrimp with achiote lime butter; slow-braised California lamb shank with white beans and bacon; and Zin's signature dish, Coq au Zin—chicken braised in zinfandel with applewood-smoked bacon, pearl onions, and mushrooms over celery-root mashed potatoes. You can choose from more than 50 zinfandels out of the 130 wines offered. *344 Center Street; 707-473-0946.* **$$$**

Wine Country lodgings encompass luxury resorts such as the Sonoma Mission Inn & Spa as well as quaint B&Bs and chain accommodations.

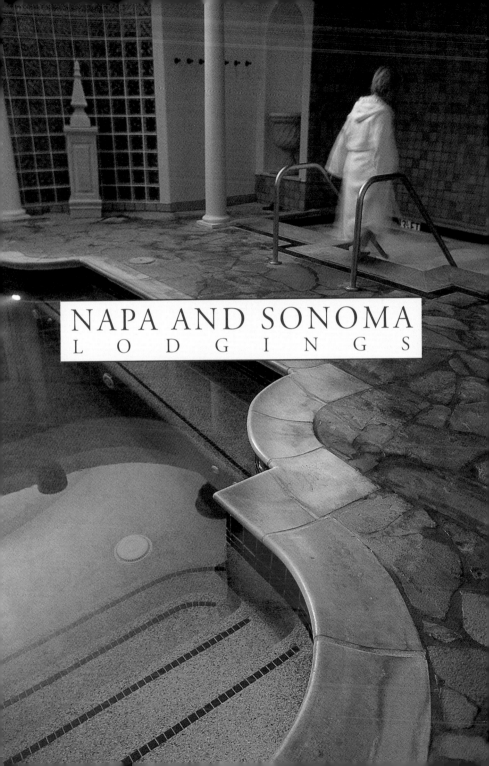

NAPA AND SONOMA
L O D G I N G S

Wine Country lodging can be very special and often as good as any lodging you might find in Europe. But like the best of the European hotels, accommodations here can be expensive, and reservations are sometimes hard to come by. Included at the end of this chapter are the names of chain accommodations, many of which are very comfortable and modestly priced. Remember that you might find a less expensive room outside the main Wine Country towns but close to the wineries and restaurants you wish to visit. For those hankering to pamper themselves in full Wine Country style, we've provided an overview of some of the top spas.

Prices designations for lodging, per couple

$ = less than $150   **$$** = $150–$249   **$$$** = $250–$400 **$$$$** = $400 plus
★ = Top Pick

■ SOUTHERN NAPA VALLEY

■ NAPA   *map pages 72 and 96*

Milliken Creek. This inn has undergone many alterations since it was built in 1857 as the Coach House, a stagecoach inn on the Silverado Trail of yore. Although the old building forms the core of the inn, it is hardly recognizable among the several newer structures flanking it. Rooms are now modern and exceedingly comfortable, with fireplaces, king-size beds, and whirlpool tubs, as well as great views of the tree-lined river. Breakfast is served in the lobby, in the garden, or in your room. There is an afternoon cheese tasting in the lobby, and guests can sip local reserve wines and vintage port. At night, housekeeping transforms rooms with candles and rose petals. Spa services at Milliken Creek include the opportunity of getting a massage by the river. *1815 Silverado Trail; 707-255-1197 or 888-622-5775.* **$$$–$$$$**

Oak Knoll Inn. Hidden by gardens and surrounded by 600 acres of chardonnay vines, this is the quintessential Wine Country retreat. It has just four large suites, with tall French windows, fieldstone walls, and cathedral ceilings. There's a pool to help you cool off on hot summer days. A delicious breakfast is included in the rate, as are afternoon wine tastings, which are often attended by local winemakers. Innkeeper Barbara Passino arranges for her guests to visit wineries that are not generally open to the public, and she has connections at restaurants where reservations are hard to get. If you need help creating an itinerary, she will be glad to help. *2200 East Oak Knoll Avenue; 707-255-2200.* **$$$–$$$$**

The decor has changed greatly since the time when Milliken Creek was a stagecoach inn.

■ **YOUNTVILLE** *map page 72*

Napa Valley Lodge. It is often difficult to get a room in this comfortable hacienda-style lodge on the outskirts of Yountville. The 55 rooms are spacious (upper ones have vineyard views), and there's a large pool area. *2230 Madison Street; 707-944-2468.* **$$$–$$$$**

■ **NORTHERN NAPA VALLEY**

■ **CALISTOGA** *map page 103*

Fanny's. This Craftsman cottage a couple of blocks off Calistoga's busy main street is as quiet as a place can be in this bustling spa town. The two-room inn has a full-length front porch complete with rocking chairs and lounging cats. Bedrooms have private baths and window seats, and the delicious breakfasts alone are worth the reasonable rates. Owner-innkeeper Deanna Higgins knows the valley, its wineries, and vintners well and is ever willing to help plan forays. She's also a good hiking guide. *1206 Spring Street; 707-942-9491.* **$**

Mount View Hotel & Spa. This hotel on Calistoga's main drag first opened in 1917. The 20 regular rooms have feather beds, cable TV, and direct-dial phones, and the nine suites and three cottages contain additional amenities. The hotel's highlights include the Cajun-style Catahoula restaurant (one of Calistoga's best dining spots), a very fine spa, and a heated outdoor pool. A Continental breakfast is delivered to each room. Within walking distance of Calistoga's attractions, the Mount View is nonetheless rarely noisy, perhaps because the town quiets down quickly after dark. *1457 Lincoln Avenue; 707-942-6877 or 800-816-6877.* **$$–$$$**

■ RUTHERFORD   *map page 103*

Auberge du Soleil. The Napa Valley's most famous lodging, set in an old olive grove, is renowned for its stunning views, sophisticated ambience, and popular restaurant. The rooms (the lowest-priced ones are on the small side) and suites have French doors, terra-cotta tiles, and private terraces. The more deluxe accommodations have fireplaces and whirlpool baths. *180 Rutherford Hill Road; 707-963-1211.* **$$$$**

■ ST. HELENA   *map pages 103 and 112*

Ambrose Bierce House. America's favorite literary curmudgeon, Ambrose Bierce, lived here until 1913, when he became bored with the peaceful wine valley and vanished into Pancho Villa's Mexico, never to be seen or heard from again. The ambience at his namesake inn is blast-from-the-past Victorian—yellow tones and a generally lacey feel—but the amenities in the two rooms and single suite are strictly up-to-date. *1515 Main Street; 707-963-3003.* **$$–$$$**

El Bonita Motel. Only in the Napa Valley could the prices on rooms in a gussied-up classic motel start at nearly $200 a night in high season, but El Bonita nevertheless has a few things going for it, including its pleasingly pastel decor and very convenient location between Rutherford and downtown St. Helena. Some of the 41 rooms have hot tubs. *195 Main Street; 707-963-3216.* **$$**

Inn at Southbridge. This 21-room hotel at the south end of St. Helena is within walking distance of shops and restaurants. Merryvale winery is next door, and the beloved Tra Vigne restaurant is on the same block. The rooms have an almost Scandinavian feel—clean and spare with light-colored wood details—though the overall effect is a tad corporate (and indeed business meetings take place here).

Complimentary wine and fruit are offered in the afternoon; breakfast, served on the ground floor in a common area, includes fresh fruit, bottled water, croissants, and yogurt. *1020 Main Street; 707-967-9400 or 800-520-6800.* **$$$–$$$$**

★ **Meadowood Resort.** A mild wisp of 1920s nostalgia pervades this upscale resort, which attracts an active clientele with amenities such as its nine-hole golf course, short hiking trail through oak woods, professional croquet course, seven tennis courts, two pools, and spa, whose practitioners are trained in all the latest therapies. For the more sedentary, there's a wine tutor who instructs guests in the arcane secrets of local wines. The 85 accommodations here—some of them cottages and others rooms and suites in lodge-like structures—are arranged in small clusters all over the property, which is within walking distance of downtown St. Helena. There are two restaurants at Meadowood, but if you want to head out, the concierge can often get guests reservations at restaurants that claim to have no room available. At night, the place becomes so quiet you can hear owls and distant coyotes. *900 Meadowood Lane; 707-963-3646.* **$$$$**

White Sulphur Springs Inn & Spa. This resort feels more like a mountain retreat than a Wine Country lodging, even though it is a short drive from the center of St. Helena. The 37 accommodations include rooms (with shared baths) in a lodge squeezed between the narrow road and a steep mountainside, rooms (with private baths) in an inn, and rustic creekside cottages. The atmosphere here is refreshingly unpretentious. *3100 White Sulphur Springs Road; 707-963-8588.* **$–$$**

■ SONOMA VALLEY

■ **GLEN ELLEN** *map page 180*
★ **Gaige House Inn.** This Queen Anne home, built in 1890 for the wealthy town butcher, is a bed-and-breakfast with modern paintings, art objects, and gorgeous greenhouse-quality orchids. The 15 rooms in the house and surrounding buildings are bright and airy, and all have private bathrooms. There's a swimming pool in the large garden, which runs down to Swan Creek. Outrageously good breakfasts, prepared by a professional chef and large enough to be considered brunch, are served either in the dining room or out on the terrace. Gaige House is exceedingly well run, yet the service never seems fussy. *13540 Arnold Drive; 707-935-0237 or 800-935-0237.* **$$–$$$$**

The Sonoma Mission Inn: pink, expensive, and popular.

■ **SONOMA** *map pages 169 and 180*

★ **El Dorado Hotel.** Facing the Sonoma Plaza, this 26-room hotel was built in 1843 as the home of Gen. Mariano Vallejo's never-quite-respectable brother, Salvador. It debuted as a hotel in 1851 and after a few other incarnations became one again in 1890. The rooms are generally small except for the newer ground-level suites beyond the patio and pool, which are not only large but also luxurious. Breakfast is best enjoyed under the courtyard fig tree. The El Dorado is within easy walking distance of everything. *405 First Street West, 707-996-3030.* **$$**

Sonoma Mission Inn & Spa. Pink, expensive, and popular, this 170-room inn run by the Fairmont chain has a large pool, tennis courts, two restaurants, and a world-class spa. The rooms are chic and luxurious, and some of the suites have large whirlpool tubs. But walls are thin, so if any of the neighboring guests take a shower at 6 A.M., it becomes your alarm clock. *100 Boyes Boulevard, off Highway 12, Boyes Hot Springs, Sonoma; 707-938-9000.* **$$$$**

■ RUSSIAN RIVER REGION

■ FORESTVILLE *map page 193*

Farmhouse Inn and Restaurant. In a wooded glen right off River Road, this hostelry built in 1873 consists of eight cottages—five with one room and three with separate bedrooms—tucked into a mossy hillside and half hidden by late-blooming roses and tall calla lilies. A rough trail runs back into the woods, where the fragrance of jasmine gives way to the spicy scent of native laurels draped with mosses and ferns. Although the setting of the Farmhouse Inn is very woodsy, the interior is anything but rustic. All of the well-appointed rooms have private bathrooms with whirlpool tubs, and most have private saunas. There's a swimming pool here, and the inn offers full spa services, including several kinds of massage. *7871 River Road; 707-887-3300.* **$$–$$$**

■ GUERNEVILLE *map page 193*

★ **Applewood Inn & Restaurant.** A truly great lodging, Applewood is a combination of three pink Mediterranean-style villas fitted snugly into the landscape of redwoods and apple trees. There are 19 rooms, all splendidly comfortable. Nine are in the historic 1920s Belden House, and the remainder are in the Piccola Casa and the Gate House, built within the last decade or so. Those in the seven-room Piccola Casa, spacious and private, are the best choice. A superb breakfast is served each morning in the restaurant. The owner, Jim Caron, is an expert on local wines, and he can direct you to small, virtually unknown wineries of the Russian River Valley. *13555 Highway 116; 707-869-9093.* **$$–$$$**

■ NORTHERN SONOMA COUNTY

■ HEALDSBURG *map page 199*

★ **Camellia Inn.** Built in 1869 in the Italianate style, this nine-room inn only a couple of blocks from the shops and restaurants of Healdsburg Plaza once served as a doctor's office and as Healdsburg's first hospital. The several-dozen varieties of camellias on the property were planted a century or more ago by the renowned horticulturist Luther Burbank, a friend of the then owners. The rooms have private baths, and several have private entrances (one has a private porch), whirlpool tubs, or gas fireplaces. The breakfasts served here are so hearty you may find yourself skipping lunch. Innkeeper Ray Lewand, an accomplished winemaker, knows his way around the Wine Country—you'll learn more about local wineries during happy hour on the swimming pool terrace than you will on many winery tours. *211 North Street; 707-433-8182.* **$–$$**

Healdsburg Hotel. Huge overstuffed couches grouped around a fireplace warm up the minimalist concrete lobby of northern Sonoma County's grandest lodging. Locals proudly point out that the Healdsburg Hotel looks like a New York or San Francisco establishment, and in one respect they are right: as in many urban hotels, the 49 rooms here are on the small side—nowhere near the size of rooms at other local inns (though the six suites here are suitably roomy). The hotel overlooks the town plaza, one of the most pleasant urban spaces in the Wine Country. *25 Matheson Street; 707-431-2800 or 800-889-7188.* **$$$–$$$$**

Healdsburg Inn. This 10-room bed-and-breakfast occupies a former stagecoach stop built in 1900 (and shortly thereafter rendered obsolete by the automobile). The well-preserved architectural detailing is all in the grand Victorian style, and the furnishings—claw-foot tubs, quilts, curtains, and beds—echo the period feel, creating a cozy and highly romantic atmosphere. The special touches here include a full champagne breakfast and early-evening wine tastings. *110 Matheson Street; 707-433-6991 or 800-431-8663.* **$$–$$$**

Honor Mansion. The most beautiful inn garden in Healdsburg is among the charms of this elegant 1883 Italianate mansion. Tall trees shade an outdoor sitting area and a koi pond, and there's a swimming pool out back. The 10 rooms and suites (there's also a cottage) have private baths, antiques, and featherbeds and are adorned with fresh flowers. The rates include a full breakfast, a sumptuous spread that will more than fortify you for a day of wine touring. Serious wine aficionados stay here, so you may even pick up some tips while you dine. *14891 Grove Street; 707-433-4277 or 800-554-4667.* **$$–$$$$**

Guests relax in minimalist style at the Healdsburg Hotel.

LIVING THE SPA LIFE

by Karen Croft

When you travel to Napa and Sonoma Counties you are, of course, interested in the wine. But along with the enjoyment of the grape, you should experience other pleasures: delectable food, exquisite scenery, and hedonistic spas.

Although it may be difficult to indulge in spa treatments without feeling guilty about pampering yourself, the only way to fully appreciate them—and to get your money's worth—is to relax and allow the people you've hired to make you feel good do just that. Don't hesitate to tell a practitioner what you want and need—more pressure, less heat, attention to a sore back, a sip of water, a cool towel for the forehead—and don't be afraid to ask questions. A good practitioner will explain all procedures and should ask if you have any special sensitivities, injuries, or needs.

It is important to plan your day around your spa appointment. You'll be relaxed but drained when your treatment is complete, so don't plan a 10-mile hike for later in the day. And if you have a massage, wrap, or water treatment with heat, which can be dehydrating, drink a lot of water and avoid alcohol afterward. Don't have your hair styled before a treatment; it will need to be redone afterward anyway.

In choosing a spa, you need to decide whether you want to be royally pampered in an atmosphere of heightened tranquillity or are more in need of rustic delights. There is a big difference between the utilitarian mud-bath regimens of Calistoga's low-end spas and the luxury that unfolds at Spa at Silverado. You'll wind up rejuvenated whichever you try, but the session will vary greatly.

On a recent series of visits to Wine Country spas, I had a basic massage, a deep tissue massage (which helps sore muscles), aromatherapy (which can energize you or put you to sleep), and a hot-oil massage (which definitely puts you to sleep). You might also try the burrito-like wrap, for which you are rubbed with grape-seed or lavender lotion, then covered in layers of linen, heated towels, and a blanket. This is not for the claustrophobic—or for those with runny noses—because your hands are not free for at least 20 minutes. Not for you? Nearly everyone can relish the outdoor whirlpools common to most spas. There is something comforting about being immersed in hot water while fresh air circulates around you and blue sky looms above.

Below are some of the Wine Country's best spots to rejuvenate, revitalize, relax, and refresh your body and soul.

SOUTHERN NAPA VALLEY

Spa at Silverado

The Spa at Silverado is designed to meet every whim of its high-end clientele. People come to the Silverado Resort to golf, and with a "golf widow" treatment package that lasts all day, the whole place is geared toward gals whose men are on the links. The spa is a 5- to 10-minute walk across a road from the rooms, so you can request a golf-cart ride over and back if you don't want to mitigate your glow. The facilities are spacious, but the lockers are small, so don't bring too much gear. The outdoor pool is large, and there is a lovely patio with a whirlpool, great on a sunny day. There are private showers and lots of cucumber water and iced face towels outside the sauna.

The Spa at Silverado: a haven of high-end pampering.

I tried the couples massage with a girlfriend. The wrap comes first, with a rose-scented lotion, hot linen towels, and blankets. After a restful few minutes, you put on a robe and must sit in the waiting room until the tables are prepared for the massage (it would be nicer if there were a private room off the couples room for this). I chose the ginger jasmine lotion, because the scent was invigorating and I had planned a dinner out. The therapist asked if I wanted the pressure hard or soft and what areas to concentrate on. I said hard, and shoulders, which she promptly ignored and gave me a massage that was good but generic. My friend had the same experience of being asked and then ignored. But the demeanor of the practitioners was gracious—my gal even said she considered it an honor that people allowed her to touch them.

The sauna here is a fine one, and the manicures and pedicures are done very carefully. Towels are plentiful, and the staff is alert to your every need. *1605 Atlas Peak Road, Napa; 707-257-5555.*

Villagio Inn and Spa

The Villagio is a large Tuscan-style property in the tiny town of Yountville. The spa here is relatively small, and the locker room needs to be enlarged—you shouldn't have to wait for a turn at the one shower!—but the massages are good, especially the deep tissue. The simple treatment rooms are painted in earth tones and decorated with black-and-white photographs of Italian statuary.

Spa users have exclusive use of an outdoor heated pool with whirlpool. Your experience is enriched by the beauty and fragrance of Meyer lemon bushes and white roses, which are in abundance on the property. In good weather you can request a massage al fresco. *6481 Washington Street, Yountville; 707-944-8877.*

Northern Napa Valley

Health Spa Napa Valley

This spa, associated with the adjacent Inn at Southbridge, plays down the fancy iced towels, body products, and rose petals prevalent at more luxurious places and concentrates instead on healing and rejuvenating the whole body. The well-organized layout includes small rooms that look out on a garden filled with lavender, rosemary, and water features that create a soothing sound.

I had a grape-seed mud wrap here, and it caused a nice tingle on my skin as I lay there like a burrito wrapped in warm towels and had the pressure points on my face and neck gently massaged. I prefer this treatment to the regimens of Calistoga. You don't dip into a tub of this French fine mud but rather have it applied like a paste.

At Meadowood you can sip tea on the porch before or after your treatment.

After a shower in that same room, I moved to the waiting room for some cucumber water and a rest before my Abhyanga, a relaxing four-handed hot oil treatment that heats and moisturizes your body. At first, the feeling of hot oil being poured on your skin is a bit shocking, but when you get used to the feeling it's supremely relaxing—especially on a cool day. The only drawback to this process is that if one of the practitioners has a slightly harder touch than the other, you might detect the asymmetry. There is an optional hot-oil-in-ear finish that I declined. *1030 Main Street, St. Helena; 707-967-8800.*

Meadowood
A sprawling but secluded New England–style retreat for the well-heeled, Meadowood has tennis courts, a golf course, and even a croquet field with resident pro. The high-caliber spa has private showers with rustic handmade tiles. You can sit out on the porch drinking hot tea while browsing through the spa's bird-watching guide.

I enjoyed a Valley Stone Massage, for which the therapist uses heated and cooled stones to relax and invigorate your body. Grape-seed oil is applied to your skin, and the stones are worked up and down your arms, legs, and back. The feeling was sooth-

(opposite) A mud bath at Indian Springs. (above) The resort in the mid-1940s.

ing, and the weight of the stones on the back and tummy were very grounding. It is important to tell your therapist if the stones are too hot or too cold—the shock of either can diminish the massage's benefits. A shower is needed afterward, because oil left on your skin can be sticky. Although the stones add to the overall effect of the massage and warm the body, those who like deep tissue work may find that fingers do a better job. *900 Meadowood Lane, St. Helena; 707-963-3646.*

Restorative Mud in Calistoga
The hot springs of Calistoga have attracted spa-goers since the 19th century, and the town is famous these days for its mud baths. The best choice in this category is **Indian Springs** (1712 Lincoln Avenue; 707-942-4913), where you're immersed in 100-percent volcanic ash for 10 minutes or so, after which you proceed through a regimen that includes a mineral bath, steam, and a blanket wrap. A massage is optional. Indian Springs, which has tidy little bungalows for overnight stays, costs a lot less than Silverado or Villagio, and you can go even further downscale at the motel-style **Calistoga Spa Hot Springs** (1006 Washington Street; 707-942 6269), **Golden Haven** (1713 Lake Street; 707-942-6793), and several other places where the treatments are similar to those at Indian Springs but the volcanic ash is mixed with peat. Count me among the folks who find the entire concept of mud baths yucky, but aficionados swear by their restorative powers.

SONOMA COUNTY

Sonoma Mission Inn

The routine is seamless at the 40,000-square-foot Sonoma Mission Inn's spa: fruit and water everywhere, carefully timed treatments, centralized waiting room, and large locker area. This is Gatsby done by Disney, however, and on a busy summer weekend, you can end up feeling like a sheep being herded into a massage pen.

The site's hot springs have been exploited commercially since 1840, but there are now three outdoor pools and two indoor thermal plunges adjacent to the sauna and steam room. The treatments offered are standard—basic massage, aromatherapy massage, facials, salt scrubs, and herbal wraps. If you are sensitive to scents, ask to sample products before they are applied. The scented lotion used in the popular Vanilla Float treatment is reminiscent of drugstore candles, and should you not care for the spa's signature apricot products, you're out of luck—they're everywhere.

For patrons here to revive their relationships, the spa provides couples massage, couples instructional massage, relationship reading (I have no idea what this might be and don't want to find out), and a couples wine and roses "Kur," in which you take a bath together while sipping wine and then are given a grape-seed massage.

In the lap of luxury at the Sonoma Mission Inn.

The aromatherapy massage, with your choice of invigorating grapefruit or calming chamomile oil blends, is a good basic choice here. My massage therapist was strong and businesslike, his touch more therapeutic than relaxing. The relaxing part for me came with the Bathing Ritual—an exfoliating shower, dips in warm and hot soaking pools, time spent in a eucalyptus steam room and a dry sauna, and a cooldown shower. You can spend as much time as you want in these areas before and after a treatment, and there are lounge chairs on the patio for relaxing in between. *100 Boyes Boulevard, off Highway 12, Boyes Hot Springs, Sonoma; 877-289-7354.*

MacArthur Place Country Inn and Spa

This quaint operation is a collection of bungalows surrounding a small spa and outdoor pool. Breakfast is served in a separate dining room done up with saddles, horse imagery, and lots of wood. The spa's tiny waiting area is part of the spa shop.

I chose the lavender experience here. This included a bubble bath (which could have been warmer) strewn with rose petals (lavender was somehow not available), followed by a lavender body mask with wrap, which was instantly calming. After about 20 minutes, I showered that off and then had a deep massage from a woman who listened to me when I told her my shoulders needed more attention than my legs. She was also good about keeping me completely covered and warm. *29 East MacArthur Street, Sonoma; 707-938-2929.*

Spa Hotel Healdsburg

The overall feel of this small white-walled spa is one of gentleness. It is a kind of Zen retreat in the middle of a rustic, though gentrifying, northern California town. The focus here is on natural aromatherapy and marine-based and herbal products.

I had the signature massage, a basic all-body treatment for which you can choose one of several aromatherapy oils, each associated with either air, water, earth, or fire and each scented for either energizing or soothing results. The treatment rooms are on the small side and were a bit cool during my session.

A small pool and a whirlpool are just outside the treatment rooms. Hot tea or cold water are available, and the practitioner will freely offer advice on how to care for your specific aches and pains at home. (Mine told me how to use a tennis ball in a sock as a makeshift massage tool.) This spa is part of a modern hotel decorated in gray, light green, and brown tones; the hotel's big windows bring in lots of light. *25 Matheson Street, Healdsburg; 707-433-4747.*

—Karen Croft is a senior editor at Salon.com.

■ CHAIN AND MOTEL LODGINGS

Calistoga
Calistoga Spa Hot Springs. *1006 Washington Street; 707-942-6269.*
Calistoga Village Inn & Spa. *1880 Lincoln Avenue; 707-942-0991.*
Comfort Inn–Napa Valley North. *1865 Lincoln Avenue; 707-942-9400.*
Golden Haven Spa Hot Spring Resort. *1713 Lake Street; 707-942-6793.*
Hideaway Cottages. *1412 Fair Way; 707-942-4108.*

Geyserville
Geyserville Inn. *21714 Geyserville Avenue; 707-857-4343.*

Healdsburg
Best Western Dry Creek Inn. *198 Dry Creek Road; 707-433-0300.*
Travelodge. *178 Dry Creek Road; 707-433-0101.*

Napa
Best Western Inn. *100 Soscol Avenue; 707-257-1930.*
Chablis Lodge. *3360 Solano Avenue; 707-257-1944.*
Discovery Inn. *500 Silverado Trail; 707-253-0892.*
Napa Valley Budget Inn. *3380 Solano Avenue; 707-257-6111.*
Napa Valley Marriott. *3425 Solano Avenue; 707-253-7433.*
Napa Valley Travelodge. *853 Coombs Street; 707-226-1871.*
Wine Valley Lodge. *200 South Coombs Street; 707-224-7911.*

Rutherford
Rancho Caymus Inn. *1140 Rutherford Road; 707-963-1777.*

St. Helena
Vineyard Country Inn. *201 Main Street; 707-963-1000.*
Wine Country Inn. *1152 Lodi Lane; 707-963-7077.*

Santa Rosa
Best Western Garden Inn. *1500 Santa Rosa Avenue; 707-546-4031.*
Santa Rosa Courtyard. *175 Railroad Street; 707-573-9000.*
Santa Rosa Motor Inn. *1800 Santa Rosa Avenue; 707-523-3480.*
Travelodge Downtown. *College and Mendocino Avenues; 707-544-4141.*

Sonoma
Best Western Sonoma Valley Inn. *550 Second Street West; 707-938-9200.*

The golden hills and green fields of a Napa Valley vineyard.

PRACTICAL INFORMATION

■ AREA CODES AND TIME ZONE

The area code for the Napa, Sonoma, and Mendocino wineries is 707; Clarksburg, 916; Lodi, Acampo, and much of the Sierra Foothills, 209; Placerville, 530; Santa Cruz and Monterey, 831; San Luis Obispo County and Santa Barbara County, 805. All of California is in the Pacific time zone.

■ METRIC CONVERSIONS

1 foot = .305 meters   1 mile = 1.6 kilometers   1 pound = .45 kilograms
Centigrade = Fahrenheit temperature minus 32, divided by 1.8

■ CLIMATE/WHEN TO GO

The Wine Country climate generally follows a pattern of sometimes-heavy winter rainfall and summer drought accompanied by often stifling heat. The region's northernmost climes are particularly hot in summer, though coastal fogs cool things off. In summer the hills are brown and dry, and in winter they're green. The sea fogs and varied terrain of the Wine Country create myriad microclimates, which in turn create prime conditions for a variety of grapes.

Winter is a beautiful time to visit California's wineries: the hills are green with velvety grass, the first wildflowers are spreading beneath the oaks, and the air smells fresh and invigorating. At this time of year winemakers are more likely to have time to discuss their wines with visitors. Though the tasting rooms, wineries, and inns of Napa and Sonoma are busy, they are slightly less so in winter than at other times of the year.

Spring is another great time to visit the wine regions, because it brings more wildflowers, beginning in the Santa Barbara County and Sierra Foothills vineyards, but soon reaching the northernmost hillsides. Golden poppies, buttercups, blue and cream irises, and red, white, blue, and yellow lupines raise their bright banners and dominate the roadsides.

Winemakers stick close to their cellars, because this is not only the season when last vintages begin to be bottled, but also a time of dubious weather, when late frosts can descend on the vineyards and kill the tender buds. The crowds of visitors are beginning to swell, especially on weekends, but there are still quiet moments to be enjoyed.

Summer days are hot and the air is dusty. The wineries are thronged with visitors now, and so are the hotel swimming pools. At night, when cooling breezes waft in from the ocean, diners fill the courtyards and terraces of restaurants. This is a season for wine festivals and county fairs. If the weather is favorable, the first of the grapes, those destined for crisp white wines and sparkling wines, will be harvested as early as August.

Fall is both the busiest and most exciting season. This is the time of harvesting and crushing the grapes, of fermenting and punching down the juice, of racking and fining the new wine. The air is heavy with the aroma of must. The winemakers are busy checking on the wines and racing out to the vineyards to see if the next crop of grapes is ripe.

■ GETTING THERE AND AROUND

■ BY AIR

San Francisco International Airport (SFO) is the area's largest airport and is served by most international and domestic airlines. The airport is 14 miles south of San Francisco. *Off U.S. 101, 650-876-7834; www.flysfo.com.*

Oakland Airport (OAK) is served by many domestic carriers and some international airlines. The airport is closer to the Napa-Sonoma Wine Country than SFO. *Hegenberger Road, off I-880; 510-563-3300. www.flyoakland.com.*

San Jose International Airport (SJC), 2 miles north of downtown San Jose and served by 14 major airlines, is the closest large airport to the Santa Cruz Mountains, Carmel Valley, and Salinas Valley regions and is within comfortable driving distance of the other Central Coast wineries. *Airport Boulevard, off Highways 85 and 87; 408-501-7600; www.sjc.org.*

Sacramento International Airport (SMF) is served by many domestic carriers and some international airlines. This is the closest major airport to the Sierra Foothills, Clarksburg, and Lodi wine regions. *Off I-5, northwest of downtown; 916-929-5411; www.sacairports.org/passenge.htm.*

Santa Barbara Airport (SBA), 8 miles from downtown and about 30 miles south of Santa Barbara County's wine region, is served by the feeder airlines of several major carriers. *500 Fowler Road, off U.S. 101; 805-683-4011; www.flysba.com.*

■ BY CAR

To reach the Napa and Sonoma Wine Country from San Francisco, cross the Golden Gate Bridge and head north on U.S. 101, east on Highway 37, then north on Highway 121 into the **Carneros Region.** Continue on Highway 121 to Highway 29 north to reach the **Napa Valley.** To enter the heart of the **Sonoma Valley,** turn north from Highway 121 onto Highway 12. To get to the **Russian River Valley** wineries, stay on U.S. 101 north to Highway 116 west. To reach the **Dry Creek** and **Alexander Valley** wineries, stay on U.S. 101 all the way to Healdsburg. From the East Bay, head north on I-80, which has connections to Highway 29.

The **Anderson Valley** can be reached from the Bay Area by taking U.S. 101 north and Highway 128 west. From coastal Highway 1, head east on Highway 128.

Take Highway 12 east from Napa to reach the **Clarksburg Wineries,** which lie along Highway 160, south of Sacramento. Continue east on Highway 12 to the **Lodi** wineries, which are on or near Highway 99, also south of Sacramento, and can be accessed from I-5. Wineries in the **Sierra Foothills** region are off U.S. 50 and Highways 49 and 4, southeast of Sacramento.

You will need to head south of San Francisco on I-280, Highway 1, or U.S. 101 to reach the **Central Coast** wineries, which are spread out from the Santa Cruz Mountains all the way to southern Santa Barbara County. Many of the wineries covered in the Central Coast chapter are on or near U.S. 101; see the Santa Cruz Mountains, Monterey County, San Luis Obispo County, and Santa Barbara County sections for specific directions.

■ DRIVING TIPS

As you cruise down winding Wine Country lanes and highways, drive carefully. You may be on vacation, but the people who live and work here are not, so avoid rush hours (generally between 7 and 9 in the morning and 4 and 6 at night). Traffic can be especially bad on Friday and Sunday afternoons, when weekenders add to the mix.

This is not only true for the suburban North Bay, but for the Sierra Foothills, the Lodi area, Monterey County, and the Paso Robles area as well. Some drivers in Napa and Sonoma, especially workers in a hurry during the harvest and crush season, will pass over double yellow lines before blind curves to get past slow drivers. Don't let other drivers push you. Pull over at a safe turnout and let them pass.

Don't overindulge as you "taste" wine, and don't drive if you've overindulged. It is sometimes difficult to realize that you've had one too many, but the local cops can tell, and they're waiting. On big festival weekends, the California Highway Patrol sends extra troopers into the Napa Valley to catch intoxicated drivers. If you can, have a designated driver who is not allowed to drink alcohol (some wineries provide free nonalcoholic beverages for designated drivers).

■ SHIPPING WINE

Sending wine home from the wineries you visit is getting easier. As a result of legislative actions and court decisions, more states are liberalizing the rules for shipping wine interstate. In 2003, additional states opened their borders to direct-to-consumer shipments of wine from other states. Texas now allows shipments, though only to "wet" counties. Laws regarding the purchase of wines online have also begun to liberalize, and, depending on the outcome of several court cases, online wine shipping could expand. Because laws about interstate shipping of wine vary so greatly from state to state, and because the penalties for noncompliance in some states can be severe, if you're going to ship wine home, it is wise to do so either through the winery or a professional shipper.

■ OFFICIAL TOURISM INFORMATION

Amador County. *209-223-0350; www.amadorcountychamber.com.*
Calaveras County. *209-736-0049; www.visitcalaveras.org.*
El Dorado County. *530-621-5885; www.eldoradocounty.org.*
Healdsburg. *707-433-6935; www.healdsburg.org.*
Lodi. *www.visitlodi.com.*
Mendocino County. *866-466-3636; www.gomendo.com.*
Monterey County. *888-221-1010; www.montereyinfo.org.*
Napa Valley. *707-226-7459; www.napavalley.org.*
San Luis Obispo. *805-781-2531; www.sanluisobispocounty.com.*
Santa Barbara County. *805-966-9222; www.santabarbaraca.com.*
Santa Cruz County. *831-425-1234; www.scccvc.org.*
Sonoma Valley. *707-996-1090; www.sonomavalley.com.*

■ **USEFUL WEB SITES**

Amador Wine Country/Amador Vintners. *www.amadorwine.com.*

Anderson Valley Winegrowers Association. *www.avwines.com.*

Calaveras Wine Association. *www.calaveraswines.org.*

Central Alexander Valley/Geyserville. Winery, dining info. *www.geyserville.com.*

Fodors.com. Wine Country sightseeing, online booking, itineraries, and features. *www.fodors.com.*

Lodi Appellation Winery Association. *www.lodiwines.com.*

Mendocino Online. Restaurant and lodging reviews, maps, things to do, places to see. *www.mendocino.org.*

Mendocino Winegrowers Alliance. *www.mendocinowine.com.*

Monterey County Vintners & Growers Association. *www.montereywines.org.*

Napa Valley Vintners Association. *www.napavintners.com.*

Napa Valley Wine Train. Dining aboard a train while rolling through the Wine Country. *www.winetrain.com.*

NapaValley.com. Spas, wineries, hotels, restaurants, sports facilities, and recreational activities. *www.napavalley.com.*

Northern Alexander Valley/Cloverdale. Wineries, dining, lodging information. *www.cloverdale.net.*

Russian River Wine Road. *www.wineroad.com.*

Santa Barbara County Vintners Association. *www.sbcountywines.com.*

Santa Barbara Wine Country Info. *santabarbara.winecountry.com.*

Santa Rosa Press Democrat. Sonoma County's main daily paper. *www.pressdemocrat.com.*

Sonoma County Farm Trails. Where to buy fresh fruit and produce in season. *www.farmtrails.org.*

Wines.com. Wine information, plus Wine Country travel and tourism tips. *www.wines.com.*

■ FESTIVALS AND EVENTS

■ JANUARY

Santa Cruz Wine Country Passport Program. The first of four yearly events (that also take place in April, July, and November); provides the chance to visit many wineries not usually open to the public. *831-479-9463.*

Winter Wineland, at Russian River Wine Road wineries. Seminars, tastings, entertainment. *800-723-6336; www.wineroad.com.*

■ FEBRUARY

Annual Barrel Tasting Weekend, Amador County. Taste wines of the near future. *209-267-2297; www.amadorwine.com.*

Cloverdale Citrus Fair. Gourmet food show and wine tasting. *707-894-3992; www.cloverdale.net.*

Napa Valley Mustard Festival. Valley-wide art, wine, and food celebration, with a bow to the blooming wild mustard. Continues into March. *707-259-9020; www.mustardfestival.org.*

President's Wine Weekend, Calaveras County. Tastings and special events. *209-376-6722; www.calaveraswines.org.*

■ MARCH

Barrel Tasting Preview, Alexander Valley. Wineries offer food and wine pairings, discounts on wines. *707-433-1944.*

Heart of the Valley Barrel Tasting, Kenwood and Glen Ellen. Wineries open their cellars to visitors and offer tastes. *707-433-1944; www.heartofthevalley.com.*

Lodi Spring Wine Show. Hors d'oeuvres, music, entertainment, and tastings of wines from more than four dozen wineries. *209-369-2771; grapefestival.com.*

Paso Robles Zinfandel Festival. Takes place at area wineries. *805-239-8463.*

Russian River Wine Road Barrel Tasting Weekend. About seven dozen wineries participate. *800-723-6336; www.wineroad.com.*

The California golden poppy is the state flower and blooms from early spring through June.

■ **APRIL**

Monterey Wine Festival. Fun event sponsored by the American Restaurant Association. *800-656-4282; www.montereywine.com.*

Passport to Dry Creek. A popular weekend of tastings and other events; sells out early. *707-433-3031; www.wdcv.com.*

■ **MAY**

Healdsburg Country Fair. This event includes a livestock show and chili cook-off. *707-431-7644.*

Luther Burbank Rose Parade Festival, Santa Rosa. Parade through town and tours of famous horticulturist's gardens. *707-542-7673.*

Pinot Noir Festival, Anderson Valley. *707-895-9463; www.avwines.com.*

Russian River Wine Festival, Healdsburg Plaza. Wine tastings, food, music. *800-723-6336; www.wineroad.com.*

Santa Cruz Mountains Wine Auction. Takes place throughout the Silicon Valley. Rare chance to sample many area wines in one place. *831-479-9463.*

Vines to Wine, Lodi. This wine celebration has a down-home feel. *209-368-4793.*

■ JUNE

Annual Ox Roast, Sonoma Plaza. A fun event, with big barbecue and plenty of wine. *707-938-4626; www.sonomavalley.com.*

Napa Valley Wine Auction, St. Helena. Tickets sell out early for the nation's premier food and wine event. *707-942-9775; www.napavintners.com.*

Santa Cruz Mountains Vintners Festival. Two-weekend event includes food, music, art exhibits, winery tours, and barrel tastings. *831-479-9463.*

Sausage & Wine Festival, Lodi Grape Festival Grounds. Entertainment, wine tastings, crafts—and lots of sausage. *209-367-1374.*

■ JULY

Napa County Fair, Calistoga. A chance to see the real Napa Valley at its rustic and laid-back best. *707-942-5111.*

Salute to the Arts, Sonoma Plaza. A major festival, with music, wine tastings, and plenty of eats. *707-938-1133; www.salutetothearts.com.*

■ AUGUST

Shakespeare at Buena Vista, Sonoma. Every Sunday in August and September; bring a picnic, buy a bottle of wine, and enjoy the show. *707-938-1266; www.buenavistawinery.com.*

■ SEPTEMBER

Santa Cruz County Fair, Watsonville. Wine competition, tasting, and other events take place at the fair. *831-479-9463.*

Soroptimists Annual Beer & Sausage Tasting, Healdsburg Plaza. Local sausages, local mustards, and beer from more than two dozen breweries. *707-433-0773; www.sihealdsburg.org.*

Valley of the Moon Vintage Wine Festival, Sonoma Plaza. This is one of the most fun and least snooty wine festivals anywhere. Good food too. *707-996-2109; www.sonomavinfest.com.*

Winesong, Mendocino Botanical Gardens, Fort Bragg. The North Coast's top wine and food festival. Not to be missed, if you can get a ticket. *707-545-4203.*

■ OCTOBER

Paso Robles Harvest Wine Tour. Winemaker dinners, barrel samples, seminars, barbecues, music, winery tours. *805-239-8463; www.pasowine.com.*

Sonoma County Harvest Fair, Sonoma County Fairgrounds. The hilarious grape stomp and the "tallest weed" contest are among the events at this showcase for Sonoma County produce. *707-545-4203 or 707-545-4200; www.harvestfair.org.*

■ NOVEMBER

Evening of Wine and Roses, Santa Cruz County Fairgrounds. Wine auction and food and wine tastings. *831-479-9463.*

Great Winery Escape, Monterey. A splendid weekend of winery open houses, winemakers' dinners, and other events. *831-375-9400; www.montereywines.org.*

Napa Valley Wine Festival, Town & Country Fairgrounds, Napa. On the first weekend of the month. *707-253-3563.*

Russian River Wine Road—A Food and Wine Affair. Food and wine pairing along the wine road. *800-433-4335; www.wineroad.com.*

■ DECEMBER

Russian River Christmas Crafts Fair, Guerneville. *707-869-9000.*

G L O S S A R Y

Acidity. The tartness of a wine, derived from the fruit acids of the grape. Acids stabilize a wine (i.e., keep it from going flat), serving as a counterpoint to its sugars (if there are any) and bringing out its flavors. Acid is to wine what salt is to cooking—a proper amount is necessary, but too much spoils the taste. Tartaric acid is the major acid in wine, but malic, lactic, and citric acids also occur, in greatly variable concentrations.

Aftertaste. The way a wine lingers on the palate after you have swirled it around in your mouth. Good wines have a long-lasting aftertaste of many complex flavors and aromas.

Aging. The process by which wines react to oxygen at a very slow rate. Wine is most commonly aged in oak vats or in old or new oak barrels, slowly interacting with the air through the pores in the wood. If properly stored, some wines improve with aging, becoming smoother and more complex and developing a pleasing bouquet. New oak contains tannins and flavoring elements that the wine leaches from the wood. Too much exposure to these oak extracts can overpower the varietal character of a wine. Most wines do not age well. Even a small amount of oxidation can spoil lighter wines, which are much more enjoyable when young and fresh. When aged for just a short time, they may lose their fruit and thus their appeal. Their color dulls: whites turn brownish, rosés orange, reds brown. Today even some of the wines once made in a heavier style, such as cabernet sauvignon, are sometimes made to be drunk after 5 to 10 rather than 20 to 50 years.

Alcohol. Ethyl alcohol is a colorless, volatile, pungent spirit that not only gives wine its stimulating effect and some of its flavor but also acts as a preservative, stabilizing the wine and allowing it to age. A wine's alcohol content must be stated on the label, expressed as a percentage of volume, except when a wine is designated table wine (*see below*).

American Viticultural Area (AVA). A region with unique soil, climate, and other grape-growing conditions designated as such by the Alcohol and Tobacco Tax and Trade Bureau. It is more commonly called an appellation. When a label lists an appellation—Napa Valley or Chalone, for example—85 percent of the grapes used to make the wine must come from that region.

Appellation. *See* American Viticultural Area.

Aroma. The scent of young wine derived directly from the fresh fruit. It diminishes with fermentation and is replaced by a more complex bouquet as the wine ages. The term may also be used to describe special fruity odors in a wine, like black cherry, green olive, ripe raspberry, or apple.

Astringent. What a layman might call "sour," though experts use the term "sour" only for a spoiled wine.

AVA. *See* American Viticultural Area.

Balance. The harmony of elements in a wine. A well-balanced wine has a special mouth feel, an appeal to the olfactory, gustatory, and tactile senses that is difficult to describe verbally.

Barbera. An Italian wine grape from the Piedmont. It grows well in several California microclimates, where it produces deeply colored, full-bodied wines with tarry, spicy, earthy character and a backbone of balancing acid. It goes very well with Italian food.

Barrel. A cylindrical storage container with bulging sides; usually made from American, French, Slavonic, or Baltic oak. A full barrel holds the equivalent of 240 regular 750 ml bottles.

Barrel Fermenting. The fermenting of wine in small oak barrels instead of large tanks or vats, allowing the winemaker to keep grape lots separate before blending them. This method, traditionally used by small European wineries, has recently become common among California winemakers. The trend may or may not survive the spiraling cost of oak barrels.

Big Wine. A wine with considerable body, high alcohol, and forward aromas (those that hit you in the nose as soon as you pour a glass of the wine as compared to more subtle aromas that develop as the wine meets the air). A big wine is not necessarily a good wine, since this excess can translate into a wine that is merely coarse and heavy.

Binning. Cellaring bottles of wine at the winery for aging. The bottles are laid on their sides to keep the corks moist, since dried-out corks may allow air to leak in, spoiling the wine.

Blanc de Blancs. A term denoting wine made from white grapes; often used to distinguish sparkling wines made solely from white grapes from those made from pinot noir grapes (and called Blanc de Noirs).

Blending. The mixing of several wines to create one of greater complexity or a more enjoyable one, as when a heavy wine is blended with a lighter one to make a more approachable medium-bodied wine.

Body. The wine's substance as experienced by the palate. A full body is an advantage in the case of some reds, a disadvantage in many lighter whites.

Bordeaux Blend. A blend of red-grape varieties native to France's Bordeaux region—cabernet sauvignon, cabernet franc, malbec, merlot, and petit verdot.

Bottle Sizes. Metric sizes have replaced the traditional bottle sizes of gallon, quart, fifth, et al., though the old names linger:

Tenth . . . . .375 ml of wine

Fifth . . . . .750 ml (25.4 oz)
The most commonly used wine bottle

Magnum . . . . .1.50 liters (50.72 oz)

Half Gallon . . . .1.75 liters (59.2 oz)

Double Magnum . . . . .3.0 liters
also called Jeroboam

Rehoboam . . . . .4.5 liters (approx.)
The equivalent of five 750 ml bottles

Other, larger-sized bottles include the approximately 9-liter Salmanzar and the Nebuchadnezzar, which holds from 13 to 15 liters of wine, depending on where, when, and by whom it was made.

Bouquet. The different odors a mature wine gives off when opened. They should be diverse but pleasing, complex but not confused, and should give an indication of the wine's grape variety, origin, age, and quality.

Brix. A method of telling whether grapes are ready for picking by measuring their sugars. Multiplying a grape's Brix number by .55 yields the potential alcohol content of the wine (though the finished wine may be slightly higher or lower).

Brut. A dry sparkling wine (*see also* demi-sec, sec).

Burgundy. The English name for Bourgogne, a French region where red and white wines are made. Also refers to the wine from that region. The term is sometimes used on labels of inferior California red wines to indicate a cheap, generic red wine.

Cabernet Franc. This noble grape of France's Bordeaux region produces aromatic red wines that are softer and more subtle than those of the closely related cabernet sauvignon and that age more quickly. Cabernet franc is often blended into cabernet sauvignon to soften the wine of that somewhat harsher grape.

Cabernet Sauvignon. The noble red-wine grape that has made the clarets of Bordeaux renowned grows very well in parts of California. Its wine is deeply red, tannic, and requires a long period of aging to become enjoyable. For this reason it is often blended with cabernet franc, merlot, and other related red varieties, to soften the resulting wine and to make it enjoyable earlier.

Case. A carton of twelve 750 ml. bottles of wine. A magnum case contains six 1.5-liter magnum bottles.

Cask. A wine container, commonly made from oak staves.

Chablis. A prime French wine-growing region making austere white wines. It is sometimes used on labels of inferior California wines to indicate a cheap, generic white wine, though it is also used to describe cheap pink wines.

Champagne. *See* Sparkling Wines.

Chardonnay. The noble French grape variety making the great white Burgundies of Montrachet, Meursault, and Chablis, as well as the lesser whites of Pouilly-Fuissé and Mâcon. It is also one of the principal varieties of the Champagne region.

Chenin Blanc. This noble old French white-grape variety has fallen from grace in California because it does not make big wine, the way chardonnay does.

Chianti. An Italian red wine made primarily from the sangiovese grape; it goes beautifully with Italian food.

Claret. A name formerly applied to red wines from Bordeaux that were shipped to British connoisseurs. The term came into disrepute when it was applied to California bulk wines. It is, however, regaining respect as a name several California premium wineries are bestowing on their red Bordeaux blends.

Clarity. The lack of particles—both large and minute—floating in a wine; a requirement for a good wine. Wine should always be clear (though it can be dark or dense); it should never be cloudy.

Cloudiness. The presence of particles—often minute—that do not settle out of a wine, causing it to taste dusty or even muddy. To correct it, set the bottle at a slant or upright in a place where it will not be disturbed, then let the sediments settle. This could take from a few minutes to several hours depending on the wine. Decant the clear liquid on top and discard the sediments. If the wine remains cloudy, get rid of it—it has been badly made or is spoiled.

Complexity. Layers of different flavors and aromas in harmony with the overall balance of a wine, and perhaps, in an aged wine, a pleasing bouquet and a lingering aftertaste.

Controlled Fermentation. The process used to ferment white grapes at low temperatures, in chilled tanks, to preserve the fruit and the delicacy of the grape flavors and aromas. Reds may undergo uncontrolled fermentation, which results in high temperatures that help extract tannins and pigments from the grape skins, but this is undesirable for whites.

Cooperage. A collective term used to describe all the containers of a winery in which wine is stored and aged before bottling. It includes barrels, casks, vats, and tanks of different materials and sizes.

Corky or Corked. Used to describe a wine affected by off flavors and aromas created by a leaky cork or cork infection. The contact between the wine and the air that leakage allows will, with time, spoil the wine.

Crush. The California vintners' term for the grapes in a particular year used to make wine. Not all of the grapes grown in the state go into wine—some go to fresh markets, others are made into grape juice. These are not part of the "crush" but are counted as part of the grape harvest.

Cuvée. A sparkling wine that is a blend of different wines and sometimes different vintages. Most sparkling wines are cuvées, although in very good years some are vintage dated.

Decant. To slowly and carefully pour an aged wine from its bottle into a decanter. Decanting need be done only with old wines that have a sediment, which when stirred up by careless handling might cloud the wine. Careful decanting leaves the sediment in the bottle.

Demi-sec. Although *sec* means "dry," in the convoluted language of sparkling wine, *demi-sec* is sweet. More specifically, wine that contains 3.5 to 5 percent sugar.

Dessert Wines. Sweet wines that are big in flavor and aroma but may be quite low in alcohol, or wines that have been fortified (*see* fortification) with brandy or neutral spirits and may be quite high (17–21 percent) in alcohol.

Dry. The term used to describe a wine

that is not sweet, although it may contain some residual sugar. The American wine industry's long fight to wean consumers away from sweet wines has turned "dry" into an important enological concept.

Estate Bottled. A term indicating that both the winery and the vineyards from which grapes were harvested are in the same appellation (which must be printed on the label), that the winery owns or controls the vineyards, and that all the wine-making processes, from crushing to bottling, were done at a single facility.

Fermentation. The process—in which enzymes generated by yeast cells convert the grape sugars into alcohol and carbon dioxide—by which grape juice becomes wine.

Fermenter. Any vessel, small or large (such as a barrel, tank, or vat), in which wine is fermented.

Filtering, Filtration. A purification process in which wine is pumped through filters to rid it of suspended particles. If mishandled, filtration can remove much of a wine's flavor.

Fining. A method of clarifying wine by adding crushed eggshells, isinglass, or other natural substances to a barrel. As these solids settle to the bottom, they take suspended particles with them, clarifying the wine. A slower, more tedious process than filtering, but one that makes better wine.

Flat. Said of a wine that lacks acid and is thus dull; also of a sparkling wine that has lost its bubbles.

Fortification. A process by which brandy or natural spirits are added to a wine to stop fermentation and to increase its level of alcohol, making it more stable—less subject to spoilage and to separation of the solids from the liquids—after a bottle has been opened, than a regular table wine.

Foxiness. The odd flavor of native American grapes such as *Vitis californica* that grow wild in the woods and thickets of the Napa and Sonoma Valleys. Wines made from these grapes are an acquired taste.

Free Run. Juice that runs from the crushed grapes before pressing. It is more intense in flavor than pressed juice and has fewer (or no) off flavors.

Fruity. Having aromatic nuances of fresh fruit—fig, raspberry, apple, et cetera. Fruitiness, a sign of quality in young wines, is replaced by bouquet in aged wines.

Fumé Blanc. Term coined by the Napa Valley's Robert Mondavi to describe a dry, crisp, oak-aged sauvignon blanc. It is now used so indiscriminately that it has lost its special meaning.

Gamay. Also called Gamay Beaujolais, this vigorous French red-grape variety is widely planted in California. It produces pleasant reds and rosés that should be drunk young. There is some confusion as to which California plantings are the true gamay and which are instead clones of pinot noir.

Gewürztraminer. A German-Alsatian pinkish grape variety that makes excellent aromatic, almost spicy white wine in Mendocino County's Anderson Valley. It is also planted elsewhere in California.

Green. Said of a wine made from unripe grapes, with a pronounced leafy flavor and a raw edge.

Grenache. A southern French red-wine variety of Spanish origin *(garnacha)*, with limited plantings in California, where it makes good rosés. Its popularity has increased with the rise of the new Rhône-style blends.

Grey Riesling. Not a Riesling, but a grape of dubious origin that makes indifferent wine yet is popular with some consumers.

Horizontal Tasting. A tasting of wines of the same vintage from several wineries.

Johannisberg Riesling. *See* Riesling.

Late Harvest, Select Late Harvest, Special Select Late Harvest. Wine made from grapes harvested later in the fall than the main lot, and thus higher in sugar levels. These terms are vague, however, and have no legal meaning in California; at worst, they may simply indicate that the grapes grew too ripe and that the resulting wine is sweet and cloying.

Lees. The spent yeast and grape solids that have dropped out of suspension while a wine ages in a barrel or tank. White wine left on the lees for a time improves in complexity; this method has become a popular way of aging chardonnay and sauvignon blanc.

Maderized. A term applied to a white or rosé wine that is past its prime and has become oxidized with an undesirable flavor and aroma of Madeira, the Portuguese fortified wine.

Malbec. A red Bordeaux grape, malbec makes deeply colored, somewhat tannic wine. Less aromatic than cabernet sauvignon, it is softer and ages earlier and for this reason is commonly blended with cabernet in Bordeaux reds and Meritage wines (*see* Meritage).

Malolactic Fermentation. A secondary fermentation in the tank or barrel that changes harsh malic acid into softer lactic acid and carbon dioxide, making the wine smoother. Because it lowers the perceptible level of a wine's acids, malolactic fermentation is frowned upon in regions where wines, especially whites, tend to have low acid to begin with. In cool regions, where wines have a high natural acidity, it is a boon to the winemaker, because it rounds out the wine, making it less acidic and more complex at the same time.

Marsanne. A white-wine grape of France's northern Rhône Valley that can produce a full-bodied, overly heavy wine unless handled with care. It makes very good wine in California.

Meritage. High-quality red or white wines blended from Bordeaux varietals in which none of the component grapes reaches the level of 75 percent required by law in order to designate the wine as being made of a particular grape. The term Meritage, a combination of "merit" and "heritage," was coined by winemakers to allow them greater flexibility in blending their wines. Most Meritage wines are in no way inferior to varietal wines, and most carry vintage dates. A few wineries use proprietary names such as Insignia or Trilogy instead of, or in addition to, the Meritage designation.

Merlot. Known in its native France as *merlot noir,* for the dark, blue-black color of its berries, this grape is more productive than cabernet and yields a softer, more supple wine that may be drunk at a younger age. Until recent years, merlot was not widely planted in California, but it has experienced a boom.

Méthode Champenoise. The traditional, time-consuming method of making sparkling wines in which the wine is fermented in individual bottles. This helps create small bubbles that are diffused throughout the wine and are released only slowly after a bottle is opened. When the wine finishes fermentation, it is disgorged (that is, each bottle is opened and its sediments are removed) before a dosage of yeast and sugar is added to induce a secondary fermentation that creates more bubbles. This method was developed in Champagne, France, and is used for making the highest quality sparklers. The labels of wines made this way state that the wine was *fermented* in this bottle rather than simply "made in the bottle," which is a simpler, cheaper process that involves filtering the wine and results in less complex wines with fewer bubbles.

Meunier (also called Pinot Meunier). A relative of the pinot noir whose dusty-black grapes are made mostly into white or off-white sparkling wine. Though more productive than pinot noir, its quality is not as high. There are limited plantings of meunier in California.

Mourvèdre. This red-wine grape was once moderately popular in California under its Spanish name, *mataro,* but it has gained a new following under this French name and has been made into Rhône-style wines. Wine made from mourvèdre is alcoholic, deeply colored, very dense, and at first harsh, but it mellows with several years of aging.

Muscat Blanc. Also called muscat canelli, this aromatic grape may have been brought to France by Greek colonists who settled Provence before the Roman Empire. Planted in California since the mid-19th century, but never on a large scale.

Must. Crushed grapes or their juice, either ready to be or in the process of being fermented into wine.

Nebbiolo. The great red-wine grape of Italy's Piedmont region, where it makes renowned wines such as barolo, barbaresco, and gattinara. One of the greatest red-wine grapes in the world, it is now widely planted in California. It produces full-bodied, sturdy wines that are fairly high in alcohol and age splendidly.

Noble. A term that, applied to grapes and wines, denotes both inherited status and quality. A noble grape variety produces good (or, in the right hands, great) wine almost everywhere it is planted. A noble wine—either varietal or blended—is one whose combination of flavors, aromas, mouth feel, and finish even a novice can identify as special.

Noble Rot. *Botrytis cinerea,* a beneficial fungus mold that attacks certain ripe grapes, perforating their skin. This shrivels the grapes through dehydration and concentrates the sugars and flavor elements in the remaining juice while preserving the grape's acids. This helps keep the resulting sweet wine from becoming cloying.

Non-Vintage. Having no date on the label, usually indicating that the wine is a blend from different vineyards, growing regions, and even years. This is not always evidence of poor quality and can represent an attempt to make wine of a consistent quality from year to year.

Nose. The overall fragrance (aroma or bouquet) given off by a wine; the better part of its flavor.

Oak. The most popular wood for making wine barrels, because, if used properly, it can impart desirable flavors to the wine that is stored in it and can add to the wine's complexity. If abused, it can make a wine taste woody and oaky.

Oaky. Said of a wine that has been aged in new oak for too long and tastes more of the vanilla-like flavors of the wood than of the grape. Once praised as a virtue in California chardonnays; now considered a fault.

Oxidized. Condition of a wine that had too much contact with the air, either as juice or through faulty wine making or a leaky barrel or cork. Most often occurs with white wine, although it does happen to reds too. An oxidized wine has lost its freshness and is on the way to becoming maderized. Depending on how far the oxidation has progressed, such a wine should be either drunk immediately (preferably with strongly seasoned food) or discarded.

Petite Sirah. A noble red-wine grape of California whose origin is shrouded in mystery. It was once thought to be the true *syrah* grape of France, but it is not. Because it is a true vinifera grape, it may be a hybrid that occurred in a mid-19th-century California vineyard—much like the equally mysterious zinfandel.

pH. An indicator of a wine's acidity. It is a reverse measure: the lower the pH level, the higher the acidity.

Phylloxera. A disease caused by the root louse *Phylloxera vastatrix,* native to the central and eastern United States. It attacks grapevine roots, first weakening, and ultimately destroying them. It was transported to France when the French experimented with native American grape varieties such as concord and muscadine.

Pinot Blanc. A white-wine grape variety that evolved from pinot gris, which in turn evolved from pinot noir. Pinot blanc, when treated properly, makes a wine much like chardonnay.

Pinot Gris. This is the classic white grape of Alsace, Italy (where it is called pinot grigio), and Germany (Ruländer); a white mutation of pinot noir. It has grayish-rose skin when ripe and can yield full-bodied, full-flavored, and complex white (or pinkish) wine in cool growing regions. (It can become flabby and flat in hot climates.)

Pinot Noir. An ancient French grape variety that under perfect conditions makes some of the best red wine in the world. Until quite recently, it rarely made more than ordinary wine in California. But recent wines made from new plantings in the cooler growing regions of the Carneros District, the Russian River Valley, and Paso Robles, combined with improved vinification methods, hint that pinot noir will have a great future in California.

Pinot Noir Blanc. White wine made from the black pinot noir grape, most commonly as sparkling wine. "White" is relative here, since the wine, more often than not, has a rosy pink tinge.

Pomace. The spent skins and grape solids from which the juice has been pressed, commonly returned to the fields as fertilizer.

Racking. Moving wine from one tank or barrel to another to leave deposits behind; the wine may or may not be fined or filtered in the process.

Residual Sugar. The natural sugar left in a wine after fermentation. When grape juice is fermented into wine, the sugars are converted into alcohol. If the fermentation is not interrupted, all of the sugar will be transformed. The winemaker can interrupt the process to make the wine lightly sweet. Also, if the must has very high sugar levels, the yeasts may not convert all the sugar before they are killed by the alcohol being created. Since the average human palate cannot detect sugar levels of less than 0.5 percent, any residual sugar falling below that level is simply ignored and treated as though it does not exist. In the 1990s, it became popular to leave some residual sugar (often as much as one percent or more) in white and red table wines, because consumers, while claiming to like dry wines, actually prefer slightly sweet ones.

Riesling. Also called Johannisberg Riesling or white Riesling, the noble white-wine grape of Germany was introduced to California during the middle of the 19th century by immigrant vintners. This cool-climate grape has rarely made great wine here, although at times it has made very sweet ones.

Rosé. French term for pink wine, usually made from black (red-wine) grapes whose juice has been left on the skins only long enough to give it a tinge of color. Rosés can be versatile food wines, especially when made from premium grapes like cabernet sauvignon, grenache, or pinot noir.

Rounded. Said of a well-balanced, complete wine—a good wine, though not necessarily a distinctive or great one.

Roussanne. A noble white-wine grape of France's Rhône Valley that gives a full-bodied, distinguished wine. It makes very good wines in California.

Sangiovese. The main red grape of Italy's Chianti district and of much of central Italy. Depending on how it is grown and vinified, it can be made into vibrant, light-bodied to medium-bodied wines, as well as into long-lived, very complex reds (such as Italy's renowned *Brunello di Montalcino*). Sangiovese was once widely planted in California—it went into the famous Tipo Chianti made by the Italian Swiss Colony before Prohibition—but has made a comeback only recently.

Sauvignon Blanc. This may well be the wild grape of the Bordeaux region. It most likely thrived on the banks of the Gironde estuary long before the Romans introduced viticulture to southwestern France. Sauvignon blanc does very well in the California Wine Country and makes more interesting wine than the more popular chardonnay. A dry, austere wine made from this grape is sometimes marketed as fumé blanc.

Sauvignon Vert. A simple white-wine grape that is not a true sauvignon but makes a pleasant, easily drinkable wine. It is made as a varietal by only one winery, the Napa Valley's Nichelini Vineyards.

Sec. Although *sec* means "dry" in French, in speaking about wines sec indicates one that has from 1.7 to 3.5 percent sugar. In the language of sparkling wine, drier than demi-sec but not as dry as brut.

Sediment. Deposits that most red wines throw as they age in the bottle, thus clarifying their appearance, flavors, and aromas. Not a defect in an old wine or in a new wine that has been bottled unfiltered.

Sèmillon. A white Bordeaux grape that, blended with sauvignon blanc, has made some of the best sweet wines in the world. Like the Riesling grape, it can benefit from the noble rot, which concentrates the juices and intensifies the flavors and aromas.

Sparkling Wines. Wines in which carbon dioxide is suspended, making them bubbly. Sparkling wines were invented in Champagne, the northernmost wine district of France. Grapes in this area tend to be a bit acidic because they do not always ripen fully; thus, sparkling wines have traditionally been naturally tart, even austere. The term Champagne is often used in America to denote sparkling wines of local origin, but this is frowned on by the French (and illegal elsewhere in the world).

Sugar. Occurring naturally in grapes, sugar is the food the yeasts digest to make alcohol. The higher the sugar of the grape, the higher the potential alcohol of the wine. Fermentation stops when all the sugar has been digested or when the alcohol level becomes high enough (from 15 to 16 percent) to kill off the yeast. In France it is legal to add sugar to unfermented grape juice in order to raise the alcohol level of a wine; in California it is not.

Sylvaner. A white-wine grape from Central Europe that makes good, rather than great, wine. The wine is greenish yellow in color and has a light body and aroma. In the past, much of California's sylvaner wines were labeled "Riesling," a practice that benefited neither wine.

Syrah. A red-wine grape from France's hot-climate Rhône region, syrah produces the best wine when grown in austere soils; it loses its noble qualities when planted in fertile, irrigated bottomlands. At its best, the wine made from this grape is big-bodied and complex and needs to be aged to bring out its qualities. California's petite sirah is not of this variety. Plantings of true syrah were once very limited in California but have increased in recent years, partly due to the new popularity of Rhône-style wines, partly because of the success syrah has had in Australia, where it is called shiraz.

Table Wine. A wine that has at least 7 percent but not more than 14 percent alcohol by volume. Wines so labeled need not state their exact alcohol content. (The term is sometimes used, incorrectly, by consumers to denote an inexpensive wine.)

Tank. A very large container, usually upright and cylindrical, in which wine is fermented and stored. Tanks are commonly made of stainless steel, though they may also be made of wood or concrete (the latter are usually straight-sided cubicles) and lined with glass.

Tannins. Naturally occurring compounds in grape skins, seeds, and stems, and in barrel oak, that taste astringent and make the mouth pucker. Because tannins settle out in the natural sediments that red wine throws as it ages, older reds have fewer tannins than do younger ones.

Tartaric Acid, Tartrates. The principal acid of wine, some of which is deposited in the form of crystals (tartrates) as the wine settles in a cask. Sometimes, in unstable wines, tartrates are also deposited in the bottle, and since they look like tiny shards of glass (though they are not harmful), consumers may complain of "broken glass" in the wine.

Terroir. The French term for soil, used to indicate that the soil of a specific vineyard imparts a special taste to its grapes and, through them, to the finished wine. The term is also used—colloquially, and not altogether correctly—to indicate a specific microclimate.

Varietal Wine. A wine that takes its name not from a town, district, or vineyard—as in much of Europe—but from the grape variety from which it is made: chardonnay, merlot, sangiovese, and so on. According to law, a wine labeled as a varietal must contain at least 75 percent of wine made from the grape variety printed on the label.

Vat. A large container of stainless steel, wood, or concrete, often open at the top, in which wine is fermented or blended. The term is sometimes used interchangeably with "tank."

Vertical Tasting. A tasting of one or more varietals from the same winery but of different vintages, generally starting with the youngest and proceeding to the oldest.

Vinifera. The great wine grapes of the Old World, which—despite their widely varying character—all belong to a single species, *Vitis vinifera.* Many varieties of vinifera grapes have been successfully transplanted to the New World, and they produce our best wines. The native grapes of the New World tend to have odd flavors.

Vintage. The grape harvest of a given year, and the year in which the grapes are harvested. In California the term "crush" may be used for the harvest as though it were synonymous with vintage. A vintage date on a bottle always indicates the year in which the grapes were harvested—never the year in which the wine was bottled.

Viognier. A white-wine grape of France's Rhône Valley that produces a unique, distinguished golden wine with a fruity bouquet.

Viticultural Area. *See* American Viticultural Area.

Woody. A pejorative term, said of a wine that has been stored in a wood barrel or cask for too long and has picked up excessively musty wood

A perfect vineyard.

aromas and flavors. A woody wine has the mouth feel you get when you have chewed on a wooden toothpick for too long. Unlike "oaky," the term "woody" is always a negative.

Yeasts. Minute, single-celled fungi that germinate and multiply rapidly as they feed on grape sugars, creating alcohol with the help of enzymes and releasing carbon dioxide. Because different yeasts vary in quality and flavor, winemakers must exercise care in their selection. The yeast cells die after fermentation—after they have run out of food—and slowly drift to the bottom of the wine barrel, where they make up a part of the lees left behind when the wine is racked or filtered.

Zinfandel. A red-wine grape especially popular on the West Coast. Much has been written about its origin, but though scientists have traced it to an obscure Croatian grape, winemakers agree that the American variety has unique qualities and makes better wine than does its European ancestor. Whatever its origin, this grape can give complex, well-balanced wine that ages as well as the best French clarets.

VINTAGES 1994–2002

I'm a bit reluctant to give you vintage evaluations, because these work best for small, self-contained districts, such as France's Chablis or Germany's Rheingau. Large, sprawling wine regions, such as those of northern California, have too many microclimates with unique conditions ever to allow their wines to be neatly categorized on a definitive vintage chart. Knowing the grower and winemaker and knowing about local conditions is much more important than knowing the vintage.

For example, in late August 2003, just before the early harvest for sparkling-wine grapes got under way, the Yountville, Oakville, and Rutherford areas of the Napa Valley were soaked with rain for a day. Newspapers ran stories about vintners wringing their hands in despair, but overall, the precipitation caused no damage. This being California, in general rain is quickly followed by sunshine, and the vines and grapes dry out before mildew spoils the vintage. Not only that, when it does rain, the precipitation does not affect every wine region. During the 2003 harvest, the Carneros and northern valley, for example, received nary a drop.

So keep in mind that vintage descriptions are a rough guide and should never be a substitute for tasting the wine. Even in France, where wineries often lower their prices in off-years (something that has yet to happen in California), you can find some great wines among a sea of average ones. In other words, once the vintage description has pointed you into a specific direction, you must still visit a winery and sniff, taste, and make up your own mind.

1994 A cool growing season without heat surges. The overall crop yield was down, but there were high yields at harvest for some wineries. Fruit quality was excellent, with almost perfect acid levels. It was an excellent year for all types of grapes in many diverse growing regions. A long, cool harvest allowed some growers to pick cabernet sauvignon and merlot in October, and chardonnay and sauvignon blanc as late as November. Viognier and some of the other new varieties planted in Sonoma County did very well. A great year for Sonoma County zinfandel. The zinfandel crop was down 30 percent to 40 percent, making for intensely flavored wines that should develop beautifully with age. A vintage to enjoy—either now or in the next few years.

1995 The end of the drought. Heavy spring rains washed out some vineyards but hardly affected others, because they fell when the vines were still dormant. Cold weather and rains during bloom caused low fruit set, making for an exceptionally small, although excellent, crop and causing wineries to scramble for extra grapes. Expect wine prices to go higher as the wines mature and become even richer and more complex. Connoisseurs who expected great things from this vintage have been proved right. Although many of the best wines from all growing regions have not yet reached their full potential, they are developing beautifully in the bottle, with the exception of merlot and chardonnay, which should be drunk now. Still, be sure to keep a few cases of this vintage cellared for even greater joys in years to come.

1996 A strange year with low yields but good fruit. Rain during blossoming of the vines and fruit set cut quantity in many areas, but a warm fall and summer made up for much of that. Even so, this seems to have been a vintage that ripened very late. Some red-wine grapes were picked as late as November. Most winemakers seem very happy with the results. Chardonnays are drinkable now, and should not be kept for much longer, lest their beauty fades; viognier, marsanne, and perhaps sangiovese should also be drunk now. Cabernet sauvignons and zinfandels could be cellared for several more years, but some, especially the zinfandels, are ready to drink now, while the bigger ones can be held for another three to five years. Decide by tasting and by winery.

1997 Everybody's dream vintage. Yields were up (Napa had its biggest harvest ever) but so was quality. Some wineries had to hire tank cars to store all that bounty. Grapes for sparkling wines saw their earliest harvest ever. Rains in late summer worried some growers, but everybody came out just fine, making 1997 one of the great vintages of the decade. Chardonnay, viognier, and marsanne should be drunk now, but could be held for another year or two. Sangiovese also shows signs of early maturity. Cabernet and zinfandel are surprisingly enjoyable. Even though several wines seemed to mature early and were enjoyable while quite young, they also appear to have staying power and the ability to age and improve, until 2006 or beyond.

1998 This turned out to be the most controversial "vintage of the century," because it included some great as well as some awful wines. Where the rains struck seems to have played a key role. The Lodi and Central Coast vineyards largely escaped the rains (and the resulting grape rot and off-flavors). Napa, Sonoma, and the North Coast did not fare as well, though here too there were vineyards that escaped the damage. It appears that quite a few northern wines were augmented with Central Coast and Lodi grapes to improve their quality. Fortunately, many of the 1998s were drunk early and will not be around to haunt us in years to come.

1999 With the exception of pinot noir, this was indeed a "vintage of the century." Although the crop was small, quality was high, especially in Sonoma and Napa Counties. Among the reds, cabernet sauvignon, merlot, and zinfandel fared best; pinot noir suffered from a cooler than normal growing season in the north but made some very nice wines in Santa Barbara and San Luis Obispo County. Italian and Rhône varieties did well in the Sierra Foothills, Lodi, and on the Central Coast. Chardonnays were rich and well-structured, not only on the North Coast but also in Lodi and on the Central Coast as well.

2000 There were some rains, but they did not affect the vintage, and the grapes did not suffer from mildew. Cabernet sauvignon and merlot ripened somewhat erratically, though some good wines were made. Pinot noir was of variable quality: Central Coast vineyards did better with pinot noir than those in the Carneros and Russian River regions. The cool weather did affect some heat-loving zinfandel, making for uneven quality. Chardonnays are well balanced, though they may lack some depth. Lodi did better than average with all of its grape varieties because of the consistency of its growing climate. Sierra wines of this vintage are showing good backbone. Santa Barbara produced both good quantity and quality. (It seems that in dubious years like this, the grapes of the rain-deprived Central Coast—which are hardened against mildew by frequent fogs—do better than the coddled Napa and Sonoma grapes.)

2001 Early indicators make this a very good year, but it is still too soon to know for sure. Some growers claim that this was a year of great richness and could rival 1997 and 1999 in quality. Chardonnays from this vintage seem to be developing beautifully, as do some of the pinot noirs from the Central Coast.

2002 Opinions are varied, but growers seem to agree that quality was higher than expected, but yields were lower than normal.

RECOMMENDED READING

Americans and the California Dream, 1850–1915 (1973), by Kevin Starr. A state historian wrote this delightful analysis of why the Wine Country is the way it is and how the region fits into California as a whole.

Angel's Visits (1991), by David Darlington. The author of this book got his hands stained in a winery to learn what makes great zinfandel.

California: A Literary Chronicle (1968), by Lee W. Storrs. An especially good resource for information about the early years of wine making, this book contains excerpts from writings about California.

California's Napa Valley: One Hundred Sixty Years of Wine Making (1999), by William F. Heintz. One of northern California's most distinguished wine historians interviewed longtime vintners and new arrivals in shaping this beautifully illustrated chronicle of the Napa Valley's rise to enological prominence.

A Cultivated Life: A Year in a California Vineyard (1993), by Joy Sterling. A proprietor of the Iron Horse winery wrote this account of what it takes to make a winery successful.

The Far Side of Eden: The Ongoing Saga of Napa Valley (2002), by James Conaway. Conaway's second book on the Wine Country picks up where the first, *Napa (see below)*, left off.

Guide to California Wines (1955, et cetera) by John Robert Melville. The original edition and several revisions between 1960 and 1978 provide a glimpse into the Wine Country just before it became the famous region it is today.

Historical and Descriptive Sketchbook of Napa, Sonoma, Lake and Mendocino Counties (1873), by Campbell Augustus Menefee. A reporter's biographical sketches of pioneer vintners are enhanced by descriptions of the countryside while it still lay primarily untilled.

Napa (1992), by James Conaway. The Wine Country lifestyle and local politics undergo intense scrutiny in this behind-the-scenes exposé.

Napa Stories (2003), by Michael Chiarello and Janet Fletcher. Chiarello, a noted Napa Valley chef, and Fletcher, a writer, profile famous vintners and other Napa players in this book, which is photographed beautifully by Stephen Rothfield.

Napa Valley: The Land, the Wine, the People (2003), by Charles O'Rear. St. Helena resident Charles O'Rear captures the best of the valley in this lushly photographed book.

Napa Wine: A History from Mission Days to the Present (1994), by Charles L. Sullivan. This comprehensive history of the Napa wine industry contains many historical photos.

Silverado Squatters (1883), by Robert Louis Stevenson. The author of *Treasure Island* and other classics recalls the days he and his wife, Fanny, spent in the Wine Country.

A Tale of Two Valleys (2003), by Alan Deutschman. The author, a well-known journalist, focuses on the behind-the-scenes rivalry between residents of the Napa and Sonoma Valleys.

The University of California/Sotheby Book of California Wine (1984; various editors). In this valuable book, historians, enologists, and vintners write about the topics they know best, from the early days of California wine to the 1980s.

Vines in the Sun: A Journey through California Vineyards (1949), by Idwal Jones. This small book, though not always accurate, is loaded with anecdotes, character sketches, and descriptions of places as they looked in the 1940s.

The WPA Guide to California (1939), by the Federal Writers' Project. This Depression-era snapshot of the state contains some vivid writing about the Wine Country.

Wild mustard blooms amid the vines on a hazy late-winter day.

INDEX

ACKNOWLEDGMENTS

■ FROM THE AUTHOR

A book is the product of more than a single mind. I would therefore like to thank the many people who have made it possible. Christopher Burt and Kit Duane asked me to write it—I thank them and Julia Dillon and Debi Dunn for making me feel like I could do it. I would especially like to thank Daniel Mangin and Paula Consolo for doing such a great job editing the current edition and for making it seem so easy. My thanks also to Fabrizio La Rocca, Geraldine Sarmiento, and Victor Lau for the many graphic features added this time around.

I would like to express my special gratitude to Zita Eastman, formerly of the Sonoma County Wine Library in Healdsburg, for easing the travails of historical research, and to Mildred Howie for answering questions that popped up at unexpected moments. I would like to thank Antonia Allegra for showing me the real Wine Country, the homespun community behind the facade of visitors' attractions.

My thanks to Madeleine Kamman for showing me that great Wine Country food can indeed be simple. I also appreciate the way Pam Hunter and Ann Marie Conover have kept me updated on wineries and Wine Country happenings during the last decade, and I am indebted to Lee Hodo and Tom Fuller for keeping me involved.

Special thanks go to the vintners and winery staff whose wines have warmed my soul and whose smiles have made me feel welcome. These include, among many, Marty Bannister, Forrest Tancer, the Cakebread family, Virginia Van Asperen, Charlie Abela, Mark Swain, Revelee Hemken, John Williams, Bob Iantosca, Francis and Francoise DeWavrin-Woltner, and Nyna Cox.

I'm profoundly grateful to Marie Gewirtz for introducing me not only to fine Sonoma County wines but also to that gastronomic paradise's great foods. I would also like to thank Jim Caron and Darryl Nutter, as well as Michele Anna Jordan, for guiding me to Sonoma County food producers, and to thank Alan Hemphill for giving me glimpses of the business side of wine.

Last, but not least, I thank my wife, Victoria, for the patience and understanding with which she has supported yet one more book project.

■ From the Publisher

Compass American Guides would like to thank Karen Croft for her reviews of Napa and Sonoma spa resorts, Joan Keener for copyediting this book, Ellen Klages for proofreading it, Joan Stout for indexing it, and Catherine Christenberry for her many editorial contributions. And we are extremely grateful to Robert Holmes and Charles O'Rear for the use of their photographs:

Robert Holmes, pages 71, 76, 78–79, 81, 86, 101, 114, 120, 132–133, 137, 145, 146–147, 153, 156, 160, 164–165, 167, 173, 179, 185, 187, 188, 189, 197, 200, 202, 208, 210 (top and bottom), 214, 217, 219, 221, 224–225, 230, 234, 237, 241, 246, 252–253, 258, 262, 263, 270, 271, 273, 275 (top and bottom), 276–277, 279, 281, 287, 292–293, 305, 317, 318, 320.

Charles O'Rear, pages 9, 12 (top and bottom), 13, 20, 22–23, 40 (second row, second from left) 42, 43, 45, 47, 48, 52, 56, 57, 62, 69, 84, 85, 90, 106, 110, 118; 141, 144, 149, 159, 170, 171, 177, 186, 191, 201, 205, 206, 207, 213, 296, 303, 323, 330, 347, 353.

Compass would also like to thank the wineries that provided labels and photographs for "How Fine Wine Is Made" (page 51), the wine-bottle collage (pages 64–65), and "How to Read a Wine Label" (page 67). And we thank the following individuals and organizations for the use of their photos or illustrations:

Stepping into History
Pages 16–17, Bancroft Library, University of California, Berkeley (#1988.103:11)
Page 19, Bancroft Library (POR 13)
Page 24, Buena Vista Winery
Pages 26–27, Bancroft Library (Banc Pic 1963.002:0665–C)
Page 30, Wine Institute of California
Page 31 (all photos), Wine Institute of California
Page 32, Wine Institute of California
Page 35, Caroline Martini
Page 36 (top), Trustees of the Ansel Adams Publishing Rights Trust 1961 (courtesy of Mumm Napa Valley, Rutherford)
Page 36 (bottom), Trustees of the Ansel Adams Publishing Rights Trust 1961 (courtesy of Sterling Vineyards, Calistoga)
Page 37, Trustees of the Ansel Adams Publishing Rights Trust 1961 (courtesy of Mumm Napa Valley, Rutherford)
Page 40 (top row, first from left), Robert Mondavi Winery
Page 40 (top row, second and third from left), Beringer Vineyards
Page 40 (top row fourth from left), Bancroft Library (#1)
Page 40 (second row, first from left), Buena Vista Winery